THE AFRICAN AMERICAN CHILD

YVETTE R. HARRIS, PhD, an associate professor of psychology at Miami University in Oxford, Ohio, received her doctorate in psychology from the University of Florida with a specialization in cognitive development. For the past 17 years her research has focused on exploring the environmental contributions to preschool and school age cognitive development, and more recently has taken on applied focus examining the learning/teaching patterns of African American mothers transitioning from welfare to work. She has presented her work at both national and international conferences, her research has appeared in a variety of educational and developmental journals, and her work has been funded by the National Science Foundation, Proctor and Gamble, Miami University, and the Harvard/Radcliffe Murray Research Center.

JAMES A. GRAHAM, PhD, is an associate professor at The College of New Jersey (TCNJ), Department of Psychology. Dr. Graham received his BA from Miami University; and his MS and PhD from the University of Memphis. He is a developmental psychologist whose work explores the social-cognitive aspects of children's relationships. Currently, he is the Coordinator of the Developmental Concentration in Psychology at TCNJ. He has published articles on the roles of race and sex in children's friendships, children's evaluations of social situations, children's relationship to media, and program evaluation. During the summer, he teaches graduate education and psychology courses in Johannesburg, South Africa through The College of New Jersey's Graduate Global Program.

The African American Child

Development and Challenges

Yvette R. Harris, PhD and James A. Graham, PhD

SPRINGER PUBLISHING COMPANY
NEW YORK

Springer Publishing Company, LLC
11 West 42nd Street
New York, NY 10036
www.springerpub.com

Acquisitions Editor: Sheri W. Sussman
Production Editor: Matti Salomaki
Cover design: Joanne E. Honigman
Composition: Apex Publishing, LLC

07 08 09 10/ 5 4 3 2 1

Library of Congress Cataloging-in-Publication Data

Harris, Yvette R.
    The African American child : development and challenges / Yvette R. Harris and James A. Graham.
        p. cm.
    Includes bibliographical references and index.
    ISBN-13: 978-0-8261-2756-3 (alk. paper)
    ISBN-10: 0-8261-2756-8 (alk. paper)
    1. African American children—Social conditions.   2. African American children—Health and hygiene.   3. African American children—Education.   4. Child development—United States.   5. Developmental psychology.   I. Graham, James A., Ph.D.   II. Title.

HQ792.U5H27 2007
305.23089'96073—dc22   2006038960

Printed in the United States of America by Bang Printing.

Contents

List of Figures and Tables   xi

Preface   xiii

Acknowledgments   xv

CHAPTER 1   Demographics: A Portrait of African American
            Children   1

            Overview

            Section One: Population Statistics on African American Children

            Section Two: Living Arrangements of African American Children

            Section Three: Economic Conditions of African American
            Children and Their Families

            Perspectives on Demographics and African American Children

            Additional Readings

CHAPTER 2   Research Issues With African American Children   15

            Overview: The Importance of Studying Developmental
            Research Methods

                Insider's Voice: The Need for More Research on African
                American Children

            Section One: Problems: Methodological Constraints in
            Research Designs

                Insider's Voice: Where Have We Gone Wrong?

            Section Two: Conducting Culturally Relevant Research With
            African American Children

                The Need for Culturally Sensitive Research With
                African American Children

                Conceptual Frameworks and Interdisciplinarity

                The Role of Context in African American Child Development

                The Relationship to African American Child Development and
                Central Characteristics in Developmental Psychology

                Ethical Considerations With African American Child Participants

            Section Three: Theories

                Vygotsky's Sociocultural Theory

                Bronfenbrenner's Bioecological Systems Theory

                Integrative Conceptual Model of Child Development

Perspectives on Research and Theories

Chapter Summary

Additional Readings

CHAPTER 3   African American Children and Health Issues   39

Overview

Section One: Health Challenges

Infant Mortality

Insider's Voice: Infant Mortality

Maternal Risk Factors

Initiatives Designed to Reduce African American Infant Mortality Rates

Physical Challenges Beyond Infancy

AIDS

Treatment of AIDS

Plumbism

Insider's Voice: Plumbism

Treatment of Plumbism

Sickle-Cell Anemia

Insider's Voice: Sickle-Cell Anemia

Treatment of Sickle-Cell Anemia

Asthma

Treatment of Asthma

Obesity

Treatment of Obesity

Section Two: Access to Health Care

Perspectives on the Health Status of African American Children

Chapter Summary

Additional Readings

CHAPTER 4   Mental Health Issues and Racial Identity   65

Overview

Section One: Mental Health Issues

Insider's Voice: African American Children and Mental Health Issues

Risk Factors

Assessment and Diagnosis

Treatment of Mental Health Disorders

Section Two: Racial Identity

Perspectives on Mental Health and Racial Identity

Chapter Summary

Additional Readings

CHAPTER 5   Education and African American Children   83

Overview

Section One: School Desegregation and African American Children

Insider's Voice: Resegregation of America's Public Schools

Desegregation and African American Children

Section Two: Schools That Work for African American Children

Public School Models

Independent Black Schools (IBS)

Section Three: African American Children and Early Intervention Programs

Head Start

High/Scope Perry Preschool Project

The Abecedarian Project

Perspectives on Education and African American Children

Chapter Summary

Additional Readings

CHAPTER 6   Language and Literacy   111

Overview

Section One: The Controversy

Insider's Voice: The Oakland School Board Ebonics Resolution

Section Two: Language Learning and African American Children

Section Three: Language and Literacy Issues

Section Four: Language and Literacy Intervention Programs for African American Children

Section Five: Language Assessment and African American Children: Distinguishing Dialect From a Speech Language Disorder

Perspectives on Language Learning and Literacy and African American Children

Chapter Summary

Additional Readings

CHAPTER 7   Moral Development   133

    Overview

        Insider's Voice: What if Heinz Were Black?

        The Issues

    Section One: Theories of Moral Development

        Piaget's Theory

        Kohlberg's Theory: The Ethic of Justice

        Criticisms of Piaget's and Kohlberg's Theories

        Gilligan's Theory: The Ethic of Care

        Gibb's Sociomoral Reasoning Model

        Humphries' Culture and Empathy Model

        Turiel's Domain Theory: Moral Rules and Social Conventions

    Section Two: Prosocial Behavior and African American Children

        Possible Factors Influencing Prosocial Behavior in African American Children

        Morality and Racial Identity Development

    Section Three: Moral Development and Community Violence

        Insider's Voice: Dissecting the 'Code of the Street'

    Perspectives on African American Children and Moral Development

    Chapter Summary

    Additional Readings

CHAPTER 8   Social Contexts in the Lives of African
            American Children: Family and Peers   165

    Overview

        Issues

        Insider's Voice: The Negro American Family

    Section One: Models of the African American Family

        Pathological Model

        Cultural Equivalent Model

        Emergent Model

        Ecology Models of the Family

        Guiding Principles of Family Systems Theory

        External Systems Affecting the Family

    Section Two: African American Family Structure and Child Development

        Nuclear Family

African American Single-Parent Families
Augmented Families
Section Three: The Peer Group
African American Children's Peer Relationships
African American Children's Friendships
Perspectives on African American Children and Social Contexts
Chapter Summary
Additional Readings

CHAPTER 9   Epilogue: Where Do We Go From Here?   185
Poverty
Cultural Diversity Within the African American Population
Family Constellation
Health Care
Education
Violence

References   189
Index   215

List of Figures and Tables

FIGURES

1.1	Percentage of White children and Black children in 1960s.	2
1.2	Percentage of children in the United States, 2004.	3
1.3	Number of African American children from 1990–2004.	3
1.4	Percentage of African American children residing in two-parent family and mother-headed households from 1960–2004.	4
1.5	Percentage of children living in father-headed households.	5
1.6	Percentage of African American children living in grandparent-maintained homes from 1960–2004.	6
1.7	Percentage of children formally adopted, 2004.	7
1.8	Percentage of children awaiting adoption, 2004.	8
1.9	Percentage of African American families and White families with incomes below the poverty level.	9
2.1	Developmental designs.	18
2.2	Factors in multidimensional development.	26
2.3	Continuity and discontinuity in development.	27
2.4	Bronfenbrenner's bioecological systems theory.	33
2.5	A phenomenological variant of the ecological systems theory (PVEST).	34
2.6	Integrative model for the study of developmental competencies in minority children.	35
3.1	Infant mortality statistics for African American infants and White infants.	41
3.2	Infant health status and maternal risk factor model.	43
3.3	Percentage of mothers receiving late or no prenatal care, 2002.	47
3.4	Number of newly diagnosed AIDS children.	50
3.5	Asthma incidence among children under 18 by race.	57
3.6	Body mass index comparisons.	58
4.1	Resiliency model.	67
4.2	Barbarin's resiliency model.	68
4.3	Racial identification model.	73
4.4	Racial preference study outcomes, 1940-1980.	74

5.1   Fourth Grade Reading Proficiency Test Scores 1992–2005   90
5.2   Fourth Grade Writing Proficiency Test Scores 1984–2003   90
5.3   Fourth Grade Math Proficiency Test Scores 1990–2005   91
7.1   Cultural and empathy model for moral reasoning.   142
7.2   Race distribution of violent felons in the 75 largest U.S. counties,
       who were under 18 years old at date of arrest, 1990–2002.   147
8.1   Family stress model.   174
8.2   Barker and Hill's family functioning behaviors.   179

TABLES

2.1   Threats to Internal Validity With African American Child
       Samples   20
2.2   Threats to External Validity With African American Child
       Samples   22
2.3   Methodological Characteristics of Articles on African Americans
       in Six APA Journals (1970–1989)   23
3.1   Infant Mortality State Rates (FY 2002)   42
3.2   Initiatives to Improve the Health Status of African American
       Children   60
5.4   Guidelines for Nondiscriminatory Assessment   93
7.1   Kohlberg's Ethic of Justice Theory of Moral Development   137
7.2   Gilligan's Ethic of Care Theory of Moral Development   140
7.3   Moreland and Leach's Common Themes Between Moral
       Development and Racial Identity Theories   146
8.1   Bronfenbrenner's Ecology of the Family as a Context for Human
       Development   171
8.2   Poverty Rates (Percent Below Poverty Level) in 1999 for Children
       Under 18 Years by Race and Hispanic Origin and Living
       Arrangements   173
8.3   Percent of Children Under 18 Years With Single Parents and
       Cohabiting Parents   175

Preface

The desire to write this book developed when the first author was teaching a course one semester on African American Child Psychology. While putting together the material for the course, she realized that there was a need for a comprehensive text on African American children. This book is designed to fill that need and introduce social science students (developmental psychology, social work, sociology, Black World Studies) and other related disciplines (family sciences, education, and nursing) to African American child development.

We had four goals in mind while writing this book. First, we wanted to introduce students to issues that impact the lives of African American children that typically are not discussed in child development textbooks or are relegated to a paragraph in most developmental textbooks. Second, we wanted to present a balanced discussion of the challenges that impact the lives of African American children as well as emphasize their strengths and their resiliency. Third, we wanted to familiarize students with a sampling of research that moves beyond a deficit view of the development of African American children and takes into account the historical, cultural, and social factors that influence developmental outcomes for African American children. Fourth and perhaps most importantly, we wanted to stimulate critical thinking in social science students about future directions for research on African American children and their families.

The book is divided into nine chapters. Each chapter begins with an overview of the material to be covered, continues with an Insider's Voice, which offers a personal story or a personal view point about the issues discussed in the section or chapter and concludes with a discussion of current perspectives on African American child development, and suggestions for additional readings.

Acknowledgments

We would like to take this opportunity to acknowledge the many people who helped to make this book possible.

Many thanks to our family and friends for their love and encouragement. We appreciate your belief in our dream to create this textbook and thank you for keeping our heads above the water as we navigated our way through the various stages of writing this book.

We would like to extend our thanks to the authors and publishers whose works are included in this text. We appreciate your courage to investigate topics on African American children. Your work served an instrumental role in the creation of this text.

A special thanks to Dr. Elijah Anderson from the University of Pennsylvania, Dr. Katrina Bledsoe and Dr. Ruth Hall from The College of New Jersey, Dr. Anthony Thompson from the University of Central Florida, and Dr. Gloria Oliver Carpenter from the University of Cincinnati Children's Medical Center for their thoughtful discussions and suggestions on the direction of the book; a special thanks to Dr. John Rothgheb, and Dr. Augustus Jones from Miami University for their encouragement during the initial phases of this project and to the many Miami University students who served as the research assistants, the sounding boards, the readers, and the arms and legs of the project.

We would also like to thank our respective universities (Miami University, College of New Jersey) for providing us with the time and resources to complete such an undertaking.

This text could not have been written without the support of many people. We thank Neil Salkind and Studio B agency for their invaluable assistance in finding a publisher for our book. Editorial support was provided by Alana Stein and Sara Yoo.

Our special thanks and appreciation to our editor, Sheri W. Sussman, at Springer Publishing Company LLC. This book could not be possible without your editorial feedback, guidance, and belief in our work. We greatly appreciate your assistance.

CHAPTER 1

Demographics: A Portrait of African American Children

OVERVIEW

The word *dynamic* aptly describes the socio-environmental-economic changes that have occurred in the lives of African American children for the past 40 years. One focus of this chapter is to describe those changes, specifically highlighting changes in the population demographics, changes in their living arrangements, and changes in the economic conditions of their families. This 40-year time period has been selected because the changes that occurred represent a pivotal and important time period in the sociopolitical history of the United States (i.e., Civil Rights Movement, Black Power Movement). Furthermore, these sociopolitical changes have had a profound impact on the quality of life experienced by African American children.

The chapter is divided into four sections. Sections one through three provide statistical information on African American children, focusing on their numbers relative to their peers from other racial and ethnic groups, their living arrangements, and the economic conditions of their families. The data presented in this section come from a variety of statistical sources including Statistical Abstracts of the U.S., Demographic and Government Documents, Statistical Record of Black Americans, and Statistical Abstracts of Children. Section four, Perspectives on Demographics and African American Children, posits the question what do the changing demographics tell us about African American children for the new millennium? The chapter ends with an overview of the topics to be covered in the book.

We now begin with a discussion of population statistics on African American children.

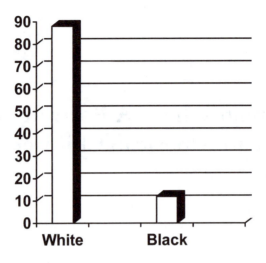

FIGURE 1.1   Percentage of White children and
Black children in 1960s.
Source: U.S. Census Bureau, Statistical Abstracts of
the United States, 1993.

SECTION ONE: POPULATION STATISTICS
ON AFRICAN AMERICAN CHILDREN

In 1960, there were 55,723,000 children under the age of 15 in the United
States. White children represented 88% of that number and African American
children represented 12% of that number (data were not available on children
from other ethnic groups during that time period; see Figure 1.1).

In the past 46 years, the number of children under the age of 15 in the
United States has increased to 71,341,000 (U.S. Census Bureau, 2006). Of
that number, White children comprise 65%, Hispanic children 16%, Asian
American children 3%, Native American children 2% and African American
children 13% (see Figure 1.2).

The African American population in general and the population of African
American children in particular have grown at a faster rate than the national
average for the past 10 years.

During the 1990s, the number of African American children under the
age of 15 steadily increased (see Figure 1.3). As illustrated by the figure,
in 1990, there were 8,296,000 African American children under the age
of 15. That number increased by 632,000 to 8,828,000 in 1995; and increased by 675,000 to 9,606,000 in 2000. Currently, there are 9,415,000
African American children in the United States. The population growth rate
for African American children is due in part to the swell in the number
of children who were either born to parents of African descent from the

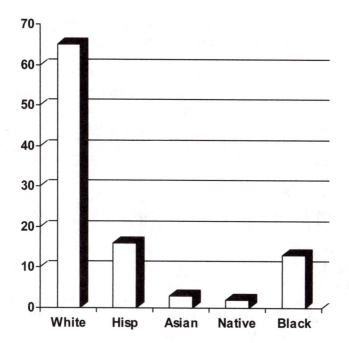

FIGURE 1.2   Percentage of children in the United States, 2004.
Source: U.S. Census Bureau, Population Estimates and Projections 2006.

Caribbean, South America, or Africa, or who immigrated to this country with their parents.

Demographers and population growth experts predict that this population growth rate will continue for the next several decades, and that by 2040, African American children and Hispanic children will constitute the majority of American children.

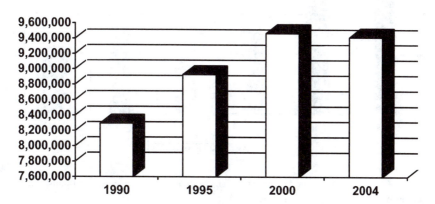

FIGURE 1.3   Number of African American children from 1990–2004.
Source: U.S. Census Bureau, Statistical Abstracts of the U.S. 2001, 2006.

SECTION TWO: LIVING ARRANGEMENTS
OF AFRICAN AMERICAN CHILDREN

While the living arrangements of all children in the United States have undergone significant changes since the 1960s, the changes in living arrangements of African American children have been the most dramatic.

We begin our discussion of living arrangements with a focus on comparing mother-headed households with two-parent households. Figure 1.4 provides an illustration of the changes that occurred in those living arrangements from 1960 to 2004.

As shown in the figure, in 1960, the majority of African American children (67%), lived in homes with both parents whereas 20% of African American children lived in mother-headed households. In 1970, over half (58%) of African American children lived in homes with both parents compared to the 30% living in mother-headed households.

The increase in the number of African American children living in mother-headed households and the decrease in the number of African American children living in two-parent families did not begin until the 1980s. As the figure shows, in 1980, 42% of African American children lived in two-parent family homes and 43% in mother-headed households. However, the dramatic change in their living arrangements did not occur until 1990, where 37% of African American children lived in homes with both parents and 51% of African American children lived in mother-headed households.

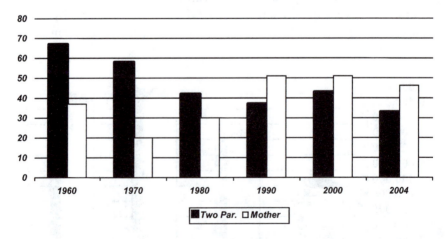

FIGURE 1.4   Percentage of African American children residing in two-parent family and mother-headed households from 1960–2004.

Sources: Bureau of Census Internet website:www.census.gov/population/socdemo/ms-la/tabch-4.txt; U.S. Census Bureau Statistical Abstracts of the U.S., 2006.

At present, 48% of African American children live in mother-headed households; this percentage has remained steady for more than a decade. This compares to 16% of White children, and 26% of Hispanic children living in mother-headed households (U.S. Census Bureau, Statistical Abstracts of the U.S., 2006).

What factors have contributed to the increase in the number of African American children living in mother-headed households? Brewer (1988) states that a multiplicity of factors, including the increase in divorce rates, and the increase in the number of African American children born out of marriage, contribute to the increase.

Father-headed households have also become a common living arrangement for African American children in the past 40 years. For example, in 1960, 2% of African American children resided in father-headed households. This percentage increased to 2.3% in 1970, but decreased to 1.9% in 1980 and increased to 3.5% in 1990 and to 4.4% in 2000 and then in 2004 increased to 5.8% (see Figure 1.5).

How do these statistics compare to the statistics of children from other racial and ethnic backgrounds? In 1960, only 1% of white children lived in father-headed households. That percentage decreased to less than 1% in 1970, increased to 1.6% in 1980, to 3% in 1990 and to 4.4% in 2004. A similar pattern is evident for Hispanic children. In 1980, 1.5% of Hispanic children lived in father-headed households, 2.9% in 1990 and 4.4% in 2004 (U.S. Census Bureau, Statistical Abstracts of the U.S., 2006).

While this pattern suggests that more children, independent of race, are living with their fathers, the findings become more relevant for African American fathers because of the myths that surround their low level of involvement in the lives of their children.

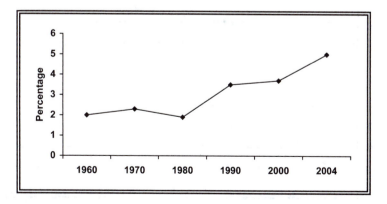

FIGURE 1.5   Percentage of children living in father-headed households.
Sources: Bureau of Census Internet website:www.census.gov/population/socdemo/
ms-la/tabch-4.txt; U.S. Census Bureau Statistical Abstracts of the U.S., 2006.

During the past 40 years, African American grandparents have also assumed a more prominent care giving role in the lives of their grandchildren and this living arrangement constitutes a more common alternative living arrangement for African American children than do father-headed households. Comparatively, African American children are more likely to be reared by their grandparents, usually their grandmothers, than are their counterparts from other ethnic and racial backgrounds (Ross & Aday, 2006). These grandparents have assumed custodial care for a variety of reasons ranging from death of a parent, incarceration of a parent, parental mental illness, parental drug abuse, child abuse, divorce, family violence, and unemployment issues (Burton, 1992).

As depicted in Figure 1.6, in 1960, 9.5% of African American children lived with their grandparents. In 1990, 12% of African American children lived with their grandparents in comparison to 4% of White children and 6% of Hispanic children.

Presently, 9% of African American children are raised in grandparent-maintained homes. Unfortunately, some of these grandparent-maintained homes experience some form of economic hardship.

Foster care and formal adoptive arrangements represent another family constellation for many African American children. This is due in part to the crack epidemic of the 1980s, and in the 1990s, due in part to parental incarceration, death and a variety of neighborhood and social factors (Burton, 1992). Current and accurate data on the percentage of African American children residing in foster care and adoptive families are sparse, especially for the past 40 years.

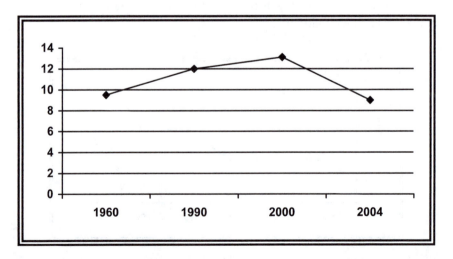

FIGURE 1.6   Percentage of African American children living in grandparent-maintained homes from 1960–2004.
Sources: U. S. Census Bureau, 1993, 2000, 2003.

Based on the available data, from the U.S. Department of Human Services, Administration for Children and Families Report (2006), in 2004 there were 517,000 children in foster care; approximately 34% of children in foster care were African American children. This percentage tends to vary by state. In states such as New Jersey, Louisiana, and Delaware, over 50% of children in foster care were African American and in major urban areas about 80% were African American (McRoy, Oglesby, & Grape, 1997).

The experiences of African American children in foster care differ significantly from their White counterparts. According to Roberts (2002), racial disparities exist at every level in the child welfare system for children of color in general and African American children in particular. That is, they enter foster care at higher rates, remain in foster care longer, experience multiple foster care placements; receive fewer services and have fewer contacts with caseworkers than their White counterparts.

To begin to address this issue, a Consortium on Racial Equality in the Child Welfare was formed by a collective of African American social workers who were concerned with the disparate treatment of African American children in the welfare system. The goal of this consortium is to monitor the treatment of children of color in the welfare system, provide cultural competence training to social workers and others who work with African American children, and to assist in the development of community initiatives on adoption and placement of African American children.

In 2004, 52,000 children were formally adopted from the public foster care system. African American children represented 32% of that number. Figure 1.7 provides comparative information on the percentage of children formally adopted in that year.

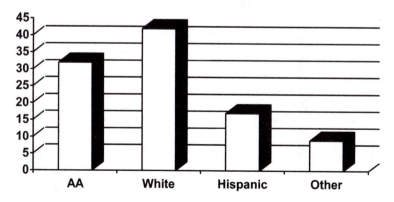

FIGURE 1.7   Percentage of children formally adopted, 2004.
Source: Administration for Children and Families: Adoption and Foster Care Analysis and Reporting System (2006).

In that same year, 118,000 children awaited adoption; 39% of the children were African American. Figure 1.8 provides comparative information on children awaiting formal adoption.

For many years, members of the African American community engaged in the practice of informal adoption of African American children. However, precise information on the percentage of African American children adopted informally, as well as information on the existing status of this practice is virtually unknown.

Presently, African American parents legally adopt the majority of African American children; however, a small percentage of African American children are adopted by White parents. This form of interracial adoption began in the U.S.; after World War II and between 1962 and 1967, approximately 10,000 African American children were transracially adopted. The National Council for Adoption estimates that 12% of all adoptions in 1993 were transracial adoptions, and current estimates suggest that approximately 1,000 African American children are adopted annually by White parents. Unfortunately few states keep detailed statistics on transracial adoption and the federal government issued the last report on transracial adoptions in 1975.

Transracial adoptions are not without controversy and have generated a great deal of debate for the past three decades. Opponents argue that White parents are ill equipped to socialize African American children about racial issues, and as a consequence, their ability to develop a healthy racial self-esteem is compromised (Taylor and Thornton, 1996). Supporters contend that the basic ingredient for healthy psychological development is a stable and healthy relationship with one's parents and not the race of the parent.

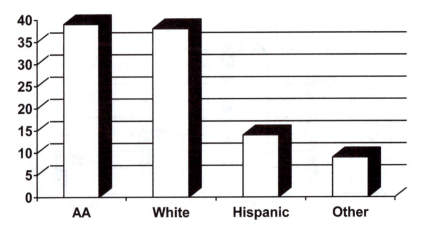

FIGURE 1.8   Percentage of children awaiting adoption, 2004.
Source: Administration for Children and Families: Adoption and Foster Care Analysis and Reporting System (2006).

SECTION THREE: ECONOMIC CONDITIONS OF AFRICAN AMERICAN CHILDREN AND THEIR FAMILIES

The economic status of African American children and their families has undergone significant changes since the early 1960s. Although the overall economic condition of the nation has improved significantly in the last 40 years (the number of families living below the poverty level decreased from 22.4% in 1960 to 12.7% in 2003), this has not been the case for African American children and their families, especially for African American children residing in mother-headed households.

Figure 1.9 provides information on the percentage of African American families with incomes below the poverty level from 1960 to 2003.

As the figure indicates, in 1960, 55% of African American families lived below the poverty level, this compares to 20% of White families; in 1970, 41.5% lived below the poverty level, in contrast, to the 10.7% of White families living below the poverty level.

In 1980, 28.9% of African American families lived below the poverty level, in contrast, only 8% of White families lived below the poverty level; in 1990, 29.2% of African American families lived below the poverty level, whereas only 8.1% of White families lived below the poverty level. In 2003 the percentage of African American families living below the poverty level decreased to 22.3%, compared to 8.1% of White families living below the poverty level. However, when those percentages are contrasted with the percentages for White families, they suggest that in any given decade, African American families are 2 to 4 times more likely than White families to be poor.

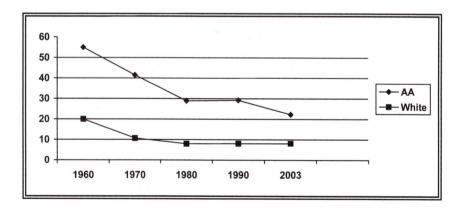

FIGURE 1.9   Percentage of African American families and White families with incomes below the poverty level.

Sources: Bureau of Census Internet website:www.census.gov/population/socdemo/ms-la/tabch-4.txt; U.S. Census Bureau Statistical Abstracts of the U.S., 2006.

The percentage of African American children living in poor families tends to vary by family structure, parental gender, and child age. That is, the majority of African American children (47.4%) who reside in mother-headed households are poor. This compares to 11% of African American children living in two-parent family homes; 20% living in grandparent homes and 27.5% living in father-headed households. African American children under the age of three are more likely than older African American children to reside in homes with incomes twice below the poverty level (U.S. Census Bureau, 2004). Furthermore, they are more likely than their counterparts from other racial and ethnic backgrounds to experience long-term or persistent poverty (Ellwood, 1990). Consequently, they are at risk for physical, academic, social, emotional and behavioral problems (Hogan & Lichter, 1995).

What factors have contributed to the change in the economic status of African American children? Some social scientists believe that this change in the economic status of African American children and their families corresponds to an increase in the number of African American children residing in mother-headed households. They contend that these households are poor, because the mother is undereducated and must rely solely on public assistance for income (O'Hare, Pollard, Mann, & Kent, 1998). The reduction in cash assistance, and the temporal restrictions placed on the receipt of cash assistance are thought to be contributing factors as well.

It may be that independent of family structure, the number of African American children residing in homes with incomes at or below the poverty level is a result of geographical factors (i.e., African American families tend to live in regions that have experienced the most economic decline), employment opportunity factors (i.e., African American children tend to reside in regions where there are few opportunities for employment for their families) and wage level factors (i.e., African Americans tend to live in communities with lower wage levels; see Box 1.1). Perhaps, a more plausible explanation is that an interaction of all of these factors has contributed to the current economic status of African American children and their families.

BOX 1.1

WHO ARE THE WELFARE FAMILIES?

The racial composition of welfare families has changed over the past 10 years. In 1990, 38% of whites, 40% of blacks, and 17% of Hispanic families were recipients of welfare support. Today, 31% of Whites, 38% of Blacks, and 25% of Hispanics are recipients of welfare.

While a disproportionate number of African American children live in families with incomes at or below the poverty level, the number of African American children residing in middle- and upper-middle-class families has increased. This is due to the improving economic conditions for some African American families and due to the increase in the number of college-educated African American parents (McAdoo, 1992). Social science research rarely focuses on the experiences of African American children from upwardly mobile or middle-class African American families (McAdoo, 2000).

PERSPECTIVES ON DEMOGRAPHICS AND AFRICAN AMERICAN CHILDREN

What does the demographic pattern just described in the preceding section tell us about African American children?

In general, the pattern informs us of the obvious as stated at the beginning of the chapter: the lives of African American children have been dynamic and undergone noteworthy changes in the past 40 years. It is our hope that these demographics will serve to frame and guide research on African American children in this new millennium.

Research on African American children, regardless of the issues, must be grounded in theories germane to African Americans. A full discussion of those theories is presented in chapter 2. Furthermore, in order to accurately assess the experiences of African American children, measures and designs must be selected for their cultural relevance as well as their internal and external validity. Finally, future educators, scholars, and practitioners must become familiar with the political, historical and contextual factors which influence the functioning and development of African American children.

The goal of this book is to stimulate thinking, reflection, and action in students of human development, who will eventually become the researchers and practitioners involved in the lives of African American children in the 21st century.

The remainder of the book is divided into eight chapters.

Chapter 2, Research Issues with African American Children, begins with a discussion of the problems inherent in current research on African American children, continues with descriptions of how different data collection methods (e.g. interview, survey, naturalistic observations) and designs (e.g. cross sectional, longitudinal, ethnographic) may influence the research conducted on African American children as well as the interpretation of the results and concludes with a discussion of issues of reliability, validity and ethics as they pertain to African American children and their families.

Chapter 3, African American Children and Health Issues, is divided into two major sections. The first section provides information on the health challenges that confront African American children and the second section discusses access to health care.

Chapter 4, Mental Health and Racial Identity, is divided into two broad sections. Section one identifies the risk factors that predispose African American children to mental health problems, and includes a discussion of resiliency, assessment, diagnosis, and treatment for some African American children. The last half of the chapter focuses on the development of racial identity in African American children.

Chapter 5, Education and African American Children, presents information on the education of African American children. The chapter starts with a discussion of the impact of desegregation on their educational attainment. The chapter continues with a discussion of both private and public schools that enable African American children to excel academically. The chapter concludes with a discussion of African American children and early educational programs.

Chapter 6, Language and Literacy, begins with a discussion of the controversial decision by the Oakland School Board to use African American Vernacular English (AAVE) as a tool to improve students' standardized test performance. The chapter includes a comparison of the features of AAVE and Standard English, a discussion of the specific language and literacy issues confronting African American children, and a description of the language and literacy intervention programs designed for African American children. The chapter concludes with a discussion of language assessment and children and perspectives on language issues.

Chapter 7, Moral Development, begins with a general discussion of the pros and cons of using Piaget's, Kohlberg's and Turiel's theories to explain the moral development/behavior of African American children. This chapter includes sections on the prosocial, aggressive, and violent behavior among African American children. The chapter concludes with a discussion of the sociopolitical ramifications of moral development, especially as it relates to African American juvenile delinquents and incarcerated youth.

Chapter 8, Social Contexts in the Lives of African American Children: Family and Peers, presents information on the various theoretical perspectives guiding research on African American children and their families, including a discussion of the research on African American children within their family and peer groups.

The book finishes with chapter 9, Epilogue: Where Do We Go From Here?, which highlights the critical issues discussed in the text and offers suggestions for future research on African American children in the 21st century.

ADDITIONAL READINGS

Briggs, L. (2003). Mother, child, race, nation: The visual iconography of race and the politics of transnational and transracial adoption. *Gender & History, 15,* 179–200.

Children's Defense Fund, The State of American's Children Yearbook (Washington, DC: Children's Defense Fund, 2003)

Hollinger, J. (1998). A guide to the Multiethnic Placement Act of 1994 as Amended by the Interethnic Adoption Provisions of 1996. (Washington, DC, ABA Center on Children and the Law).

Roberts, D. (2002). *Shattered bonds: The color of child welfare.* New York: Basic.

Routh, D. K. (1994). Impact of poverty on children, youth and families. *Journal of Clinical Child Psychology, 23,* 1–10.

CHAPTER 2

Research Issues With African American Children

OVERVIEW: THE IMPORTANCE OF STUDYING DEVELOPMENTAL RESEARCH METHODS

A major criticism of developmental research has been its focus on Eurocentric values in theories and methodology. Contemporary developmental psychology has begun to recognize the importance of culture in child development. Unfortunately, most developmentalists are not trained to examine the role of culture in child development (Greenfield & Cocking, 1994). As a result, many developmentalists promote research that derives from their own cultural perspective (often middle-class and Eurocentric), or from the dominant Eurocentric perspective that is perpetuated by many mainstream psychology journals. Thus, the result is that our knowledge base in developmental psychology is founded largely upon the perspective of middle-class European-American children. It is just as important to value the unique perspective of African American children within the field of developmental psychology. This chapter provides a systematic and objective focus of research issues in African American child development. First, we present some of the major problems associated with different research designs and we discuss the effects of using these particular research designs with African American children. Second, we provide recommendations on how to conduct research with African American children that is both culturally and ethically sensitive. Third, we highlight the central questions in developmental science and discuss a few developmental theories that are particularly relevant to African American children.

INSIDER'S VOICE: THE NEED FOR MORE RESEARCH ON AFRICAN AMERICAN CHILDREN

Despite the trend towards interdisciplinarity, research on the positive impact of the cultural context in African American child development remains relatively sparse. The reason for this is not clear, and many child development researchers agree there is an apparent need for more research involving the life stories of children of color. Even with this agreement and the persistent calls to action for more research involving various racial and ethnic groups (Comer, 1988; Dumas, Rollock, Prinz, Hops, & Blechman, 1999; Ogbu, 1992) there is a continuing struggle to find published psychological literature highlighting cultural issues in the lives of African American children (Graham, 1992; Sue, 1999).

Systematic investigations of research concerning African American children are limited. However, McLoyd (1991), and Belgrave and Allison (2006) note a range of historical and ongoing concerns regarding the methods used in studies of African American child development.

SECTION ONE: PROBLEMS—METHODOLOGICAL CONSTRAINTS IN RESEARCH DESIGNS

Much of child development research that uses African American subjects has several methodological limitations, such as deficiencies in internal and external validity. Some of the common threats to validity in research with African American children will be discussed within the context of race-comparative, cross-sectional, and longitudinal designs.

From the standpoint of experimental design, race-comparative studies are flawed. We cannot randomly assign children to majority or minority status groups, thus the research is confounded in a number of ways, such as education, socioeconomic status, and language.

Race-comparative studies compare children of different racial groups on a set of measures or factors, whereas race homogenous studies descriptively examine factors within a single racial group to describe how members of a single racial group behave and develop (Belgrave & Allison, 2006). In general, the percentage of studies based on a race-comparative model has declined since the early 1980s (McLoyd & Randolph, 1985). However, an examination of studies published from 1970 to 1989 found the number of race-comparative articles in two of the leading psychology journals *Developmental Psychology* and *Journal of Educational Psychology* was 65% and 78%, respectively (Graham, 1992). The race-comparative model has influenced race-homogeneous studies. Numerous articles published between 1927 and 1977 in leading social science journals, with samples of exclusively African American children, used standardized measures normed on European-American children (Myers, Rana, & Harris, 1979). Some argue that the use of standardized norms on African American children was justified because it allowed for the direct comparison of findings from studies based on European-American samples.

Cultural deficit models based on comparative research have long been in studies to identify, analyze, and explain similarities and differences across societies. Typically, the race-comparative model is not criticized for highlighting parallels and disparities between groups, but rather it is disparaged because of its failure to understand the underlying causes of these differences (McLoyd, 1991). According to psychologists Carolyn Tucker and Keith Herman (2002), several problems arise when researchers apply a race-comparative research design to African American children. Researchers deny the importance of culture when they attempt to use a universalist one-size-fits-all cultural model to children of varying ethnic and racial groups (Nagayama Hall, 2001). Thus, researchers who adopt a universalist approach may fail to develop culturally sensitive hypotheses and measures (Nagayama Hall, 2001), or they may overlook meaningful socioeconomic status differences (Betancourt & Lopez, 1993), or they may portray differences as deficits that need to be corrected (Oyemade & Rosser, 1980) to match the non-Latino White American middle-class standard from which the majority of the psychological literature is based.

> In sum, comparative studies are criticized for the following three reasons. First, they point to the ways in which African American children do not behave rather than how they do behave, yielding data that are limited in their informative value, virtually useless in generating theory and ultimately, capable of supporting only superficial analyses of individual differences and their determinants among African Americans (Howard & Scott, 1981; Myers et al., 1979). Second, they foster indirectly the views that African American children are typically interpreted, if not by the author, by a significant portion of the readers, as deficiencies or pathologies in the former rather than in cultural relativistic or systemic terms (Hall, 1974; Myers et al., 1979; Washington & McLoyd, 1982). Finally, they promote person-blame interpretations of social problems rather than thoughtful treatments of the roles of situational and systemic factors, since they emphasize the race of the subjects or personal characteristics associated with the race (Caplan & Nelson, 1973).
>
> (McLoyd, 1991, p. 424)

Typically, developmental psychologists are concerned with fundamental issues in development: (1) the normative changes that occur in developing indi-

Cross-sectional design				
Age groups (in years)	5	7	9	11
Date of birth	2001	1999	1997	1995
Time of assessment	2006			

Longitudinal design				
Age (in years)	5	7	9	11
Date of birth	2001			
Time of assessment	2006	2008	2010	2012

FIGURE 2.1   Developmental designs.

viduals and (2) individual differences in these developmental functions (Baltes & Nesselroade, 1979). In general, developmental designs, such as cross-sectional and longitudinal (see Figure 2.1), focus on three variables: age, cohort, and time of assessment (Schaie, 1965). However, each design has its own strengths and weaknesses. In the following sections, we will examine the use of cross-sectional and longitudinal designs and discuss some of the unique challenges researchers might encounter when using these designs with African American samples.

The cross-sectional design is popular among developmental researchers. A cross-sectional design compares different cohorts that differ in age groups of individuals on a measure at one point in time. This design has many advantages such as efficiency, minimal attrition and practice effects, and imperviousness to any changes in the field of child development.

There are many disadvantages in using cross-sectional designs, including the threat to internal validity, which refers to the extent to which changes in the dependent variable can confidently be attributed to the influence of the independent variable rather than the potential influence of confounding variables (Stangor, 2004). These threats may affect research findings on African American children in unique ways, such as selection bias, history confound, and reactivity. Table 2.1 provides a sample of some of these concerns.

One should be particularly sensitive with using standardized assessments based on a cross-sectional design due to selection biases. There is not a problem when an individual is compared to himself, but many measures have historically been normed on middle-class White samples. African American children are integrated only to the extent to which they represent a stratified sample based on the larger American demographic context. Although this inclusion allows comparisons between individuals and the overall American norms for all children, considering the diversity within and between cultural groups, it is often difficult to fully understand the implications of comparisons of individual African Americans to overall national norms (Belgrave & Allison, 2006).

Cross-sectional studies do not permit researchers to uncover findings about how change occurs in development nor does it measure individual stability over time (Miller, 1998). It is not possible to determine if differences between two groups are due to typical developmental changes or due to historical or cultural effects resulting in a history or cohort confound. Because of the historical and cultural impact that race and ethnicity has on the lives of African American children, the findings in many cross-sectional studies that use age norms for specific measures of development remain questionable.

An additional threat to internal validity in cross-sectional studies is reactivity. This confound occurs when the research environment causes changes in a participant's behavior or thinking. Reactivity may occur in a lab setting or in field research. Some African American children may be uncomfortable or pay more attention to unfamiliar laboratory settings and equipment, and the strange people. As a result, it is important to be sensitive to the complexities of race, class, and culture of the group being studied in order to structure the research setting in such a way to eliminate as much subject reactivity as possible.

Research that utilizes the longitudinal design compares the same individuals in a single age group on various measures over time. This design has many advantages such as the ability to document actual change within a particular group over time (no selection bias), and it allows for predictions about future behavior. The focus on intraindividual development make the longitudinal design better suited to assess individual stability or individual change.

Unfortunately, many of the advantages of the cross-sectional design are potential disadvantages in the longitudinal research design, such as practice effects and changes to the field of child development. Furthermore, many of the potential problems, such as instrumentation and history-age confounds, noted in cross-sectional designs may actually be enhanced by the use of longitudinal designs with African Americans (see Table 2.1).

Longitudinal studies are not as common as cross-sectional studies for many reasons. They require a large time-commitment on the part of the participants, they are more expensive to carry out, and the theoretical relevance and instruments used may become outdated. Another threat to internal validity based on longitudinal designs including African American samples must be noted. Selective dropout (attrition) is a common threat, especially among studies involving low income African Americans and their children. Many of the social and economic factors affecting this population (i.e., lack of social services and financial support, and residential mobility) may make it challenging for researchers to keep track of these individuals over an extended period of time (Belgrave & Allison, 2006).

TABLE 2.1   Threats to Internal Validity With African American Child Samples

		Cross-sectional	Longitudinal
Selection bias	Participants come from nonequivalent settings. Are differences between comparison groups attributable to preexisting conditions or by exposure to the variable of interest?	√	
History/cohort/age	Individual differences and experiences between participants. Did participants' earlier experiences produce an effect or is it due to the manipulation of an independent variable (IV)?	√	√
Selective dropout (attrition)	Participants with certain characteristics may select to withdraw from the study at different rates. Are differences due to effect of the IV or to differential drop out rates?	√	√
Instrumentation	Unintended changes in measures and/or research settings. Are observed changes due to the instrument or experimenters' behaviors over the course of the study or are they a result of changes from exposure to the IV?		√
Reactivity	Unintended changes in participants, usually from problems with instrumentation or researchers. Did participants' interactions with the measures and the experimenters produce a change or is it due to the manipulated variable?	√	√
Testing	Repeated exposure to same measure may affect performance. Did familiarity with the instrument produce changes in the dependent variable (DV)?		√
Race/social class	Assumption that low socioeconomic status (SES) African American children is comparable to middle-SES European American children. Are outcomes due to IV or a result of race or SES differences?	√	√
Experimenter race	Postulation that race of experimenter is not influential. Does race of experimenter contribute to error variance?	√	√

Sometimes the internal validity in a study is threatened by a race-social class confound. A large percentage of developmental research with African Americans largely centers on lower-income and urban samples, rather than middle-class or rural groups (Belgrave & Allison, 2006). As a result, many race-comparative studies compare lower income African American children with middle-class and/or lower income non-Hispanic white children. This creates a serious confound between race and social class.

The failure to account for the race of the experimenter (i.e., examiner, interviewer, and therapist) is another major threat to the internal validity of many published studies on African American child development (Graham, 1992; McLoyd, 1998; and McLoyd & Randolph, 1984; 1985). The concern here is more about the methodological errors, which may be a result from the absence of this information, rather than the negative impact that White experimenters have on the behaviors and cognitions of African American children. Some work has indicated that White researchers do not negatively affect performance (Graziano, Varca, & Levy, 1982), and an examination of the presence of an African American experimenter on performance in African American children is warranted. Without the proper specification of race it is challenging to examine its influence. This is a complex and pertinent issue in child development research that is in need of further consideration.

INSIDER'S VOICE: WHERE HAVE WE GONE WRONG?

Our modus operandi is to assume that the work is universally applicable; the burden of proof is placed on researchers concerned about race, ethnicity, and bias to show that there are ethnic differences. Whatever happened to the scientific notion of skepticism, where little is taken for granted, where conclusions are drawn from evidence and not from assumptions? We have not followed good scientific principles in assuming that findings from research on one population can be generalized to other populations.

Stanley Sue (American Psychologist, 1999)

The external validity, which is the ability to generalize the results beyond your sample, of many studies on African American children, is questionable regardless of the type of research design. A major reason for low external validity is due to the lack of research on African American children. The demand for internal validity far outweighs the expectations for external validity in the majority of published research (Alloy, Abramson, Raniere, & Dyller, 1999). Attempts to increase internal validity often enhances the scientific rigor of the research study, but it often comes at a price—a decrease in external validity. This demand for internal validity makes it more challenging to conduct scientifically rigorous research with some African American populations. Researchers who work with ethnic minority populations may encounter difficulties with recruiting participants, developing valid measures, using valid theories, and training research assistants to be culturally sensitive (Sue, 1999). These factors may discourage many scientists to initiate research that aims to uncover the complexity of African American child development, which fuels the problems associated with external validity.

Past research views the African American child from a homogenous perspective, rather than heterogeneously. More research is needed to uncover the complexities of African American child development, but it is just as important to create a knowledge base that extends beyond the stereotypical urban, lower income community of color. We need to create a more balanced representation of the African American child, one that includes varying social classes, educational experiences, and residential communities (especially suburban and rural). According to McLoyd (1998), the external validity of many studies on African American children is highly variable because of the lack of specification of the race and/or social class of the subjects (including the White comparison group). Some common threats to the external validity in research with African American children are listed in Table 2.2.

Since there is a widening divide between middle-class and lower-income African Americans, it is essential to provide an objective specification of social status given the economic, educational, and cultural complexity of African Americans, even in race-homogenous studies. As mentioned earlier, a content analysis by Graham (1992) noted trends in six APA journals (including *Developmental Psychology* and the *Journal of Educational Psychology*) over two decades (1970–1989). Appropriate social class assessment was based on direct measures (i.e., Duncan, Hollingshead, and Warner scales); and indirect measures, such as census data and school records. Inappropriate assessments were based on the researchers' subjective impressions of the participants' social class standing. As seen in Table 2.3, the percentage of articles from *Developmental Psychology* and the *Journal of Educational Psy-*

TABLE 2.2   Threats to External Validity With African American Child Samples

Lack of research	Limited amount of research on middle-class, and rural African American children.
Race of subject	Race and/or ethnicity of the subjects are not specified.
Social class	Social class of participants is not indicated.

chology that collected social class data from African American samples in an appropriate manner was 40% and 44% respectively. Unfortunately, social class was assessed inappropriately in the majority of the articles on African Americans during this period.

SECTION TWO: CONDUCTING CULTURALLY RELEVANT RESEARCH WITH AFRICAN AMERICAN CHILDREN

The Need for Culturally Sensitive Research With African American Children

Historically, the concept of culture as a source of variation in the socialization and development of American children has resulted in a complex interplay between politics and economics (McLoyd, 2004). During the 1960s and 1970s, critics often dismissed the examination of culture because it decontextualized the social and economic problems (e.g., poverty, differences in intellectual achievements, and school performance) experienced by many African American children. As a result, cultural explanations for developmental

TABLE 2.3.   Methodological Characteristics of Articles on African Americans in Six APA Journals (1970–1989)

		\multicolumn{8}{c}{Characteristic}							
		Race comparative[a]		Socioeconomic status measure[b]		Race of experimenter[c]		African American experimenter[d]	
Journal	No.	No.	%	No.	%	No.	%	No.	%
DP	111	72	64.9	40	36.0	39	35.1	24	21.6
JEP	108	84	77.8	44	40.7	24	22.2	18	16.7
JCCP	90	67	74.4	20	22.2	10	11.1	9	10.0
JAP	77	60	77.9	27	35.1	13	16.9	9	11.7
JCP	75	40	53.3	29	38.7	28	37.3	26	34.7
JPSP	65	58	89.2	16	27.6	27	41.5	21	32.3
Total	526	381	72.4	176	33.5	141	26.8	107	20.3

Note: DP=Developmental Psychology, JEP=Journal of Educational Psychology, JCCP=Journal of Consulting and Clinical Psychology, JAP=Journal of Applied Psychology, JCP=Journal of Counseling Psychology, JPSP=Journal of Personality and Social Psychology.
[a]Number and percentage of articles that were race comparative.
[b]Number and percentage of articles that reported a measure of subject socioeconomic status.
[c]Number and percentage of articles that reported experimenter race.
[d]Number and percentage of articles that included African American experimenters.
From *American Psychologist* (1992)

processes in African American children often were devalued, or were viewed as so-called cultural disadvantages or deficits (Jencks, 1992; Moynihan, 1965) in mainstream developmental research (Tulkin, 1972). In this section, we offer recommendations on how to make up for some of the negative and inaccurate research that has painted a false picture of the African American child. Our recommendations for current and future research on African American children include the following components: (1) use relevant conceptual frameworks, (2) examine development in context, and (3) analyze the central characteristics in developmental science with African American children.

Conceptual Frameworks and Interdisciplinarity

The complexity of African American culture suggests a need for expanded conceptual and research frameworks (Tillman, 2002). Research published in many mainstream child development journals claims scientific objectivity; however, in many cases there continues to be limitations in theory and interpretation of findings for African American children.

In the past couple of decades, the study of child development has become more interdisciplinary. The research in the field has focused on the interaction of a variety of disciplines, such as anthropology, biology, education, linguistics, neuroscience, and sociology. An interdisciplinary examination of child development can provide insight into various pathways of development often overlooked by a one-dimensional focus of study. The use of both quantitative research and qualitative research (e.g., case study, ethnography) approaches may also be helpful in the study of African American child development (Sue, 1999).

In spite of the increasing ethnic diversity across the United States, there is paucity of research literature focusing on ethnic minorities. It is difficult to develop culturally sensitive models of development when there is insufficient research with African Americans (Tucker & Herman, 2002). The solution to this issue is more than a matter of increasing the number of ethnically diverse participants (Dumas et al., 1999). Culturally sensitive theories are rooted in research that matches African Americans with similar socioeconomic status and values with other African Americans that the theories are targeted to (Tucker & Herman, 2002). How do we conduct research that is culturally aware? Dumas et al. 1999 purport that cultural issues must be addressed at *every* stage of the research process. We should also focus on within group (racial/ethnic) differences rather than across group differences (comparative). At a societal level, we need to increase research funding for projects on minority youth, increase minority representation among faculty and graduate students in academia, and offer more diverse courses in psychology programs at both the undergraduate and graduate levels (McLoyd, 1998; Sue, 1999).

The Role of Context in African American Child Development

Today, the majority of studies in developmental psychology occurs within a single cultural context or they ignore the role of context in the lives of children. Results published from the limited number of studies with participants varying in race and/or contextual variables (such as socioeconomic status or ethnicity) and findings are assumed to be generalizable; but generalizable to whom?

According to Robert Sternberg and Elena Grigorenko (2004), most developmental psychology research is acontextual. There are several reasons for this finding: (1) acontextual research is easier to complete and publish, (2) the findings are easier to interpret, (3) it is cheaper to conduct, (4) it may involve more sophistication that is experimental and, (5) it much easier to tease apart than a muddled contextual study.

Research needs to account for the cultural context so that we can characterize people in their everyday lives. The majority of developmental research treats children as if they exist devoid of culture; so we overlook many important points about development of all children, regardless of race and/or ethnicity. Sternberg and Grigorenko (2004) make the following statement:

> The question is whether we want the future of the field to reflect a largely middle-class North American view of North American development that is offered as something more or, instead, whether we want the future to reflect an increasingly interconnected set of cultures around the world that are diverse and that share common aspects but also retain their own aspects.

The roles of context and culture in the lives of African American children merit further examination. That is, do we envision a largely middle-class European American standard to represent continually the rich lives of African American children? We also want to see our children relish in diverse cultural experiences that are valued for their many similarities and differences.

The Relationship to African American Child Development and Central Characteristics in Developmental Psychology

Despite the great variety in the ways that researchers in developmental science approach development, they agree upon four characteristics that define developmental characteristics in children. We note the importance of these characteristics; and believe that careful scrutiny of these issues is a step in the advancement of knowledge in African American child development.

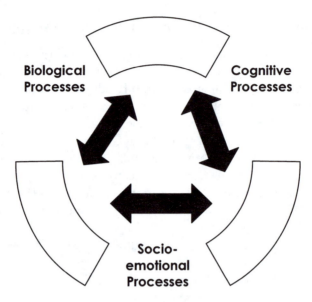

FIGURE 2.2   Factors in multidimensional development.

1. *Development is Multidimensional.* Development is comprised of biological, cognitive, and socioemotional factors. The central premise of this process is that development is multifaceted and dynamic with each dimension affecting the other. Researchers, programs, and intervention efforts in African American child development must consider the full array of needs for children in developing their goals and the strategies to achieve them as shown in Figure 2.2.

2. *Development is Continuous/Discontinuous.* As shown in Figure 2.3, is development a gradual, continuous process of change, or it is viewed as a sudden period of rapid change with the surfacing of new thought and behavior? This question may lead researchers to explore the efficacy of stage theories normed on White middle-class relationship to African American children particularly in the cognitive and social realms of their development.

3. *Development is Contextual.* The child responds to and acts on contexts that include biological heritage and physical settings, as well as historical, social, and cultural contexts. Interest and concern over the impact of contexts on childhood have prompted many developmental researchers to consider the impact of social class, racism, childcare, schooling, parenting practices, and peer interaction on African American child development. The examination of culture reminds us of how different life experiences may create different developmental niches for children, and it provides more complete conclusions regarding certain populations (Sternberg & Grigorenko, 2004).

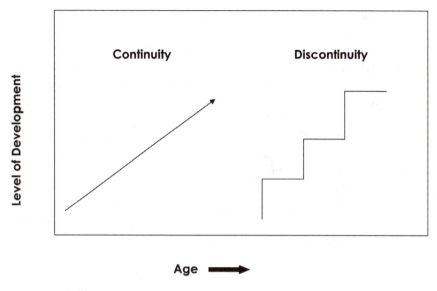

FIGURE 2.3   Continuity and discontinuity in development.

4. *Development is Plastic.* To what extent is it possible for the child to change, as the result of a purposeful intervention or an accidental exposure? Plasticity is conceptualized as within-person variability (Lerner, 1984). A critical period is a period of growth during which particular biological or environmental events must happen for so-called normal development to proceed (Cole, Cole, & Lightfoot, 2005). A sensitive period refers to a time when a child is particularly receptive to certain kinds of environmental experiences. The notion of plasticity and an examination of issues involving critical and sensitive periods in the lives of African American children warrant attention.

Developmentalists are devoted to examining these characteristics in children. The results of these processes provide insight into the developmental lives of children, and may present solid guidelines for how to promote healthy development for African American children in particular.

Ethical Considerations With African American Child Participants

Protecting the rights of research participants is a challenge because the potential for harm is often obscure (Gall, Gall, & Borg, 2005). Child development researchers must make a series of ethical decisions at every phase of the research process from conceptualization to the interpretation of findings. These decisions made at each phase are important because they determine the methodological techniques and procedures used with participants. This is important for all populations, but it merits special consideration when working with underserved or vulnerable samples of African American children. The ethical standards for research with children, as outlined by the Society for Research in Child Development (SRCD), are listed in Box 2.1.

Every researcher must weigh the risks and benefits of a research project (Graue & Walsh, 1998), which leads to the inevitable question of whether the research should be conducted or not. Today, Institutional Review Boards (IRBs) are responsible for making this decision at colleges and universities. The backgrounds (such as race, ethnicity, social class, etc.) of many IRB members may vary from the characteristics of some of the populations cited in the research protocols, and many may hold stereotypical views, which may distort their perception of ethical issues involving these populations (Scott-Jones, 1994).

Furthermore, the race-comparative framework and cultural deficit models that plagued developmental, educational, and clinical intervention research for decades may have contributed to the suspicions of many African American populations. As a result, this may be a contributing factor in the difficulty to recruiting participants for projects. If one seeks to conduct research with certain communities, then it is essential that they are treated with cultural sensitivity and are assured that the research is beneficial for both the individual (Scott-Jones, 1994) and the community.

SECTION THREE: THEORIES

There is a general understanding among developmental psychologists about the utility of various research methods, and the employment of ethical standards in child development research regardless of race or social class of the participant. However, the theoretical framework one uses is left for the researcher to decide. Developmentalists have varied historical and cultural histories that influence their theoretical orientations. As a result, it is not surprising to find that two child development researchers may interpret the high academic achievement among a sample of African American fifth graders in fundamentally different ways. There is not a single theoretical model that can account for African American child development. Thus, we propose four theories (i.e., Sociocultural, Ecological Systems, Phenomenological Variant of the Ecological Systems Theory, and the Integrative Model of Development) that are applicable to the examination of development in its cultural context among African American children. Brief descriptions of these four theories are presented in the next section.

BOX 2.1

Ethical Standards For Research With Children

SRCD Principle 1. NON-HARMFUL PROCEDURES: The investigator should use no research procedure that may harm the child either physically or psychologically. The investigator is also obligated at all times to use the least stressful research procedure whenever possible. Psychological harm in particular instances may be difficult to define; nevertheless, its definition and means for reducing or eliminating it remain the responsibility of the investigator. When the investigator is in doubt about the possible harmful effects of the research procedures, consultation should be sought from others. When harm seems inevitable, the investigator is obligated to find other means of obtaining the information or to abandon the research. Instances may, nevertheless, rise in which exposing the child to stressful conditions may be necessary if diagnostic or therapeutic benefits to the child are associated with the research. In such instances careful deliberation by an Institutional Review Board should be sought.

SRCD Principle 2. INFORMED CONSENT: Before seeking consent or assent from the child, the investigator should inform the child of all features of the research that may affect his or her willingness to participate and should answer the child's questions in terms appropriate to the child's comprehension. The investigator should respect the child's freedom to choose to participate in the research or not by giving the child the opportunity to give or not give assent to participation as well as to choose to discontinue participation at any time. Assent means that the child shows some form of agreement to participate without necessarily comprehending the full significance of the research necessary to give informed consent. Investigators working with infants should take special effort to explain the research procedures to the parents and be especially sensitive to any indicators of discomfort in the infant. In spite of the paramount importance of obtaining consent, instances can arise in which consent or any kind of contact with the participant would make the research impossible to carry out. Non-intrusive field research is a common example. Conceivably, such research can be carried out ethically if it is conducted in public places, participants' anonymity is totally protected, and there are no foreseeable negative consequences to the participant. However, judgments on whether such research is ethical in particular circumstances should be made in consultation with an Institutional Review Board.

SRCD Principle 3. PARENTAL CONSENT: The informed consent of parents, legal guardians or those who act in loco parentis (e.g., teachers, superintendents of institutions) similarly should be obtained, preferably in writing.

Informed consent requires that parents or other responsible adults be informed of all the features of the research that may affect their willingness to allow the child to participate. This information should include the profession and institution affiliation of the investigator. Not only should the right of the responsible adults to refuse consent be respected, but also they should be informed that they may refuse to participate without incurring any penalty to them or to the child.

SRCD Principle 4. ADDITIONAL CONSENT: The informed consent of any persons, such as school teachers for example, whose interaction with the child is the subject of the study should also be obtained. As with the child and parents or guardians informed consent requires that the persons interacting with the child during the study be informed of all features of the research which may affect their willingness to participate. All questions posed by such persons should be answered and the persons should be free to choose to participate or not, and to discontinue participation at any time.

SRCD Principle 5. INCENTIVES: Incentives to participate in a research project must be fair and must not unduly exceed the range of incentives that the child normally experiences. Whatever incentives are used, the investigator should always keep in mind that the greater the possible effects of the investigation on the child, the greater is the obligation to protect the child's welfare and freedom.

SRCD Principle 6. DECEPTION: Although full disclosure of information during the procedure of obtaining consent is the ethical ideal, a particular study may necessitate withholding certain information or deception. Whenever withholding information or deception is judged to be essential to the conduct of the study, the investigator should satisfy research colleagues that such judgment is correct. If withholding information or deception is practiced, and there is reason to believe that the research participants will be negatively affected by it, adequate measures should be taken after the study to ensure the participant's understanding of the reasons for the deception. Investigators whose research is dependent upon deception should make an effort to employ deception methods that have no known negative effects on the child or the child's family.

SRCD Principle 7. ANONYMITY: To gain access to institutional records, the investigator should obtain permission from responsible authorities in charge of records. Anonymity of the information should be preserved and no information used other than that for which permission was obtained. It is the investigator's responsibility to ensure that responsible authorities do, in fact, have the confidence of the participant and that they bear some degree of responsibility in giving such permission.

SRCD Principle 8. MUTUAL RESPONSIBILITIES: From the beginning of each research investigation, there should be clear agreement between the investigator and the parents, guardians or those who act in loco parentis, and the child, when appropriate, that defines the responsibilities of each. The investigator has the obligation to honor all promises and commitments of the agreement.

SRCD Principle 9. JEOPARDY: When, in the course of research, information comes to the investigator's attention that may jeopardize the child's well-being, the investigator has a responsibility to discuss the information with the parents or guardians and with those expert in the field in order that they may arrange the necessary assistance for the child.

SRCD Principle 10. UNFORESEEN CONSEQUENCES: When research procedures result in undesirable consequences for the participant that were previously unforeseen, the investigator should immediately employ appropriate measures to correct these consequences, and should redesign the procedures if they are to be included in subsequent studies.

SRCD Principle 11. CONFIDENTIALITY: The investigator should keep in confidence all information obtained about research participants. The participants' identity should be concealed in written and verbal reports of the results, as well as in informal discussion with students and colleagues. When a possibility exists that others may gain access to such information, this possibility, together with the plans for protecting confidentiality, should be explained to the participants as part of the procedure of obtaining informed consent.

SRCD Principle 12. INFORMING PARTICIPANTS: Immediately after the data are collected, the investigator should clarify for the research participant any misconceptions that may have arisen. The investigator also recognizes a duty to report general findings to participants in terms appropriate to their understanding. Where scientific or humane values justify withholding information, every effort should be made so that withholding the information has no damaging consequences for the participant.

SRCD Principle 13. REPORTING RESULTS: Because the investigator's words may carry unintended weight with parents and children, caution should be exercised in reporting results, making evaluative statements, or giving advice.

SRCD Principle 14. IMPLICATIONS OF FINDINGS: Investigators should be mindful of the social, political and human implications of their research and should be especially careful in the presentation of findings from the research. This principle, however, in no way denies investigators the right to pursue any area of research or the right to observe proper standards of scientific reporting.

SRCD Principle 15. SCIENTIFIC MISCONDUCT: Misconduct is defined as the fabrication or falsification of data, plagiarism, misrepresentation, or other practices that seriously deviate from those that are commonly accepted within the scientific community for proposing, conducting, analyzing, or reporting research. It does not include unintentional errors or honest differences in interpretation of data. The Society shall provide vigorous leadership in the pursuit of scientific investigation that is based on the integrity of the investigator and the honesty of research and will not tolerate the presence of scientific misconduct among its members. It shall be the responsibility of the voting members of Governing Council to reach a decision about the possible expulsion of members found guilty of scientific misconduct.

SRCD Principle 16. PERSONAL MISCONDUCT: Personal misconduct that results in a criminal conviction of a felony may be sufficient grounds for a member's expulsion from the Society. The relevance of the crime to the purposes of the Society should be considered by the Governing Council in reaching a decision about the matter. It shall be the responsibility of the voting members of Governing Council to reach a decision about the possible expulsion of members found guilty of personal misconduct.

The principles listed above were published in the 1990–91 Directory, except for Principles 15 and 16, first published in the Fall 1991 Newsletter from the Society for Research in Child Development.

Vygotsky's Sociocultural Theory

Lev Vygotsky (1896–1934) viewed child development as the active construction of knowledge. His Sociocultural cognitive theory underscores that children's behaviors are shaped by their social and cultural contexts. Knowledgeable members of society help children master culturally meaningful activities, knowledge, and skills. Gradually, communication in this exchange is incorporated into the child's thinking. Once children internalize the essential features of these cultural dialogues, they can use these diverse skills embedded in them to accomplish tasks of their own.

Over the past 20 years Vygotsky's theory has expanded into the fields of cultural diversity and educational practice (Kozulin, Gindis, Ageyev, & Miller, 2003). His work provides an excellent theoretical framework for examining the cultural and social variations in learning among African American children.

Bronfenbrenner's Bioecological Systems Theory

Similar to Vygotsky, Urie Bronfenbrenner (1917–2005) highlighted the importance of the interaction between factors in a child's maturing biological, peer, family, and community environments, and the societal contexts in development. Any changes or conflict in any one of the ecological contexts will affect the other layers. Bronfenbrenner believed that development occurs within five environmental systems or ecological contexts, which involve direct interactions with individuals to more global interactions with one's culture.

As shown in Figure 2.4, the five types of ecological contexts include the following: (1) the *microsystem* is the lowest level of the environment. It includes the setting for a child's behavior and the activities, participants, and roles in that setting (e.g., home with parents, home with siblings, school, and neighborhood with peers); (2) the *mesosystem* is the level of the environment that reflects the connections among microsystems (e.g. between a child's home and school); (3) the *exosystem* is the level of the environment that includes settings that children do not enter but that affect them indirectly (e.g., their parents' workplace, TV and other mass media); (4) the *macrosystem* is the most global level of the environment, which describes the consistencies in lower-level systems across a society or a culture (e.g., cultural values, customs, etc.); and (5) the *chronosystem* reflects the patterns of stability (historical) and change in children's environments over time. In other words, this level considers life transitions and its effects on children. It is interesting to note that Bronfenbrenner (1986) added the chronosystem context more than 10 years after he first proposed the Bioecological Systems Framework.

Bronfenbrenner's theory is quite useful with African American children. This model can help provide culturally sensitive assessments and intervention

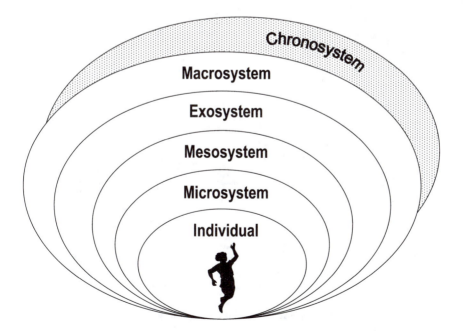

FIGURE 2.4   Bronfenbrenner's bioecological systems theory.

research strategies (Sanchez, 1995). This model challenges researchers to examine the impact of complex social/environmental problems, which in many contexts have negative consequences for African American children from various ethnic groups and social class backgrounds.

Spencer, Dupree, and Hartmann (1997) introduce a framework that combines phenomenology with Bronfenbrenner's bioecological systems approach (see Figure 2.5). According to Spencer (1982, 1985), the Phenomenological Variant to the Ecological Systems Theory (PVEST) allows for an individual's intersubjective understanding of developmental changes in social cognitive processes, and the role context in the lives of African American adolescents in particular. The findings from this model predict the importance of the relationship between perceived social supports and learning attitude, especially for African American males (Spencer et al., 1997). Thus, this model is important to the development of interventions aimed to create better life outcomes, particularly for African American adolescents.

Integrative Conceptual Model of Child Development

This proposed model integrates previously sociodevelopmental frameworks with social class, ethnicity, and race as the *nucleus* rather than the periphery of a theoretical formulation of children's development (Coll et al., 1996). As

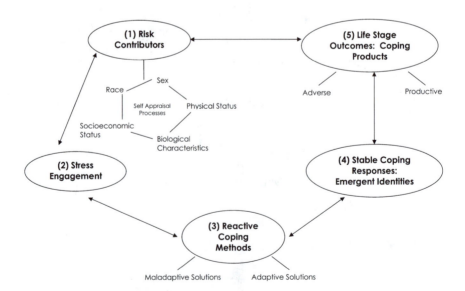

FIGURE 2.5   A phenomenological variant of the ecological systems theory (PVEST). Adapted from Spencer (1997).

seen in Figure 2.6, the Integrative Model focuses on minority children's and their families' experiences with racism, prejudice, oppression, discrimination, and segregation. Furthermore, the model focuses on the following premises: (1) the naiveté of theorists and researchers have led to the understanding of various ethnic groups; (2) the buffering role that family and kin play in the developmental processes of children of color; (3) the need to examine the roles of various contexts (outside of the family) on the development of African American and other youth of color; and finally, (4) the model emphasizes the importance of examining health and education as outcomes in development, rather than just as important contributors. This projected model serves as an alternative to traditional and culturally insensitive assessments of African American children.

PERSPECTIVES ON RESEARCH AND THEORIES

Over the past 10 to 15 years, we have witnessed an improvement in the psychological research on African American children. We have begun the process of moving past cultural deficit and pathology models to an emphasis on valuing the diversity of African American children within larger socio-ecological contexts. It is also important for developmental researchers to examine the lives of African American children, within and between groups, with a cultural lens, and they should integrate these cultural contextual factors into the creation of new models.

There is a growing trend towards interdisciplinarity in child development research. This may be particularly relevant to research on African American

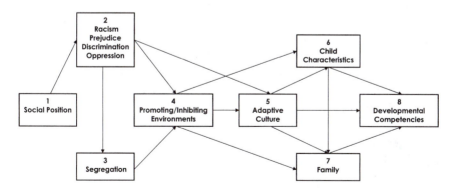

FIGURE 2.6   Integrative model for the study of developmental competencies in minority children.
(Adapted from Coll et al., 1996).

children as concepts from psychology, education, anthropology, sociology, nursing, and history may be of particular significance to this population. As a result, the types of research designs often used by developmentalists are beginning to change. Research conducted on African American children may incorporate more qualitative and applied designs (e.g., interviews, naturalistic observations, field studies, etc.), in contrast to the disproportionate use of quantitative and basic methods in past literature.

We believe that good research should highlight the positive environmental and behavioral factors in the lives of African American children. Historically, research of African American children tended to rely only on narrow examinations of the effects of negative environmental influences, such as racism, stress, and poverty. Due to the changing demographics in the United States, minority youth will be involved in the majority of developmental research within the next three decades. As a consequence of these demographic trends, we must be prepared to adequately represent these diverse experiences into future developmental scholarship.

CHAPTER SUMMARY

This chapter examines issues encountered in African American child development research. The chapter starts with a discussion of methodological limitations in race-comparative, cross-sectional, and longitudinal designs. We also explore the various threats to both the internal and external validity of a study. The second part of the chapter provides guidance in conducting culturally relevant research with African American children. In particular, we discuss the need to examine development in its cultural context. We also provide the central questions and characteristics found in general developmental psychology; however, we stress the need to examine four specific characteristics (multidimensionality, continuity, context, and plasticity) from the perspective of an African American cultural context. We also consider some possible ethical issues when working with African American populations and we include the ethical standards for working with children. The last section of the chapter focuses on a few developmental theories, namely, Vygotsky's sociocultural theory, Bronfenbrenner's bioecological systems theory, and Spencer's phenomenological variant of ecological systems theory, as well as an integrative model of development for minorities.

ADDITIONAL READINGS

Betancourt, H., & Lopez, S. R. (1993). The study of culture, ethnicity, and race in American psychology. *American Psychologist, 48,* 629–637.

Bronfenbrenner, U. (1979). *The ecology of human development.* Cambridge, MA: Harvard University Press.

Bronfenbrenner, U. (1986). Ecology of the family as a context for human development: Research perspectives. *Developmental Psychology, 22,* 723–742.

Graham, S. (1992) "Most of the subjects were white and middle class": Trends in published research on African Americans in selected APA journals, 1970–1989. *American Psychologist, 47,* 629–639.

Graue, M. E., & Walsh, D. J. (1998). *Studying children in context.* Thousand Oaks, CA: Sage Publications.

Graziano, W., Varca, P., & Levy, J. (1982). Race of examiner effects and the validity of intelligence tests. *Review of Educational Research, 52,* 469–498.

Greenfield, P. M., & Cocking, R. R. (1994). *Cross-cultural roots of minority child development.* Hillsdale, NJ: Lawrence Erlbaum Associates.

CHAPTER 3

African American Children and Health Issues

OVERVIEW

For the past two decades, initiatives at both the national, state and community levels have been implemented to ensure access to quality health care for all children in the United States. Despite these efforts, African American children are disproportionately affected by certain health conditions and have limited access to quality health care.

The focus of this chapter is to discuss the health challenges that confront African American infants and children, as well as to discuss their access to health care. The chapter is divided into two sections.

Section one begins with a discussion of infant mortality. The overall infant mortality rates have decreased, yet the rates for African American infants remain higher than the national average. The section continues with information on the health conditions that disproportionately affect African American children. Those health conditions include AIDS, lead poisoning, sickle-cell anemia, asthma, and obesity.

Section two commences with a discussion of health care coverage for African American children, a discussion of the barriers to quality health care and concludes with a discussion of federal and state initiatives designed to reduce barriers and to improve both access and the health status of African American children.

The chapter ends with a discussion of perspectives on health status and access to health care and African American children in the 21st century.

SECTION ONE: HEALTH CHALLENGES

Infant Mortality

INSIDER'S VOICE: INFANT MORTALITY

For the Love of a Child

Determined to keep babies from dying, Kathryn Hall pairs "sister-friends" with pregnant women who have nowhere else to turn.

By Bettijane Levine, *LA Times,* Feb. 1992

Sacramento—For 14 years, Kathryn Hall used the term infant mortality and thought she knew what it meant. She was after all a public health administrator, who oversaw millions of dollars of state funds. Then she held a dead baby in her arms for the first time. He was an infant who need not have died. But his mother was poor, diabetic, and often too sick to get to the clinic by bus. Hall, who heard about the woman through a public health nurse, drove to her house and took her to the clinic. But it was already too late. The baby was in extreme respiratory distress and had to be delivered by C-section. He underwent brain surgery and remained on life support until he died 10 days later.

Kathryn Hall worried about the infant death rate for years. As a state administrator, she was angered by the astonishing statistics about black babies in California. "They die at twice the rate of white babies, their birth weights are lower than all the rest," she says. Worse yet, it seemed that policy makers had begun to take the statistics for granted. "I heard them say things like maybe black babies just naturally die more, just naturally have lower weights. Those assumptions were not okay with me." She shifted into high gear and in 1988 decided to start a plan to help grow healthy black babies. She recruited Black middle class women and paired them with pregnant women. They were called sister friends and each sister friend maintained daily contact with the mother, making sure that doctor appointments were kept and medicines were taken. These sister friends saw the mother and the child until the end of the baby's first year.

Word spread that the volunteers were making dramatic differences in their sisters' lives. Birth weights were up; the death rate fell to zero. About 300 babies have been born in the project, at an average birth weight of more than 8 pounds.

Grant money for the project was secured from the Sierra Health Foundation and from the Irvine foundation.

This birthing project is not only thriving in Sacramento, but also in Los Angeles and in 34 other states as well.

Kathryn Hall's story aptly captures the severity of the problem of infant mortality that exists within the African American community.

The overall infant mortality rate in the United States has significantly decreased in the past 40 years. This is due in part to better health care available to pregnant women, and in part to the advances made in the field of neonatology. However, even with the increase in access to prenatal care, and advances in the field, the mortality rates, as well as the morbidity rates for African American infants, remain higher than the rates for White infants and infants from other ethnic groups (see Figure 3.1).

As the figure illustrates, in 1960 the infant mortality rate for African American infants was 44.3 per 1,000 live births, whereas the infant mortality rate for White infants was 22.9 per 1,000 live births. In 1970, the infant mortality rate for African American infants dropped to 32.6 per 1,000 live births and to 17.5 per 1,000 live births for White infants. For the past 20 years, the infant mortality rate for African American infants decreased, from 21.4 in 1980 to 17.4, 14.0, and 13.9 in 1990, 2000, and 2002, respectively.

Despite this decreasing trend, African American infants are 2 to 4 times more likely to die in infancy than White infants and infants from other ethnic groups.

Infant mortality rates tend to vary by state and the state rates are often higher than the national rates. As Table 3.1 indicates, states such as Wisconsin, Colorado, Nevada, Michigan, Ohio, Tennessee, and Illinois have the highest African American infant mortality rates. However, regardless of the state, the mortality rates for African American infants remain higher than the national average (Statistical Abstracts of the United States, 2003).

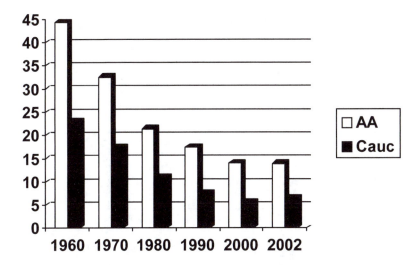

FIGURE 3.1   Infant mortality statistics for African American infants and White infants. Source: (National Vital Statistics Reports, Vol. 52, No. 3, September 18, 2003).

TABLE 3.1   Infant Mortality State Rates (FY 2002)

State	Rate
Alabama	13.9
Arizona	13.0
Arkansas	13.9
California	12.9
Colorado	21.1
Connecticut	14.2
Delaware	12.9
District of Columbia	14.5
Florida	13.6
Georgia	13.7
Illinois	16.3
Indiana	15.3
Kansas	15.2
Kentucky	14.2
Louisiana	15.0
Maryland	12.3
Massachusetts	9.1
Michigan	18.5
Minnesota	10.3
Mississippi	14.8
Missouri	17.1
Nebraska	20.8
Nevada	18.4
New Jersey	12.8
New York	9.9
North Carolina	15.6
Ohio	17.7
Oklahoma	17.2
Pennsylvania	15.1
South Carolina	15.8
Tennessee	18.3
Texas	13.5
Virginia	14.6
Washington	12.7
Wisconsin	18.9

Source: U.S. Census Bureau, Statistical Abstract of the U.S. 2006.

What accounts for this disparity in infant mortality rates? Why do more African American infants die within their first year of life?

The two primary causes frequently cited in the medical and health literature are infant health status and maternal risk factors. A conceptual model of infant health status and maternal risk factors is presented in Figure 3.2.

African American infants at risk for dying during their first year of life are those who are preterm, have low birth weight, are exposed to drugs in utero, or suffer from a host of medical problems.

Data released by Centers for Disease Control (2000), and www.cdc.org, indicated that in 1998, 6.5% of all White infants were underweight at birth, whereas, 13% of African American infants were underweight at birth; in 2002, 6.8% of White infants were low birth weight, 13.3% of African American infants were low birth weight, and in 2003, 6.9% of White infants were low birth weight and 13.3% of African American infants were low birth weight. The percentage of infants weighing less than 1,500 grams (those at greatest risk for disability) has increased to 18% for infants of African American mothers (Health United States and Healthy People Review, 2000, Child Health USA, 2004). In fact trend data suggest that the very low birth weight rates have increased for African American infants from 1985 to 2002, from 2.7 per 1,000 live births to 3.1 per 1,000 live births (Child Health USA, 2004).

As a consequence of their low birth weight and premature status, these infants are born with a plethora of medical complications, which include congenital defects such as cleft palate, (National Center for Health Statistics, 2004) and infectious diseases (Petrini, Russell, Posthman, Davidoff,

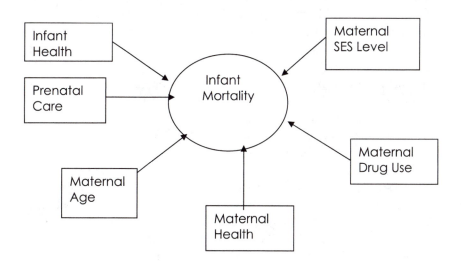

FIGURE 3.2   Infant health status and maternal risk factor model.

& Mattison, 2002). Because of their medical complications, a number of these infants do not live long after delivery (Rosenberg, Desai, & Kan, 2002).

For those infants exposed to drugs in utero, fetal addiction accompanies maternal addiction. Withdrawal symptoms such as irritability, high-pitched cries, tremors, poor feeding, and fevers are seen in 60%–90% of the infants prenatally exposed to cocaine (Coles, 1992). Once ingested, cocaine crosses the placenta and disrupts the flow of oxygen and nutrients to the fetus. As a result, intrauterine growth retardation is common in pregnancies of women addicted to crack-cocaine, and consequently the infants are often born with low birth weight or preterm, and their mortality rates are high (Jacobsen, Jacobsen, & Sokol, 1994). Those babies who survive often experience long-term physical problems or congenital abnormalities, as well as a host of behavioral and cognitive problems as a result of cocaine's influence on the development of such brain structures as the caudate nucleus, the limbic system and the cerebral cortex (Ryan, Ehrlich, & Finnegan, 1987). Cocaine also interferes with the production of dopamine, norepinephrine, and serotonin (Singer et al., 2005). Therefore, as a result of the neurological and neurochemical damage, these infants often have difficulties executing basic motor functions such as crawling, walking, reaching and grasping; they experience problems in processing and retaining information, as well as problems regulating their emotions; damage to the cerebral cortex can also produce significant language delays and problems (Singer, et al., 2005).

Alcohol, like cocaine, crosses the placenta, and prenatal exposure to alcohol can result in either Fetal Alcohol Syndrome (FAS) or Alcohol Related Neurodevelopmental Disorder (ARND) (Astley & Clarren, 2000). Infants with FAS will exhibit prenatal and postnatal growth retardation, facial malformations, behavioral and state (e.g., shifting from wake states to sleep states) problems, and mental retardation (Mattison, Schoenfeld, & Riley, 2001).

Infants born with ARND do not have dysmorphia (facial malformations), but may exhibit some behavioral and cognitive problems that often go undetected until their preschool and school age years (Astley & Clarren, 2000).

In a comprehensive study of 483 African American infants exposed prenatally to alcohol, Burden et al. (2005) observed that prenatal exposure to alcohol was related to slower information processing times and lower Bayley Mental Development Index (MDI) scores at 6 months and 12 months. At age 7, these children had lower Weschler Intelligence Scale for Children III (WISC) arithmetic and digit span scores. Teacher reports at age 7 also indicated that these children tended to be more aggressive than non-exposed children and encountered more negative peer interactions than non-exposed infants.

According to the National Organization on Fetal Alcohol Syndrome, there has been an increase in the number of infants born with FAS. In 1979, the FAS rate was one case per 10,000 births, and the rate increased in 1999 to 6.7 cases per 10,000 live births. The incidence of FAS is 6.0 per 1000 live births among African American populations (National Vital Statistics, 2000).

In addition to the aforementioned factors, in contrast to White infants, African American infants are more likely to die from Sudden Infant Death Syndrome (Weese-Mayer et al., 2003).

Maternal Risk Factors

As the model suggests, maternal age, health status, entry into prenatal care, and maternal drug use are identified as the primary maternal risk factors. More recently, Jaffee and Perloff (2003) have explored the relationship between neighborhood risk factors (i.e., high poverty levels, high violence levels) and maternal psychological functioning (i.e., depression) and adverse pregnancy outcomes. Their findings suggest that mothers who live in high crime and low income neighborhoods and experience depression are those most at risk for poor pregnancy outcomes.

Although the maternal risk factors may independently contribute to adverse pregnancy outcomes, it is plausible that they interact and increase the chances of birthing an infant who will die within the first year of their lives.

Age. African American mothers at the greatest risk are between the ages of 20 and 24, and between the ages of 35 and 54 years. The infant mortality rates for these mothers were 15.5 per 1,000 live births and 16.3 per 1,000 live births respectively in 2005 (Office of Minority and Women's Health, 2006; see their Web site, www.bhpc.dhhs.gov/omwh). Maternal death is not uncommon for these mothers and they are twice as likely to die from hemorrhage and miscarriage (Geronimus & Bound, 1990). Data released by the Centers for Disease Control revealed that in 2002, the maternal death rate for African American mothers was 24.9 per 100,000 live births, whereas the maternal death rate for White mothers and Latina mothers was 5.8 and 7.1 per 100,000 live births respectively. The gap has widened since 2000 (Child Health USA, 2004).

Socioeconomic Status and Health. Studies generally find a higher incidence of poor pregnancy outcomes among women from lower socioeconomic status (SES) groups (Grady, 2005). Poor African American mothers are highly susceptible to conditions and diseases caused by nutritional inadequacies, and inadequate medical care (Friedman, Cohen, & Mahan, 1993). Prior to pregnancy, they are more likely than non-poor mothers to be undernourished and malnourished, and during pregnancy, they tend to gain less weight, and to experience such health problems as anemia, eclampsia, diabetes and hypertension (Liberman, Ryan, Manson, & Schoenbaum, 1987).

Geronimus (1996) proposes the "weathering hypothesis" as a way of describing the link between maternal health, socioeconomic status and adverse pregnancy outcomes for older African American mothers. He argues that the cumulative effects of poverty and untreated medical conditions as well as unhealthy lifestyle, increase the likelihood of birthing an infant who will die within the first year of life. Fiscella (2003) proposes that in addition to poor health problems, maternal obesity, especially the unusually high level of obesity found in African American women, contributes to their poor health status, which ultimately contributes to adverse pregnancy outcomes.

Drug Use. During the 1980s cocaine use as well as the high incidence of other drug use among pregnant women and women in their childbearing years reached epidemic levels in the United States (Singer et al., 2005; Pursley-Crotteau, 2000). Precise statistics on the number of African American mothers abusing drugs during pregnancy is hard to obtain. Nevertheless, these women are typically polydrug users, and have a higher rate of such health problems, such as hypertension, hepatitis, and sexually transmitted diseases, all of which affect fetal growth and infant development (Jacobson, Chiodo, Sokol, Jacobson, 2002).

Prenatal Care. Receiving early and consistent prenatal care is essential in reducing the chances of birthing a low birth weight and preterm infant, in decreasing infant mortality rates and in preventing other adverse pregnancy outcomes.

Pregnant women generally initiate this care during the first trimester of their pregnancy and usually schedule one prenatal care visit per month throughout the duration of their pregnancy. During routine prenatal care visits, weight, urine, blood pressure, protein and blood sugar levels are measured and advice is given on nutrition and other pregnancy related issues (Kogan, Kotelchuck, Alexander, & Johnson, 1994)

According to data provided by Health Statistics (2003), 74% of African American pregnant women initiate early prenatal care. The 26% of pregnant African American women who fail to receive adequate prenatal care, as illustrated in Figure 3.3, are adolescent mothers and mothers older than 40.

Research has documented that a variety of internal and external barriers prevent adolescent African American women from seeking early and consistent prenatal care. For example, Lia-Hoagberg et al. (1992) observes that transportation issues as well as knowledge of the restrictions and time limits of the federal health insurance are cited by these mothers as barriers for receiving early and consistent care. York, Williams, and Munro (1993) report

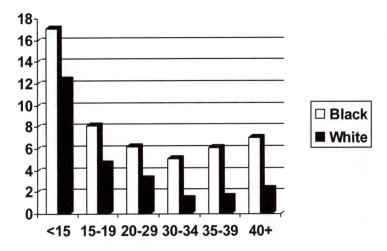

FIGURE 3.3   Percentage of mothers receiving late or no prenatal care, 2002.
Source: Child Trends Data Bank (2004).

that family functioning and child care issues emerge as barriers for this group of mothers. Reeb, Graham, Zyzanski, and Kitson (1987) found that young women experiencing family stress are less likely to receive adequate prenatal care. More recently, Paganini and Reichman (2000) found that martial status, planned versus non-planned pregnancy, city size, employment status, and maternal mental health are all factors for whether or not a woman receives prenatal care. According to Mikhail (2000), young and poor African American mothers report dissatisfaction with the quality of their prenatal care. These mothers indicate that they receive little information on nutrition and health issues during their prenatal care visits. In one report, African American mothers stated that the physician failed to inform about the risk of drinking and smoking, and the importance of good nutrition on pregnancy outcomes. This finding is consistent with recent studies showing that the quality of prenatal care services vary according to such dimensions as race and socioeconomic status (York, Tulman, & Brown, 2000).

Initiatives Designed to Reduce African American Infant Mortality Rates

Prevention and intervention programs have been designed at the federal, state, and community levels to address the problem of infant mortality in the African American community. Some programs were developed to increase access and use of prenatal care, while others were developed to reduce financial barriers. Some programs targeted teen mothers, while others targeted poor mothers, regardless of age, living in urban and rural areas (see Brown (1989) for a review of those programs).

Women Infants and Children (WIC), a federal program authorized by Congress in 1972, is designed to reach at-risk pregnant women, their infants, and their children. The goal of WIC is to provide supplemental food (e.g., milk, eggs and cheese) information on nutrition and health, and access to prenatal care for pregnant mothers. Current estimates indicate that WIC provides benefits to 4.5 million women and their children monthly and access to prenatal care for 500,000 pregnant women (USDA, 2006).

As a result of WIC, such states as Florida, Michigan, Minnesota, North Carolina, South Carolina, and Texas have been successful in decreasing the infant mortality rates, increasing the survival rates of infants born to at-risk mothers, and improving maternal prenatal care (Avruch & Cackley, 1995: Devaney, 1992).

Healthy Baby/Healthy Start is another federally funded program, implemented in 1985. Similar to WIC, Healthy Baby/Healthy Start strives to reduce the financial barriers for pregnant mothers by subsidizing medical professionals and increasing the availability of prenatal care programs for pregnant women living in the urban areas.

Programs offered at the state level provide mothers with information by distributing literature in communities, using the media, or—as in the case of our Insider's Voice—using grass roots approaches to connect young and poor pregnant women with middle-class women.

Baby Your Baby Campaign and 961-Baby are examples of state level programs. To reach as many at-risk African American mothers as possible, Baby Your Baby Campaign employs a wide range of approaches, including the dissemination of pamphlets, broadcasting advertisements on local TV channels, and community advocacy. In addition to the campaign, a 24-hour hotline service, 961-Baby was founded by the Detroit-Wayne County Infant Health Promotion Coalition in 1985 (Brown, 1989). Trained professionals are available to provide information to callers on health and social services, and make referrals to prenatal care facilities. The clientele are typically unmarried African American women under the age of 18.

Home visiting programs have been established in several southern states designed to reach high-risk mothers in rural areas. These programs use lay women from the community to discuss the importance of prenatal and perinatal care. These home visiting programs have been effective in improving maternal nutrition and in increasing the prenatal care (Brown, 1989).

Individual states have designed perinatal and prenatal program which target at-risk women. These projects differ from the media campaigns and other outreach efforts in that they provide comprehensive services (e.g., medical care, psychotherapy), and function in the role as data clearinghouses for infant mortality statistics.

Examples of those projects include a perinatal project in Alabama (Telfair, 2003), and a community based project in Michigan (Pestronk & Franks, 2003). Both of these programs involve discussions and focus groups with medical providers, community leaders and community members. As a result of the discussions, services have been targeted to those geographic areas with the highest African American infant mortality rates.

Physical Challenges Beyond Infancy

In this section we will discuss the physical challenges that African American preschool and school age children encounter. Although, many of these challenges emerge during infancy, they fully manifest themselves during the preschool and school age period and significantly impact the quality of life for preschool and school age children.

The section discusses AIDS, lead poisoning, with its effects on physical development and intellectual development; sickle-cell anemia, focusing on its incidence in the United States, describing its symptoms and physical manifestations, and discussing the psychosocial adjustment of school-aged children to the disease; asthma, with a focus on the types of medical management and community based programs available to African American children with asthma; and lastly, obesity and how obesity affects African American children in particular.

AIDS

The health concern that has the greatest impact on maternal, infant, and child survival within the African American community is AIDS. According to recent statistics released by the Centers for Disease Control, over half of all women infected with HIV/AIDS are African American and a substantial number of these women are in their childbearing years. These women are 23 times more likely to be infected with the disease than White women and accounted for the 71.8% of new HIV cases from 1999 to 2002 (Vital Statistics, 2003). Mothers infected with the virus have a 15% to 50% chance of birthing an infected infant (Bryson, 1996).

Data released by Child Trends Data Bank (2004), indicates that African American children under the age of 13 comprise 61% of all the pediatric AIDS cases diagnosed from 1985 to 2004, almost all of whom acquired the virus from their infected mothers.

Figure 3.4 suggests that the number of AIDS cases has dramatically decreased in the past 20 years, but African American children remain 2 to 3 times more likely than their counterparts from other ethnic and racial groups to be diagnosed with AIDS.

The disease proceeds rapidly in those infants who acquired the disease in utero and most of these babies are born with abnormalities of the immune system (Landry & Smith, 1998). By 6 months of age, weight loss, fever, diarrhea and respiratory illnesses are common.

The virus can also cause serious brain damage. Infants with AIDS show a loss in brain weight over time, accompanied by seizures, delayed muscle tone and movements (Pollack, Kuchik, Cowan, & Hacimamutoglu, 1996).

Treatment of AIDS

In the last few years, there has been a reduction in the perinatal transmission of AIDS as suggested by the Figure 3.4. This is in part due to the use of the zidovudine (ZDV) drug treatment during pregnancy, as well as the use of an antiviral drug therapy administered to the newborn, immediately after birth and six weeks after birth (Battle et al., 1995). However, even with these advances, the number of African American children born HIV positive and the number of African American children with AIDS represents a continuing and persistent health concern for African American preschool and school age children.

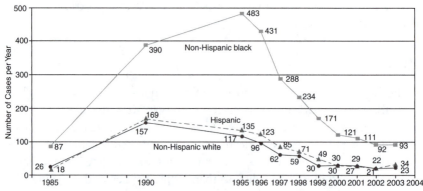

Source: Data for 1996 and 1997 from National Center for Health Statistics. *Health, United States*, 2001 *with Urban and Rural Health Chartbook.* Hyattsville, Maryland: 2001. Table 53 Data for 1998 from National Center for Health Statistics. *Health, United States, 2002 with Chartbook on Trends in the Health of Americans.* Hyattsville, Maryland 2002: Table 54. All other data from: National Center for Health Statistics. *Health, United States 2003 with Chartbook on Trends in the Health of Americans.* Hyattsville, Maryland, 2003: Table 53. National Center for Health Statistics. Health, United States, 2004 with Chartbook on Trends in the Health of Americans. Hyattsville, Mary land, 2004.

FIGURE 3.4   Number of newly diagnosed AIDS cases among children under 13, by race and Hispanic origin, selected years, 1985–2003.
Source: Child Trends Data Bank www.childtrends.org

Plumbism

INSIDER'S VOICE: PLUMBISM

Motherly Advice on Lead and Children—Courtland Milloy

Maurci Jackson will never forget the words spoken by her 15-month-old daughter that day 5 years ago. "Mommy, I ate this," Maurissa said, holding up the remains of a dried piece of lead-based paint. For Marvette Lewis, the silence of her 2-year-old twin sons spoke just as loudly. "Neither boy was saying 'Mama' or 'Daddy' or any of the easy little things that I heard other children saying," Lewis said.

It turned out that eating lead based-paint had poisoned them. What followed was a nightmare for both mothers. For the next eight months, Jackson's daughter Maurissa underwent treatment that sometimes required having two injections a day with a 4-inch needle. Medical tests showed that Maurissa's blood contained three times the safe level of lead. The twins were subjected to intensive therapy in an effort to reverse their learning disabilities.

"My sons are doing better, but they are still not on the level that normal 4-year-olds should be," said Lewis.

According to a study by the U.S. Department of Housing and Urban Development, lead-based paint is found in about 5.7 million homes and young children live in 3.8 million houses with serious lead hazards. In predominantly black urban areas with relatively poor populations, such as Baltimore and Washington, up to 50% of young children are believed to be suffering from the effects of lead poisoning. These children experience such health risks as brain damage, hearing loss, and decreased growth.

Parents are now mobilizing. Some parent groups are calling for universal lead poisoning screening and treatment. Jackson said she is optimistic that her daughter will overcome the effects of lead poisoning. But what was most important, she said, was letting other parents know that lead poisoning is preventable and that no other child need ever suffer from it again.

Plumbism (or lead poisoning), a disease primarily affecting children under the age of six, is caused by exposure to high levels of lead. Although children are exposed to lead from a variety of sources, the primary source of exposure comes from lead-based paint used in the interior of older and dilapidated homes. As stated in the Insider's Voice, it is estimated that 3.8 million children are currently living in homes that have leaded paint surfaces. Moreover, the Northeast region of the United States, which is considered to be the lead belt, has the greatest number of children living in these homes (170,000), followed by the Midwest (139,000), the Southern region (130,000), and the West (77,000) (Mushak, Davis Crocetti, et al., 1989).

Lead poisoning causes the deaths of 200 children annually and 800 are so severely impaired that they will require permanent care. Three thousand two hundred more children sustain moderate to severe brain damage (Coscia, Douglas, & Dietrich, 2003). Unfortunately a disproportionate number of these children are poor, urban African American children. Three percent of African American children in comparison to 1% of White children have elevated blood levels (National Center for Environmental Health, 2006). The prevalence is higher for children between the ages 1 and 2 (Williams, 2002).

Most children with lead poisoning are asymptomatic (not displaying symptoms). If they do exhibit symptoms, these symptoms are similar to those common to most childhood illnesses and are often misdiagnosed as such. Usually developmental delays, and persistent cognitive and physical problems, signal parents that their child is suffering from something more serious than a common childhood illness.

What are the effects of lead poisoning on physical and intellectual development? Exposure to lead results in delayed physical growth, retarded motor development, and perceptual motor coordination problems (Dietrich, Berger, & Succop, 1993). Children exposed to lead also experience such physical problems as kidney disease convulsions, sleep disturbances, blindness, and cerebral palsy (Needleman & Bellinger, 1991). Exposure to lead can also lead to mental retardation, learning disabilities, attention and concentration problems, and language and speech delays (Wigg, 2001).

Unfortunately, without early detection and treatment of lead poisoning some of these learning problems persist well into adolescence, where they manifest themselves as severe emotional and behavioral problems (Coscia, Ris, Succop, & Dietrich, 2003).

Treatment of Plumbism

Lead poisoning is currently treated by a procedure referred to as chelation therapy (Angle, 1993). Chelation therapy involves administering to the child a chelating agent, which is a drug such as Dimercaprol (BAL), Ethylene diamine tetracetic acid edetate calcium disodium (EDTA) Penicillamine or Dimercaptosuccinic (DSMA) that binds to the lead in the body. The lead is removed from the body through waste material. The type of drug used depends on the amount of lead in the body. For example, Penicillamine and DMSA (both of which are orally administered) are used with children with relatively low amounts of lead poisoning, whereas EDTA and BAL (which are injected) are used with children with higher concentrations of lead in their systems. The duration of chelation therapy varies according to the level of lead in the body; thus, treatments may range from 5 days to 6 weeks. The toxic effects of the drugs are minimal but chelation therapy provides rapid relief of acute symptoms reduces blood lead levels and results in an increase in growth velocity (Angle, 1993).

Without the complete removal of the lead from the home (lead abatement) or relocation to a lead free environment, the likelihood of lead recontamination is high.

A project sponsored by the National Safety Council's Environmental Health Center called the Lead Poisoning Prevention Outreach Program conducts meetings in the affected communities to help residents plan and execute successful lead poisoning prevention and abatement programs (see Dilworth-Bart & Moore (2006), for a review of lead abatement programs). In addition to this effort, the CDC designed the High Intensity Targeted Screening project which includes four components. The first two directly target affected children and their families. The first component is Door-to Door Screening. Homes in high risk communities are visited by health practitioners for screening and blood lead level testing. The second is intervention. Children with elevated lead levels receive treatment and homes are evaluated for lead abatement procedures. The third and fourth components focus on monitoring communities, implementing community prevention programs, and evaluating community compliance with lead abatement procedures (see CDC Web site for abatement programs, www.cdc.gov/nceh/lead).

Sickle-Cell Anemia

INSIDER'S VOICE: SICKLE-CELL ANEMIA

2 Georgia Boys May Be Proof of Sickle-Cell Anemia Cure

By Anne Rochelle
Atlanta Constitution, September 1, 1994

Normally doctors won't say they've cured an incurable disease such as sickle-cell Anemia, but they're coming close to saying it about two Atlanta-area children. The boys, ages 5 and 12, recently received bone marrow transplants and have been declared disease free, say doctors at Emory's bone marrow transplant program. The children are the first patients in Georgia and among fewer than 30 worldwide to undergo a bone marrow transplant to treat sickle-cell anemia. Seventy to eighty percent of the patients who have undergone transplants have been cured. One of the two children, Seye Arise, now goes to school, plays ball and giggles uncontrollably like any other 5 year old. But he can remember how it was before his operation last November when he received bone marrow from his older brother. "Everything hurt," he said. Seye suffered a mild stroke and was at risk for having more strokes. In the bone marrow replacement his faulty gene was replaced with a normal gene.

The second patient, 12-year-old Roger Johnson, received marrow from his older sister in April.

Researchers are hoping that with the dawn of gene therapy, it will be possible to correct a child's faulty gene without having to find a donor with a matching bone marrow. Doctors someday may be able to remove a patient's own marrow, insert a normal gene and put the marrow back, a treatment that would be applicable to a much larger percentage of patients. However, that's at least a decade away.

Sickle-cell disease is a generic term applied to a group of genetic disorders characterized by the production of abnormal hemoglobin molecules (Galloway & Harwood-Nuss, 1988). While normal blood cells are oval or round in shape, the red bloods cells of those with the disease are sickled in shape and vascular occlusion occurs when sickled red blood cells create blockages in the capillaries (Galloway & Harwood-Nuss, 1988). The disease primarily affects African Americans and current estimates indicate that one out of every 600 African American infants is born with the disease (Sickle-Cell Disease Association, 2000).

In 1974 states began screening infants for sickle-cell disease and currently 40 states make testing a routine part of their infant screening procedures (Sickle-Cell Disease Association, 2000). Screening is usually conducted on the third day after birth or on the day of scheduled discharge from the hospital. Three possible diagnoses can be made. The first is absence of the sickle-cell disease or sickle-cell traits. The second is a diagnosis of the sickle-cell disease. An infant will inherit the disease only if the gene has been inherited from both parents. The third diagnosis occurs when the newborn inherits only the genetic traits but not the manifestation of the disease from the parents. There appear to be two forms of this third trait; Sickle C Disease and Sickle Thalassemia. Neither of these two forms are severe enough to cause the pain, the discomfort, and the mortality associated with the actual disease.

Sickle-cell anemia is a lifelong disease with no known cure. Although there have been reports of death under the age of 2 (primarily caused by bacterial infections, acute splenic or sequestration crises), many with the disease often live into middle age.

One of the most serious complications of sickle-cell anemia is stroke. Statistically, about 11% of children affected with sickle-cell anemia experience strokes, which can lead to lasting disabilities.

If the diagnosis of the disease is not made at birth, most parents discover that their child has sickle-cell anemia within the first 2 years of life (Lukens, 1981). The common symptoms that parents report their children displaying include anemia, fatigue, bacterial infections, strokes, kidney dysfunction, and chronic pain in the arms, legs, back, and abdomen.

The onset and duration of the pain episodes are variable and often unpredictable. These episodes can last from one hour to several hours or days.

Although the pain of sickle-cell anemia is the most difficult to bear, the adjustment to the disease appears to be problematic for both the children and their families.

It seems that sickle-cell anemia affects family functioning in a number of ways (Armstrong, Lemanek, Pegelow, Gonzalez, & Martinez, 1993). First, the disease appears to have a negative impact on parental marital relations. In one reported case study, marital stress increased and communication decreased. Both parents expressed guilt, depression, and anxiety about their role in the child's illness. Furthermore, single mothers report feeling overwhelmed by the demands of the disease and report having more negative feelings about their children as well as being more overprotective than do intact families. Second, the disease has an impact on the child's self-esteem, peer relationships, and academic functioning. Children with sickle-cell anemia have higher levels of chronic anxiety as compared to a healthy control group of their peers (Gil et al., 1991). They tend to be excluded from peer group activities and have difficulty in developing friendships because of their frequent hospitalizations. There is some evidence suggesting that these children are less successful in school than their healthy age-mates.

Treatment of Sickle-Cell Anemia

If the pain episodes of the disease are severe, hospitalization is a common outcome. Once hospitalized, the child receives analgesics, penicillin, and fluids (to prevent dehydration).

Currently two types of medical treatments are available, both of which are new approaches and quite experimental. One treatment, as discussed in the Insider's Voice, is the bone marrow transplantation treatment. The other, which is primarily available for adults but is also currently being administered to infants and young children, is Hydroxyurea, a chemotherapy drug. Although there have been mixed results (i.e., patients have reported a significant decrease in the onset and severity of pain episodes), researchers caution that the drug is not a "cure all" for infants and young children (Powars, 2001).

To assist parents with medical management and other psychosocial issues there are several support groups available throughout the United States.

Depending on the needs of the family, these groups can function primarily as an information and referral service for the family or provide them with information on therapy and more structured support services (Armstrong et al., 1993).

There is also a national organization called the Sickle-Cell Anemia Disease Association, which serves as a clearinghouse offering information to parents and those affected with the disease on the available local and regional medical, social, and outreach services in their area (visit their website at www.sicklecelldisease.org).

The Sickle-Cell Anemia Disease Association's primary goals for the new millennium include increasing the number of states that screen for the disease in infancy, providing genetic counseling to African American parents, and targeting support services to single parent households as its.

St. Jude Children's Research Hospital is currently studying various treatment modalities for African American children who are suffering from sickle -cell anemia. In addition to conducting clinical trials for effective drug and nutrition approaches, they serve as a clearinghouse for dissemination of contemporary information on sickle-cell anemia for parents, and they provide respite care and counseling for both children and their families (Ware, 2004).

Asthma

Asthma is the most common chronic illness of childhood (Wettzman, Gortmaker, Sobol, & Perrin, 1992). The number of children diagnosed with moderate to severe asthma has increased in the past several decades and unfortunately; a disproportionate number of these children are African American (National Asthma Association, 2003; see www.lungusa.org for more information).

Presently there are 4.8 million children under the age of 18 diagnosed with asthma (American Lung Association, 2004).

The incidence of asthma is 22% higher in African American school age children than in their White counterparts and is especially prevalent in inner city African American children (Sin, Kang, & Weaver, 2005, see Figure 3.5).

According to experts, this is due to such environmental risk factors such as pollution, cockroaches, cigarette smoke, and inadequate access to health care (Izierieta et al., 2000).

African American children who suffer from severe asthma are more likely to miss school, experience frequent hospitalizations, and suffer from severe disability. They are also 4 to 6 times more likely to die from asthma than are their White age mates (Lozano, Connell, & Koepsell, 1995). African American children have an annual rate of hospitalization of 74 per 10,000 compared to

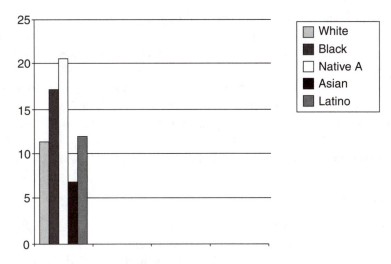

FIGURE 3.5   Asthma incidence among children under 18 by race.
Source: National Asthma Association (2003).

21 per 10,000 for White children (see National Asthma Association Web site for more information, www.lungusa.org).

Treatment of Asthma

Asthma is treated by one of two methods. One method involves the administration of anti-inflammatory agents, and the other involves the use of bronchodilators (Celand, Geller, Phillips, & Ziman, 1998). However, little information is available documenting the most effective treatment modality for African American children.

The research that exists on African American children and asthma has taken one of two foci. One focus is on school-based medical management of asthma. McEwen, Johnson, Neathelin, Millard, and Lawrence (1998) found that school-based programs which provide medication during school hours may be one way to increase the medication use, and indirectly decrease morbidity rates, emergency room visits, and the frequency of hospitalizations. They speculate that with direct and consistent supervision African American children may comply with a medication schedule.

The other body of research has focused on assessing parental knowledge and attitudes about asthma including knowledge of prevention and treatment issues. Koening and Chesla (2002) found that the majority of parents in their study were aware of asthma triggers, employed a variety of medical management strategies and used several prevention strategies; however, they were dissatisfied with medical restrictions and high cost of asthma treatments, even with co-pays. Similarly, Peterson, Sterling and Stout (2002) observed that parents were knowledgeable about the causes of asthma as well as treatment approaches.

Community-based outreach, which targets African American children with asthma, have been implemented across the United States. For example, in Seattle, Washington, a group of health care officials and school officials have created information, referral, and treatment services for African American children (National Asthma Association, 2003; Web site www.lungusa.org).

Obesity

Obesity among U.S. school age children has increased in the last 25 years (Davy, Harrell, Stewart, & King, 2004). As a result, medical practitioners as well as social policy advocates and politicians have identified this issue as a national concern for the beginning of the 21st century (Future of Children, 2006).

African American children are more likely than their White counterparts to be classified as obese during the school age period and well into adolescence. As Figure 3.6 indicates, the body mass index (BMI) for African American male and female children from ages 6 to 11 is double that of their White peers.

It seems that the health consequences of obesity are more severe for African American children than children from other racial and ethnic backgrounds. Davis (2003) found that African American children who ranked in the 95th

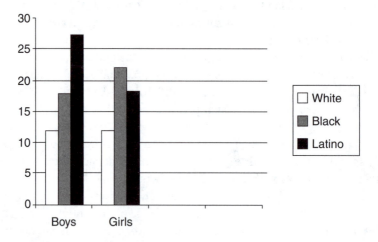

FIGURE 3.6   Body mass index comparisons.
Source: Center for Disease Control and Prevention (2006).

percentile on BMI measures were at risk for such health complications as hypertension, respiratory problems, and diabetes.

Causes identified in the scientific literature range from genetics to lifestyle issues. That is, scientists state that African American children inherit a biological predisposition to obesity as a result of parental obesity (Kumanyika & Grier, 2006). Others maintain that environmental factors such as a sedentary lifestyle, cultural preferences for food, and unsafe neighborhoods and poverty are the major contributing factors to obesity in African American children. Kumanyika (2006) expands upon the environmental contribution theory and states that the limited availability of health foods and healthy foods in urban areas constrain the types of meals and nutrition available to African American children and their families. Furthermore, coupled with environmental risk factors (i.e., neighborhoods with high crime rates), the rise of obesity rates in African American children is difficult to fight.

Treatment of Obesity

A variety of treatment approaches have been proposed. Those approaches involve dietary modifications (Shield, 2006), and increasing exercise level (Fitzgibbon, 2005). However, as Kumanyika (2006) suggests, prevention and intervention efforts for low income African American children and their families residing in urban areas may need to differ to take into account their environmental challenges and ecologies.

SECTION TWO: ACCESS TO HEALTH CARE

Having access to health care, including health care insurance and availability of a medical home, is critical in preventing, treating and managing the health challenges described in the previous section of the chapter.

According to the public health literature, African American children who lack health insurance are less likely than children with public or private insurance to visit a physician on a regular basis, less likely to have a personal physician and receive preventive services, such as routine pediatric visits, dental visits and eye exams, and more likely to use outpatient clinics and emergency rooms (Sochalski & Villarruel, 1999). Consequently, minor and acute health problems can go untreated and eventually become serious and chronic health conditions.

Fortunately, health care initiatives implemented in the past 20 years at the federal and state level have been effective in providing health care insurance for poor African American children. For example, in 1965 President Lyndon B.

Johnson established the federal program of Medicaid as a part of his war on poverty. This program provides health care insurance for the disabled, the elderly, and for single women and their children. Medicaid covers a range of services, which includes inpatient and outpatient care, periodic health check-ups, and diagnosis and treatment of health problems. Medicaid covers approximately 14,486,000 children, and African American children comprise 40% of these children (U.S. Census Bureau, 2000). At the state level, there is the Child Health Insurance Program (CHIP), implemented in 1998, and Healthy Baby/Healthy Start implemented in 2000 (Jenkins & Faulk, 2002). Both provide health care coverage to low income children and Healthy Baby/ Healthy Start offers physician referrals and other health and medical support services to poor families and their children.

Despite the federal and state level initiatives designed to provide health care coverage for poor African American children, racial disparities remain in the prevalence of certain medical conditions (Copeland, 2005). It seems that "having access to health insurance does not necessarily improve the quality of life and the overall health/well-being of African American children alone" (Cooper, 2005). Public health scholars argue that the disparities continue to exist because African American children are more likely than other children to underutilize medical services (Alio & Salihu, 2005). The reasons identified in the literature are quite diverse and range from parental attitudes and knowledge about health and well-being; structural barriers which include financial and transportation issues; to parental perceptions about the quality of medical treatment (Copeland, 2005).

What solutions have been offered and what models have been proposed to eliminate the barriers? Some national level and community level initiatives are listed in Table 3.2.

TABLE 3.2   Initiatives to Improve the Health Status of African American Children

National level	Community level
1. Inclusion of more AA children in health care research and clinical trials.	1. Increase the number of church-based health initiatives.
2. Increase funding for research on the health conditions of African American children.	2. Increase the number of health education programs located in the African American community.
3. Make health care practitioners aware of the unique challenges in the African American community.	3. Use African American community groups, fraternities and sororities as outreach vehicles.

Source: Center on Budget and Policy Priorities, 2000.

The initiatives at the national level primarily focus on improving the quality of health care for African American children by: (1) Involving African American children in medical research. African American children are rarely included in clinical trials. Consequently, there is little information available on the etiology, most effective treatment methods, and course of illnesses in African American children, or the environmental variables that might facilitate or constrain their use of medication. (2) Informing health care practitioners of the unique challenges present in the African American community. Many health care practitioners have had minimal contact with the African American culture and cannot comprehend the impact of poverty and race on such issues as health care and attitudes. (3) Increasing funding for research on health conditions that mainly affect African American children. As a result of federal funding, advances have been made in the diagnosis and treatment of sickle-cell anemia.

Currently, public health practitioners are advocating for incorporating courses that emphasize the influence of culture on health attitudes and behaviors in medical service provider coursework (Betancourt et al., 2003). In addition to this approach others have proposed a multipronged approach involving an increase in the diversity of the health care workforce to ensure that the health care workforce is reflective and representative of its patient population, along with initiating on-going cross-cultural training to health care service providers (Perloff, 2006). Horn and Beal (2004) suggest that there should be an increase in child health disparities research, which includes systematic investigations exploring the root causes of child health disparities, with the ultimate goal of developing effective intervention programs targeting families, the health system, community, and society.

The community level initiatives focus on using community groups, fraternal organizations, and churches as places to disseminate information about health insurance and health care issues to African American children and their families.

In addition to the initiatives outlined in the box, the Council on African American Affairs, a policy research organization located in Washington, DC, has identified the area of African American children and health care as one of their major policy issues for this millennium. Their primary objective is to develop strategies to eliminate the health care disparities for African American children.

PERSPECTIVES ON THE HEALTH STATUS OF AFRICAN AMERICAN CHILDREN

While there has been an increase in the number of African American mothers receiving prenatal care, the infant mortality rates for African American infants, although decreasing, still remain higher than the national average. Seemingly, the myriad of programs designed to target this population of mothers is meeting with minimal success. Why are these initiatives not producing significant changes in the infant mortality rates in the African American community? Is it the quality of prenatal care that mothers receive that place them at a higher risk for birthing an infant who will die within the first year of life? Or are there other environmental variables that need to be identified through systematic and rigorous investigations that might be associated with maternal behavior and prenatal and neonatal outcomes? Future research should focus on understanding why this problem persists.

AIDS and asthma disproportionately affect African American children. Are African American mothers aware of the drug treatment options, and are they offered the drug treatment options that reduce the chances of mother-to-child transmission? The morbidity rate for African American children from asthma is disquieting given the availability of treatment for the disease. This issue underscores the need for research that explores the causal factors for asthma and African American children.

Access to health care continues to be a pressing problem for many poor African American children. Implementing the initiatives stated in the chapter is a first step in improving access to health care and improving the health status of African American children.

CHAPTER SUMMARY

In this chapter, we have highlighted various aspects of physical development, and specific challenges and problems faced by the African American child. Some of these problems, such as lead poisoning and prenatal drug exposure, can have long-term effects beyond physical development.

The problem of infant mortality is overwhelmingly cited as a cultural problem. Higher infant mortality rates are evident in births to African American mothers living in high poverty areas in the East North Central Region of the United States.

Low birth weight and prematurity of infants are cited as causes of high infant mortality rates within the African American community.

Several biological and environmental factors contribute to low birth weight and prematurity and the increased incidence of infant mortality within the African American community. These factors, referred to as maternal risk factors, are maternal age, maternal SES, maternal health, maternal drug use, and maternal prenatal care.

Young mothers, poor mothers, mothers experiencing health problems, mothers abusing such drugs as cocaine and alcohol, and mothers receiving less than adequate prenatal care are at risk for giving birth to low birth weight and premature infants.

One major health concern within the African American community is AIDS. Mothers infected with the virus have a 30% chance of birthing infected infants. These infected infants experience several medical complications and do not live long after birth.

Several federal and state programs are targeting the problems that women face in receiving inadequate prenatal care. Programs currently implemented include WIC, Health Baby/Healthy Start, and Home Visiting Programs.

Lead poisoning, sickle-cell anemia, and asthma are three health problems that greatly impact the physical development of African American preschool and school age children. Exposure to lead poisoning comes from the paint used in the interior of older and dilapidated homes mostly located in the lead belt regions of the United States. The results of exposure to lead poisoning include physical, behavioral, and cognitive problem. Current treatment involves the administration of drugs that remove the lead from the body. Sickle-cell anemia is a blood disorder with no known cure. Diagnosis is usually made at birth and the symptoms include anemia, infection and chronic pain. Medical management involves analgesics, penicillin, and a couple of experimental procedures. Asthma, a current health problem for many school age children, disproportionately affects African American children. In comparison to their age-mates from other racial groups African American children are more likely to experience severe asthma. Little is known about the type of treatment that is most effective in managing the symptoms of asthma for African American children. However, one promising approach is school-based management and distribution of medication.

Access to health care is one way to prevent and treat the illnesses discussed in the chapter; however, many poor African American children are uninsured or underinsured. There are initiatives, both at the federal level and the community level, designed to address health care issues for African American children.

ADDITIONAL READINGS

Infant Mortality

Battle, R. S., Cummings, G. L., Barker, J. C., & Krasnovsky, F. M. (1995). Accessing an understudied population in behavioral HIV/AIDS research: Low income African American women. *Journal of Health and Social Policy,* 7, 1–18.

Foster, H., Wu, L., Bracker, M., Semenya, K., & Thomas, J. (2000). *Journal of the National Medical Association, 92,* 213–221.

Lia-Hoagberg, B. (1990). Barriers and motivators to prenatal care among low-income women. *Social Science Medicine, 30,* 487–495.

Sanders, K., & Davis, S. (1998). Improving prenatal care for low-income African American women and infants. *Journal of Health Care for the Poor and Underserved, 9,* 14–29.

York, R., Tulman, L., & Brown, K. (2000). Postnatal care in low-income urban African American women: Relationship to level of prenatal care sought. *Journal of Perinatology, 1,* 34–40.

Health Issues

Cornelius, L. J. (1993). Barriers to medical care for White, Black and Hispanic children. *Journal of the National Medical Association, 85,* 281–288.

McEwen, M., Johnson, P., Neatherlin, J., Millard, W., & Lawrence, G. (1998). School based management of chronic asthma among inner city African American school children in Dallas Texas. *Journal of School Health, 68,* 197–200.

Minority Coalition of the United Food and Commercial Workers Union (producers). (2000). Sickle-cell disease: The faces of our children. Videotape. Available from Fanlight Productions, 4196 Washington Street, Suite 2, Boston, MA, 02131.

Rand, C. S., Butz, A. M., Kolodner, K., Huss, K., & Malveaux, F. (2000). Emergency department visits by urban African American children with asthma. *Asthma and Immunology, 105,* 575–582.

CHAPTER 4

Mental Health Issues and Racial Identity

OVERVIEW

The paucity of research available concerning African American children is a reoccurring subject throughout this book, and this becomes even more evident when discussing mental health issues and African American children. There are few comprehensive studies describing the onset, etiology, and treatment of mental health disorders in African American children. This seems puzzling given that African American children are identified in the social science literature as being the most at-risk group of children and they encounter a myriad of environmental and psychosocial stressors that contribute to their poor mental health functioning.

This chapter is divided into two sections. Section one begins with a discussion of the risk factors that predispose African American children to mental health problems. The section continues with a discussion of the problems in misdiagnosing disorders in African American children. The section concludes with a discussion of the various psychotherapy interventions used with African American children.

Section two discusses racial identity development in African American children with specific attention paid to the theoretical perspectives and research on racial identity development. The chapter concludes with a discussion of Perspectives on Mental Health Issues and Racial Identity.

SECTION ONE: MENTAL HEALTH ISSUES

INSIDER'S VOICE: AFRICAN AMERICAN CHILDREN
AND MENTAL HEALTH ISSUES

1. In comparison to their White counterparts, low income African American children report experiencing higher test anxiety.
2. There is evidence to suggest that a very large percentage of African American children are at risk for clinical depression during childhood.
3. African American children are over reported as psychotic.
4. As many as 3% of African American children between the ages of 10 and 11 are diagnosed with behavior and conduct disorders.
5. A significant proportion of referrals for elementary school African American children are for academic and behavioral problems.
6. African American children are five times more likely than White children to be referred to a psychiatric facility or recommended for incarceration.

Source: Allen & Majidi-Ahi, 1988

Risk Factors

Why are African American children experiencing these disorders at higher rates than White children, and what factors are involved in making them more or less vulnerable to negative and adverse mental health outcomes?

An interaction of biological, environmental, and socio-historical factors place African American children at higher risk for the psychological impairments described in the Insider's Voice (Liaw & Brooks-Gunn, 1994).

Those biological risk factors include their birth status (e.g. low birth weight), and other childhood illnesses discussed in chapter 3. Environmental risk factors include poverty, and family constellation. African American children living in poor single-mother-headed households exhibit more symptoms of depression than those reared in two-parent family homes (Barbarin, 1993). In addition to those factors, African American children who live in families with a history of mental illness, who experience multiple moves, experience homelessness, and live in violent neighborhoods, are at a high risk for the adverse mental health outcomes discussed in the Insider's Voice (Dawson, 1991).

It seems to be when the risk factors are cumulative and persistent, the incidence of depression and other mental health problems increase and rarely abate in adolescence for some African American children (Sameroff, Seifer, Baldwin, & Baldwin, 1993).

The popular literature abounds with examples of African Americans who as children encountered difficult life circumstances, yet who were able to develop the coping strategies and survival skills that would buffer the impact of negative life circumstances.

Why and how poor children in general and African American children in particular are able to overcome the odds and prosper as adults has been the focus of research for the past three decades (Cicchetti & Garmezy, 1993). In particular, the research has addressed the basic question "what makes some children resilient in spite of their environment?" The body of literature on resiliency has identified both personal and environmental factors that are integral in overcoming the odds. One factor is temperament; children who overcome the odds are characterized as having an easygoing and flexible temperament (Garmezy, 1983). Another factor is self-esteem; children who achieve in spite of their circumstances have high self-esteem and self-efficacy. In addition to these two factors, studies show that there needs to be some external support for developing good mental health. These supports include social support—either from a teacher, a minister or through an organization (e.g., Big Brother/Big Sister); and role models (see Zimmerman, & Arunkumar, 1994 for a full discussion of resiliency models). Figure 4.1 presents a resiliency model.

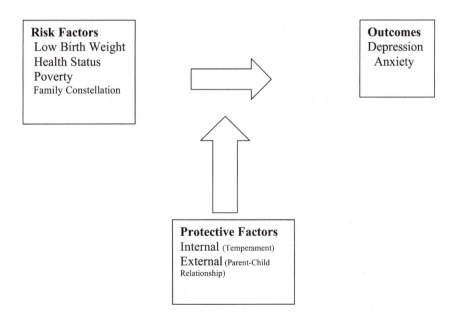

FIGURE 4.1   Resiliency model.
Source: Zimmerman & Arunkumar, 1994.

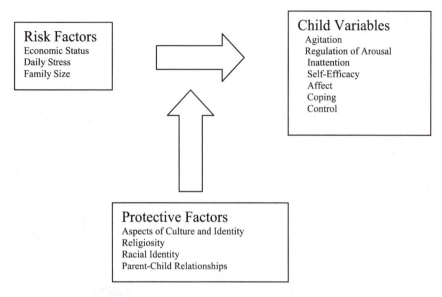

FIGURE 4.2   Barbarin's resiliency model.
Source: Barbarin, 1993.

Barbarin (1993) offers an alternative resiliency model for African American children. He argues that there is a need for such a model because little is known about the nature of the conditions that enable African American children to resist adverse circumstances. His model is presented in Figure 4.2.

The core features of his model include similar risk factors and protective factors listed in Figure 4.2, but he has expanded his model to take account of additional protective factors, such as family religiosity and racial socialization. Depending on the role they play in the caregiver's lives, these factors ultimately serve to protect African American children from adverse mental health outcomes.

Assessment and Diagnosis

For the past few decades, social scientists have voiced their concerns about the accuracy and validity of the methods and procedures used to assess and diagnose mental health disorders in African American children (Jones, 1988). They argue that the overrepresentation of African American children in certain diagnostic categories is due primarily to misdiagnosis.

Assessing mental health disorders is done through clinical interviews and the administration of personality and behavioral measures (Brems, 2004). Frequently, assessment, especially for African American children, is conducted without obtaining important environmental and social information. As a remedy,

Gopaul-McNicol et al. (1995) recommends that assessment be augmented with the inclusion of the following information: Physical appearance—an assessment of the child's physical appearance provides information on health status, affect and emotional functioning; intrapersonal issues—elicit information from the children about feelings of self-worth and value, as well as their coping mechanisms; interpersonal relationships—obtain information about peer group, and friendship relationships; family dynamics—prior to conducting the assessment it is vital to obtain information about the family system and to identify the family structure, as well as the family's attitude about mental health (e.g., what is the family's traditional pattern of help seeking). Furthermore, given the current estimates of the number of children born to parents of African descent immigrating to the United States, information on immigration history and the child's level of acculturation should be obtained. An example of a culturally relevant assessment instrument is presented in Box 4.1.

BOX 4.1

A CULTURALLY RELEVANT ASSESSMENT AND DIAGNOSTIC TOOL

Bidaunt-Russel, Valla, Thomas, Bergeron, and Lawson (1998) have developed an alternative method to assess and diagnose mental disorders in African American children. Their instrument, developed in 1981, called the Terry, is an orally administered assessment. Children are presented with pictures of Terry engaged either alone, with peers or adults, in a variety of social situations. Children are asked to respond to questions (e.g. have you ever destroyed other people's things on purpose like Terry?).

According to the authors, such diagnosis as: Depression, Dysthymia, Attention Deficit Hyperactivity Disorder, Oppositional Defiant Disorder, Conduct Disorder, Separation Anxiety Disorder, Overanxious Disorder, and Simple Phobia can be made based on the children's responses. There is also a parent component. Parents are given similar stimulus cards and asked if Terry's behavior represents the behavior of their child.

The Diagnostic and Statistical Manual (DSM-IV) is the standard manual used by clinicians to determine mental health disorders in children and adults. The DSM-IV is a multiaxial coding system that allows the clinician to rate mental health functioning according to five axes (DSM-IV, 2000). The diagnostic categories have been derived from research conducted on White populations.

Its effectiveness as a diagnostic tool for African Americans in general and African American children in particular has been a subject of controversy for many decades. The major argument is that the DSM-IV fails to take into account the cultural, socio-political, and environmental influences that contribute to the mental health functioning of African American children (Spencer, Kohn, & Woods, 1998).

There is evidence to suggest that there are differences in how individuals from different cultures experience and express symptoms of mental illness. Furthermore, the patterns of onset, duration, and the clustering of specific symptoms vary widely across cultures (Costello et al., 1996). Finally, not all expressions of mental health disorders are universal. Clinician error is also highly probable. The majority of the clinicians responsible for diagnosing disorders are White and have had little experience and training in working with African American children and their families (Neighbors, 1998).

In 1994, the American Psychological Association adopted a policy on culture and diagnosis (APA, 1994). An excerpt of the follows:

> Caution should be exercised in using the DSM with people from different cultural or ethnic groups. It is important that the clinician not employ DSM in a mechanical fashion, insensitive to differences in language, values, behavioral norms, and idiomatic expressions of distress. The clinician working in such a setting should apply DSM with open mindedness to the presence of distinctive cultural patterns and sensitivity to the possibility of unintended bias because of such differences. . . . The DSM is not based on extensive research with non-Western populations.

However, according to Johnson (1993) the policy is too vague and does not provide specific guidelines on obtaining critical information to make an accurate diagnosis.

As an alternative Johnson has proposed expanding and revising the DSM-IV to include an additional axis, called the Psychocultural Adaptive Functioning (PAF). This axis could be used to diagnosis the cultural functioning of the child as well as determine the child's coping strategies, family and environmental support. The PAF also provides detailed information on the person's racial self-esteem, locus of control, community support, family psychological availability, and cross cultural competency and allows the clinician to place the disorder in the context under which it occurs. Johnson believes that the PAF axis will ultimately lead to accurate diagnosis and effective treatment plans. He offers guidelines for evaluating and diagnosing African American children (see Box 4.2 for his guidelines).

Treatment of Mental Health Disorders

Historically, African American children and their families have underutilized mental health services (Davis & Ford, 2004). Researchers have identified a variety of internal and external barriers, which contribute to their underutilization. The internal barriers include myths, attitudes, and beliefs

BOX 4.2

GUIDELINES FOR DIAGNOSING AFRICAN AMERICAN CHILDREN

1. Each step in the diagnostic process should include acknowledgement of the role that values, beliefs and practices of the African American culture attach to psychopathology.
2. Clinicians should inform patients (parents) of their right to challenge and question the diagnosis offered.
3. The Association of Black Psychology, APA, and state licensing boards should work together to assure integration of an Afrocentric perspective into graduate training programs.
4. Consultation with a senior clinician skilled in diagnosis and treatment of African Americans is critical.
5. The clinician's diagnostic hypotheses should always prompt a series of questions so that the patient responds only with symptoms relevant to the hypothesis. The hypotheses and questions must elicit Afrocentrically related diagnostic issues.

Source: Johnson (1993)

about seeking mental health treatment (Snowden, 2001) and the external barriers include the economic and accessibility issues discussed in chapter 3 (e.g., limited access to mental health treatment facilities, lack of health insurance) as well as attitudes and negative interactions with mental health professionals (Hines-Martin, Malone, Kim, & Brown-Piper, 2003).

African American children are treated differently in terms of therapeutic approaches. African American children are less likely than their White counterparts to be referred for individual therapy. Rather, they are more likely to be recommended for group or peer counseling. There is ample evidence to suggest that African American children do benefit from individual counseling (Boyd-Franklin, 1989)

Allen and Majidi-Ahi (1989) suggests that therapists working with African American children and their families approach therapy from a social ecological perspective. This perspective entails an awareness of African American racial identity issues and the process of racial identity, language issues, as well as family dynamics.

Boyd-Franklin (1989) recommends that therapists working with African American children employ a multisystems approach. This approach involves including all members of the family, both nuclear and extended, who have a direct link to the child in the therapeutic process. Therapists working with

African American children and their families must expect to assume a variety of roles. Those roles may include serving as a mediator between the family and the school system or identifying and linking the family to the appropriate social service agencies.

Others working with African American children and their families have found cognitive, behavioral, and insight therapy to be effective forms of therapy (Spurlock, 1985).

Regardless of the type of therapy used, the most important factors for successful therapy are: (1) a willingness for the therapist to tailor therapy to the family's belief system and goals and; (2) an awareness of the influence of race, socio-economic status, culture, and environment on African American family functioning.

SECTION TWO: RACIAL IDENTITY

One major developmental task for African American children is the development of racial identity (Spencer, 1982). A strong racial identity is considered to be an important buffer against those racial experiences and a critical aspect of parental racial socialization behavior.

At what age do African American children begin to notice racial differences, particularly their own differences? How does this awareness affect their self-esteem? What role do parents play in socializing African American children? Just how the process of racial identity occurs has been the subject of research dating back to the1930s.

The initial investigations examining the development of racial identity in African American children were conducted by several researchers (Horowitz, 1939), but Kenneth Clark and Mamie Clark (1939, 1947) were considered to be the leading experts on racial identity development and Black children (see the *American Psychologist* [2002] for a review of their contributions to the discipline of social psychology).

Theoretically, the Clarks believed that the self, a core part of the personality, (e.g., that is who we define ourselves as, what we believe and feel about ourselves) was in part determined by our identification with a group, and in part determined by our beliefs or feelings about the status of that group. According to the Clarks, as children engage in the process of acquiring group identification, and learn about the status of their group, they become aware of racial differences; they begin to develop racial preferences and to develop a personal racial identity. Based on this theory, the Clarks conducted a series of studies to assess the development of awareness of racial differences, to determine racial preferences and racial self-identification in African American children. These studies were collectively referred to as the Doll Studies.

Two central findings emerged from their work. One, racial awareness is present in African American children as young as age 3; and two, the children consistently demonstrated a preference for the white doll in their responses. The later finding, according to the Clarks, may be an indication of "self-ha-tred." They believed that this early rejection of the colored doll was a reflection of the children's internalization of societal beliefs about the valence of being black and being white. According to the Clarks, "this struggle introduces early in the formation of the personality of these children a fundamental conflict about themselves" (see Figure 4.3).

The racial preference findings and the self-hatred hypothesis proposed by the Clarks sparked controversy and criticisms for more than five decades. The follow-ing problems were cited by social scientists. First, the validity of the measures to assess racial preferences and racial attitudes was questioned. Critics were doubtful that dolls alone would yield an accurate assessment of racial preferences and racial attitudes (Banks, 1976). Second, Banks, (1976) found in his reanalyzation of the earlier data that the children's responses conformed to simple chance responses. Thus the types of questions and the order of the presentation of the questions may have primed a response in the children. Third, Cross (1991) argues that the physical attributes and the novelty of the white doll may have contributed to the children's preference for the white doll over the black doll.

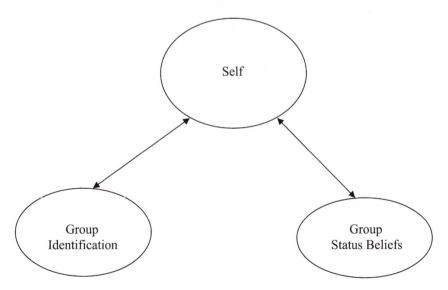

FIGURE 4.3   Racial identification model.
Source: Clark & Clark (1940).

The majority of the studies conducted since the Clarks' early investigations have examined racial preferences in African American children. These studies have spanned a 40-year period, and employed a variety of approaches to tap racial preferences. The data presented in Figure 4.4 represents a summary of the major preference findings of those studies.

As the figure indicates there was an overall increase in preference for the Black doll from 1950 to 1980. Many researchers have attributed the positive orientation to the Black doll as a result of sociopolitical movements (e.g. the Civil Rights Movement, the Black Power Movement), the positive portrayal of Blacks by the media, and the increase in the number of Black dolls available to African American children.

However, notice that the figure indicates a reversal in preference for the Black doll beginning in the 1980s. Researchers have had difficulty in interpreting this pattern, however one speculation is that the resurgence of racial intolerance that characterized the 1980s may have been a contributing factor and reflects internalized attitudes of the children.

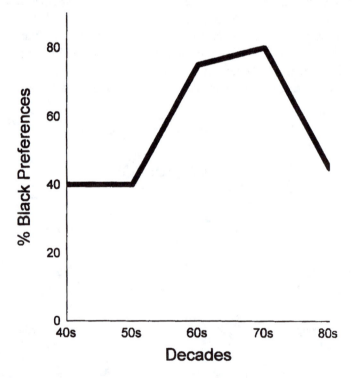

FIGURE 4.4   Racial preference study outcomes, 1940–1980.
Source: Banks (1976).

In the 1980s and the 1990s investigators took a different direction in exploring racial identification in African American children. The majority of those studies, although sparse, focused on such issues as modifying racial attitudes and racial preferences in African American children, assessing the relationship between self-concept and racial attitudes and racial preferences, and exploring cognitive models of racial identification.

Modifiability Studies. The goal of the modifiability studies was to determine if racial preferences could be changed by basic operant principles. Powell-Hopson and Hopson (1988) designed a two-phase study to test this idea. In the first phase of the study, 105 Black preschoolers and 50 White preschoolers were presented with dolls that were exactly alike except for skin color and hair texture and were asked preference questions: which doll do you want to be?; which doll do you like to play with?; which doll is a nice doll?; which doll looks bad?, which doll is a nice color?; which doll you would take home if you could?

At first, the majority of the children expressed an overwhelming preference for the white doll. The second phase of the study involved an intervention. In the intervention, the children were read a story depicting black children positively. The children were also asked to hold up the black dolls and repeat positive statements. After a 15 minute break, the children were re-administered the doll test. Posttest results indicated that the majority of the children demonstrated a preference for the black doll.

The researchers concluded that in a controlled environment, the racial attitudes of black children and white children could be modified. At some level children who incorporate negative societal messages about African Americans can be taught to change those attitudes. How these changes persist over time merits closer inspection.

Self-Concept and Racial Attitudes in African Americans. Is there a link between self-concept and racial orientation in African American children? McAdoo (1988) designed a longitudinal study to address the question. Using a methodology similar to the Clarks' to measure racial orientation, and several measures to tap self-concept, he followed a group of young children ages 3 through 6, for 5 years. His results indicated that the relationship between self-concept and racial attitudes remained statistically non-significant over the 5-year period. However, incidental findings revealed that the self-concept of these children increased over the 5 years, and their racial attitudes were initially moderately out-group oriented (e.g., they identified with a racial group other than their own) but became more in-group oriented over the 5-year period. McAdoo proposed the compartmentalization hypothesis to explain the findings. This hypothesis suggests that Black children are able to feel good about themselves independent of their favorable perception of a racial group other than their own. Therefore their racial attitudes and preferences are a reflection of their ability to effectively compartmentalize racial issues and not a reflection of their self-concept.

Cognitive Level and Racial Attitudes. McAdoo's finding that the children moved from being out-group oriented to in-group oriented over a period of 5 years points to the need to explore how their thinking, their reasoning, and their understanding of the concept of race influences their racial preferences and attitudes. Various theorists have proposed cognitive focused models for several years (Spencer, 1982; Semaj, 1980).

These theorists maintain that African American children progress from lower to higher levels of thinking, reasoning, and understanding race. This progression of their cognitive level influences their racial preferences and attitudes. It is not until the children are able to decenter, and to conserve issues about race, that they are able to understand racial differences and to have racial preferences. The central features of the cognitive models are presented in Box 4.3.

BOX 4.3

COGNITIVE MODEL OF RACIAL IDENTITY DEVELOPMENT

Stage	Characteristics
1. Racial Classification	understanding of racial differences
2. Racial Awareness	understanding that differences are limited to skin color, ability to categorize people by ethnic group
3. Racial Constancy/Stability	understanding that race is permanent
4. Racial Preferences	identification/attitudes

In addition to the cognitive factors identified above, researchers hypothesize that social and environmental factors either directly on indirectly influence the racial identity development (Marshall, 1994). Bronfenbrener's Ecological theory (1986) provides a useful framework for exploring those influences on the development of racial identity in African American children (an example of the model is presented in Box 4.4.).

Researchers have employed variants of his model to identify how social and environmental factors influence racial identity development (Dutton, Singer, & Devlin, 1998; Jaggers & Mock, 1993).

BOX 4.4

ECOLOGICAL MODEL OF RACIAL IDENTITY DEVELOPMENT

Level	Questions
Microsystem	How does the child's immediate environment influence racial identity development (e.g., parents, activities in the home, where the child lives)?
Mesosystem	As the child enters school (e.g., daycare) what experiences have an impact directly on the child's racial identity and what experiences have an impact on the parent's role or behavior in the development of the child's racial identity?
Exosystem	How do parental experiences with racial issues impact their parenting and their discussions about racial issues and racial identity?
Macrosystem	How has affirmative action/desegregation had an impact on racial identity development?
Chronosystem	How do political/societal changes impact racial identity? development?

Parents of African American children have the unique challenge of socializing their children to live a dual existence in society. That is, they must teach their children to recognize and embrace their relationship to a minority group as well as acknowledge their existence in a broader multiracial society. One particular childrearing task that parents must face is the task of racial socialization. Are there specific socialization practices and behaviors they use? The extant research on African American parents and racial socialization has increased in the past 40 years (see Hughes and Chen, 1997, for review). The research has addressed such questions as how and when do parents convey information about race to their children, what sort of information do they convey about race, and the context or situation that serves as a catalyst for discussions about race.

The conversations about race begin at an early age, around 6 or 7, the age at which most African American children have achieved a sense of racial identity. Peters (1988) found that the majority of the parents emphasize the following: (1) bicultural adaptation, (2) imparting the importance of self-respect and pride, (3) understanding the unfairness of others, (4) strong family ties, and (5) a positive orientation to one's ethnic group. Hughes and Chen (1997), on the other hand, observe that the content of those discussions can be classified into four areas: cultural socialization (discussions about ancestry, culture, heritage), preparation for bias (awareness of discrimination, unfair treatment) socialization of mistrust (distrust of people of other racial groups), and egalitarian socialization (discussions about the value and importance of people from all racial backgrounds). Hot stove encounters (see Box 4.5 for an example of a Hot Stove encounter) frequently serve as the vehicle for those discussions about race (Daniel & Daniel, 1990). These encounters are described as overt and covert racial experiences, typically negative, which African American children encounter. These experiences are unexpected, and parents often have little control over when and where those encounters will occur. According to Daniel and Daniel, parents can equip their children with skills to cope with hot stove encounters by using a variety of parenting strategies such as modeling, and providing their children with survival messages (e.g., proverbs).

Television shows and the news also provide parents with teachable moments to discuss racial issues with their children.

Thornton et al. (1990) found that there is little consensus among African American parents regarding the importance of socializing their children about racial issues. For some, race is a central concern, so therefore they directly provide information to their children. For others, race plays an insignificant role in their socialization behaviors and goals. These parents state that they hesitate to discuss racial issues for the fear that their children will become bitter and resentful. In either case, mothers tend to be the primary socialization agents.

How do these parenting behaviors influence young children's beliefs, feelings, and behaviors about racial issues? The research examining outcomes is sparse, however, of the available literature the findings suggest that an overemphasis

---

BOX 4.5

"HOT STOVE EXPERIENCES"

I can remember when I first learned that I was different—racially different that is. I was about five and I was attending Sunday school when this white boy called me a n_____. I remember coming home and running up and down the hall in our home, shouting n_____, n_____, n_____. My mother was appalled and demanded to know where I heard the word. From Sunday school I replied. From that day forward, I realized that I was different and that my parent's role in preparing me to deal with those who would not accept my difference as an African American had just begun.

on racial barriers and discrimination seem to undermine achievement and prevent the formation of interracial friendships (Christian & Barbarin, 2001; Ogbu, 1974). On the other hand, parents who chose not to provide their children with any information about racial issues leave their children with little protection (Caughy, O'Campo, Randolph, & Nickerson, 2002).

PERSPECTIVES ON MENTAL HEALTH AND RACIAL IDENTITY

If there is one area in child development that is in need of research it is the area of mental health issues and African American children. Epidemiological studies that describe the onset, duration, and characteristics of psychopathology for African American children are essential. In addition, research on effective assessment techniques, diagnostic tools, and therapeutic interventions is urgent. As discussed earlier in the chapter, some African American children are resilient and successfully emerge from the most difficult life circumstances. Barbarin's model is a first step in identifying culturally relevant protective factors. Thus, this model might prove useful for subsequent research. For example, such questions can be addressed as: do these protective factors change in their ability to buffer children?; and how do the children change developmentally?

The current consensus on the development of racial identity in African American children is that their identity development is facilitated by a host of social and environmental influences. Those influences include parents, relatives, peers, and teachers, and at some level, the media. Given that research has documented that a strong racial identity serves as a buffer against those hot stove experiences described in this chapter, subsequent investigations should focus on generating developmental models of racial identity development. Furthermore, those models should outline the relationship between different patterns of racial socialization, parenting behavior, and the psychosocial adjustment and psychosocial outcomes for African American children.

CHAPTER SUMMARY

The chapter presents an overview of the mental health status of African American children, with particular attention paid to the risk factors that predispose them to mental health problems. The chapter addresses the internal and external factors, which serve to buffer some African American children from severe mental health outcomes.

CHAPTER 5

Education and African American Children

OVERVIEW

The education of African American children has consistently generated discussion and debate among educators, social scientists, the media, and the courts. One topic in particular, desegregation, has occupied the attention of the nation for more than 40 years. The educational experience of African American children, unlike the educational experiences of their counterparts from other ethnic groups, has had a long, complex, controversial political and legal history.

The goal of this chapter is to discuss those educational experiences and to discuss the factors that impact their educational progress. The chapter is divided into four sections.

The first section of the chapter, School Desegregation and African American Children, provides information about the landmark court decision *Brown v. the Board of Education,* which changed the course of education for children of all races in the 20th century. The second section of the chapter discusses African American children in the public school system, specifically highlighting their academic performance and identifying the factors that influence their academic achievement. The third section of the chapter presents early intervention programs and information on public and private schools that work for African American children. The chapter concludes with a discussion of perspectives on education and African American children.

SECTION ONE: SCHOOL DESEGREGATION AND AFRICAN AMERICAN CHILDREN

We begin with a discussion of desegregation, education and African American children.

INSIDER'S VOICE: RESEGREGATION OF AMERICA'S PUBLIC SCHOOLS

In January 2003, an article entitled "School Segregation Growing" written by Fredreka Schouten (Gannett News Service) appeared in the *Cincinnati Enquirer*. The article discusses a disturbing trend, the resegregation of America's urban public schools. According to Ms. Schouten, a study conducted by Harvard University professor Dr. Gary Orfield and colleagues, revealed that urban public schools are becoming increasingly segregated. During the 2000–2001 academic year, more than 70% of Black and Hispanic students attended minority schools. Dr. Orfield believes that this resegregation has resulted in creating a form of "educational apartheid." "These schools tend to have fewer qualified teachers, and the students are presented with less challenging course work than students in integrated suburban schools. The tragedy is that the resegregation of public schools is undermining the quality of education that minority students receive. The trend is going to produce a deeply unequal education and a more polarized society," Mr. Orfield said.

Desegregation and African American Children

The story reported in the Insider's Voice on school desegregation is one issue that has dominated the heart of national politics and educational policies for the past 50 years. The movement from segregated schools to desegregated schools and finally to resegregated schools has been an extensive and complicated movement.

In 1954, the United States Supreme Court ruled that school segregation was unconstitutional and that schools must begin to desegregate with all deliberate speed (Gardner & Miranda, 2001). This ruling was a result of a series of court cases challenging the separate but equal educational doctrine that had operated in the United States for more than 70 years.

Prior to 1954, African American children and White children, primarily in the southern region of the United States, attended legally segregated schools. Those schools were inferior in both physical structure and educational quality. Black students were taught with outdated textbooks, lacked transportation to schools, and their school buildings were inadequately maintained (Dentler, 1991).

A collective of African American parents, educators along with the National Association for the Advancement of Colored People (NAACP), initiated legal action in both local and federal courts to protest this disparity.

According to the plaintiffs, this substandard education contributed to feelings of inferiority, lowered self-esteem, and lowered self-concept in Black children, and resulted in decreased occupational opportunities for them as adults (Irons, 1994).

On May 17, 1954, the United States Supreme Court ruled that school segregation in any form was illegal, racially identifiable schools must be eliminated and school districts must implement plans to desegregate their school districts. The legal case became known as the *Brown v. Board of Education of Topeka, Kansas* (see *Eyes on the Prize* for an excellent documentation of the case).

Resistance to school desegregation was widespread across the United States and efforts to stall desegregation were encouraged by state and local officials. In many parts of the United States, White parents and White citizens violently protested the entrance of Black students into schools. Federal troops were dispatched to provide protection for the students (e.g., Little Rock, Arkansas). It was not until passage of the 1964 Civil Rights Act that "sufficient movement was given to ensure progress in implementing the Court's ruling." The most consistent efforts to desegregate schools occurred between 1965 and 1973 (Fife, 1992). (See Box 5.1 for documentation on resistance to school desegregation).

Without specific directions and guidance from the courts, local school districts were left to develop their own desegregation plans. Those plans varied considerably from state to state and from school district to school district (Hayes, 1981).

BOX 5.1

Despite the 1954 *Brown* v. *Board of Education* ruling that required desegregation of public schools in America, one year after the decision most southern schools were still segregated and the quality of education offered to Black students was still far from equal to that offered to White students. In response, the Court ordered schools to integrate with all deliberate speed. With no definitive deadline, many states felt free to ignore the demand. In an effort to hold onto the long-standing tradition of segregation, many Whites joined the Ku Klux Klan and loosely organized groups called "White citizens councils" to terrorize and intimidate Blacks.

Chronology of Court Rulings and Efforts to Stall Desegregation

1954

The Supreme Court hands down the *Brown* v. *Board of Education* decision, stating that segregated school are inherently unequal, thus overturning the legal foundations of segregation.

School boards in Baltimore and Washington, DC, begin efforts to desegregate their systems.

1955

The Supreme Court, reacting to the slow pace of school desegregation following its *Brown v. Board of Education* decision, orders that school systems begin to integrate with all deliberate speed.

The Georgia Board of Education announces that it will revoke the license of any teacher who teaches in an integrated classroom.

1956

Three days after a Black woman named Autherine Lucy attends classes at the previously all-White University of Alabama, riots break out on campus, and threats are made on her life. In response, the school suspends Lucy. Following her court ordered re-instatement, the University expels her.

One hundred and one southern congressmen sign a "Southern Manifesto," recommending that public schools continue to ignore the Supreme Courts order to integrate. Only three members of the southern delegation to Congress—Estes Kefauver of Tennessee, Albert Gore, Sr., also of Tennessee, and Lyndon B. Johnson of Texas—refuse to sign.

1957

Governor Orville Faubus of Arkansas orders the Arkansas National Guard to block nine African American children from integrating the school. In response, President Dwight D. Eisenhower sends in paratroopers from the 101st Airborne to enforce the Supreme Court's ruling.

1961

Four high schools in Atlanta integrate without incident, earning the praise of President John F. Kennedy.

Administrators respond to student protests at Southern Louisiana University by shutting down the school.

1962

The Supreme Court orders the University of Mississippi to admit James Meredith as a student. Following a violent confrontation between White protestors and federal authorities, Meredith enters the school.

1963

Alabama governor George Wallace attempts to physically block Vivian Malone and James Hood from entering the University of Alabama.

1967

Ruling in *United States v. Jefferson County* that "the only school desegregation plan that meets constitutional standard is the one that works," the Fifth District of the U.S. Circuit Court helps speed the process of desegregation.

Source: African-American Experience on File

In the early 1960s, school districts opted to use freedom of choice and open enrollment as their desegregation efforts. Both of these methods were minimally effective in desegregating schools. At the urging of the courts, school districts turned to other methods such as pairing, rezoning, pupil placement laws, minority to majority enrollment, and reassignment from neighborhood schools via court ordered busing (see Fife, 1992 for a review).

Court-ordered busing, implemented in both the North and the South, was perhaps the most controversial facet of desegregation and caused negative and violent reactions from some parents across the nation (see Irons, 2002, for a discussion of the Finger Plan). Court-ordered busing was discontinued in the late 1970s.

During the 1980s, the desegregation process came to a standstill, and the courts ceased to monitor school districts and their compliance to the federal law.

For more than 30 years, scholars have debated whether desegregation has had a positive impact on the educational achievement of African American children. The research exploring this issue has yielded mixed results.

Systematic data collection did not begin until 1969, when the National Assessment of Educational Progress (NAEP) commissioned a study to examine the achievement test performance of African American children. From 1970 to 1984, 12 studies were conducted evaluating the impact of desegregation on the educational performance of African American children.

Few comprehensive studies have been conducted since the 1980s. Collectively, the findings from this body of research suggest two patterns: (1) Since 1971, the achievement test scores of African American elementary school children have steadily increased; and (2) despite this increase, African American elementary school children have lagged behind their White counterparts on all achievement measures by an average of 33 points (Garibaldi, 1997).

Some social scientists argue that it is difficult to determine the full impact of desegregation on the educational progress of African American children for the following reasons.

First, a decade after the *Brown v. Board of Education* judgment a significant proportion of African American students were still attending segregated schools. As late as the 1972–1973 school year, 63% of the African American children attended predominantly Black schools, and these schools remained intellectually and structurally inferior (Gadsen, Smith & Jordan, 1996).

Second, 20 years after the court ruling, there was a 70% increase in the number of African American children attending segregated schools. Some scholars question whether desegregation was ever truly implemented and contend that increases in tests scores were not an outcome of desegregation (Vergon, 1990).

Third, the methodology in each of the studies conducted on achievement and desegregation vary significantly (e.g., different outcome measure, different time of measurement, different operational definitions of desegregation). Therefore, empirically it is difficult to formulate widespread and final conclusions about desegregation, African American children, and academic achievement.

Fourth, even though studies do indicate that the achievement gap has narrowed and that high school graduation rates and college enrollment have increased, the improvements affect only a very small percentage of African American students.

For the vast majority of African American students, desegregation has had a questionable or a detrimental influence on their educational process. Black students are more likely than their White counterparts to be expelled, suspended, or pushed out of school. Garabaldi and Bartley (1989) reported that in one school district, African American students comprised 41% of the school population, but 65% of those students were suspended. African American students are often placed in lower track courses or special education courses; as a whole, they take fewer foreign language courses, advanced math, or science courses, and therefore they are often unprepared to attend a four-year college or university. They are less likely than White students to participate in extracurricular activities, such as the marching band, the debate club, or other school-related activities. The nature and the quality of their classroom experiences differ from those of their White counterparts as well (Gadsen, 1996). Teachers have lower expectations for their academic success and potential, and tend to report them more often than their White counterparts as experiencing behavioral problems (Cornbleth & Korth, 1980). Consequently, African American students drop out of school in record numbers because of the differential attention, and due to their feelings of alienation.

Brown (1994) believes that desegregation has served to undermine the academic achievement of African American children in significant ways. Many African American neighborhood and community schools were closed, and African American children were bused to predominantly White neighborhoods.

Consequently, African American children lost important academic community anchors. The racial composition of schools that remained predominantly African American changed radically. Black teachers were fired and replaced with White teachers (Bankston & Caldas, 1996). At the onset of desegregation, 6,000 Black teachers were dismissed, and 25,584 were displaced (Jones, 1994). Some White teachers viewed teaching in these schools as a less desirable assignment. The least qualified and least experienced teachers were assigned to Black schools (Bruno & Doscher, 1981). Thus, as a result of desegregation, African American children lost academic role models.

There are researchers who counter and maintain that there is ample evidence to suggest that desegregation has had a positive impact on the academic achievement of African American children. As a consequence of desegregation, the reading achievement scores of African American children have improved in the last two decades, the dropout rates for African American students have decreased in the last three decades, and there have been advancements made in interracial social relationships and job opportunities (Schofiled, 1995). Furthermore, the achievement gap between African American students and White students has narrowed considerably due primarily to desegregation (Mahard, & Crain, 1983).

Forty-eight years after the *Brown v. Board* decision, as stated in the Insider's Voice, the resegregation of African American children in the public school system is on the rise and approaching the levels of 1970. Nationally, a third of African American children attend schools where the enrollment is 90–100% minority. The concern as raised by Dr. Orfield in the Insider's Voice is that these schools do not equip African American students with the academic skills they need to succeed. Unfortunately, African American parents expressed this same concern more than 40 years ago.

Social scientists have also voiced concerns about the plight of African American children in the public school system (Trent, 1997).

African American children comprise 50% of the enrollment in 9.7% of America's public elementary schools (U.S. Census Bureau, Statistical Abstracts of the United States, 2006). They are enrolled primarily in schools located in the urban areas of the United States and schools located in areas with high concentrations of poverty.

Based on indices of academic achievement, African American children have not fared well in the public school system. On critical measures of academic achievement, African American students consistently lag behind their White counterparts. Data in Figures 5.1–5.3 compare the reading, writing, and math achievement test scores of African American fourth graders and White fourth graders. The data in the tables suggest that the performance of fourth graders on reading, writing, and math tests has been steady, with few remarkable changes in achievement for more than two decades. However, when the performance of African American children is compared to that of their White counterparts, the achievement gap is most observable in the reading achievement scores. This suggests that on the one hand, African American children are able to follow brief written directions, and engage in simple reading tasks. On the other hand, the pattern indicates that African American fourth grade children are not developing the reading skills necessary to master complex reading material.

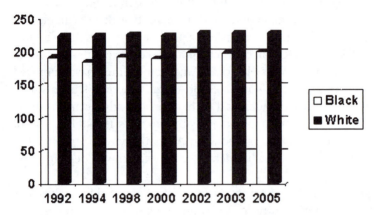

FIGURE 5.1   Fourth Grade Reading Proficiency Test Scores, 1992–2005
Source: National Center for Education Statistics, 2006.

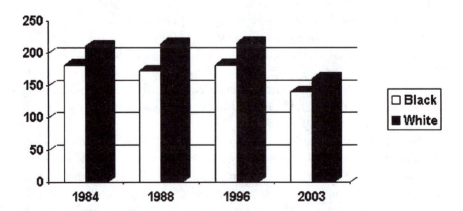

FIGURE 5.2   Fourth Grade Writing Proficiency Test Scores, 1984–2003
Source: U.S. Census Bureau, and Statistical Abstracts of the U.S., 2003.

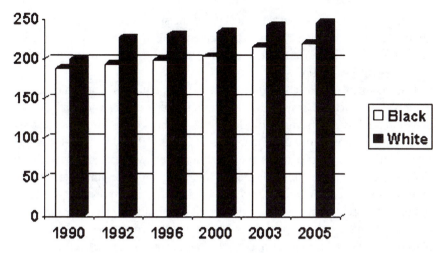

FIGURE 5.3   Fourth Grade Math Proficiency Test Scores, 1990–2005
Source: National Center for Education Statistics, 2006.

Over the past several decades, a myriad of theories have been proposed to account for the achievement gap between African American children and White children. These theories have ranged from genetic inferiority accounts (Hernstein & Murray, 1994), to environmental deprivation perspectives (Scarr & Weinberg, 1978), to socioeconomic status, to persistent economic hardship views (Duncan & Magnuson, 2005); parenting practices (Brooks-Gunn & Markman, 2005), the quality of early childhood education programs (Magnuson & Waldfogel, 2005) to cultural background (Boykin, 1986).

According to Irvine (1990), Garabaldi (1997), and Pollard (1989), the achievement gap is not a result of those factors, but due to an interaction of factors inherent in the structure of the public school system that predispose African American students for academic failure and leave them ill-prepared for college and gainful employment.

The factors inherent in the structure of the public school system include placement in special education classes, teacher attitude and expectations, peer influence, and parental involvement.

Placement in Special Education Classes. African American children are disproportionately placed in classes for the educable mentally retarded (EMR) based on their performance on intelligence tests and achievement measures.

In an analysis of 505 school districts in Alabama, Georgia, South Carolina, Mississippi, and Arkansas, over 80% of the students enrolled in educable mental retardation (EMR) classes were Black and the majority of these students were African American males. African American students comprise 16%

of the public school population, but 35% of the special education population (Harry & Anderson, 1994). These placements begin at an early age and for many African American students there are few opportunities to re-enter regular classes (Oakes, 1995).

Placement in special education classes affects students' academic performance in a variety of ways. First, the quality of teaching and teacher student interaction differs markedly from the quality of teaching and teacher student interaction found in regular classes. Oakes (1995) found that teachers of African American students in special education classes expect less of them. These expectations are often reflected in their teaching styles and interactions. During those interactions, teachers provided students with fewer opportunities to learn essential information and to build the academic skills that prepare them for high school completion and gainful employment. Second, students placed in EMR classes fail to make achievement gains. In fact, achievement test scores decrease from grades three through eight. Third, students' self-concept and peer relationships are damaged as a result of the stigma associated with placement in special education classes (Trent, 1997).

The placement of African American children in special education became a legal issue in the 1970s (Macmillian, Hendrick & Watkins, 1989). Two cases, *Diana v. Board of Education* (1970) and *Larry P. v. Wilson Riles* (1971), serve as the landmark cases, prohibiting the use of IQ tests to assign African American children to special education classes. In both of the cases, the litigants argued that standardized IQ tests used to assess African American children were culturally and racially biased; and placement in special education resulted in little remediation or efforts to improve their deficits. Consequently, these students failed to complete high school and were unable to secure employment as adults (Reschly, 1982).

The judge concurred with the plaintiffs and ruled that the method of evaluating and placing students was inappropriate in two ways: Standardized tests were discriminatory toward African American students; and the history of placing African American students in EMR classes pointed to unlawful segregated intent (Prasse & Reschly, 1986).

As a result of the court ruling, changes were implemented in both testing and placement policies, especially for African American children and other children of color. Guidelines for nondiscriminatory assessment were developed (see Table 5.1), and Public Law 94–142 was established to ensure due process and legal protection for African American children and other children of color (Gardner & Miranda, 2001).

Despite the public law, the legislation mandating changes in testing African American children, and the development of nondiscriminatory guidelines,

TABLE 5.1   Guidelines for Nondiscriminatory Assessment

1. A student must be assessed in their native language.	5. Every student identified as having a disability must be re-evaluated every 3 years.
2. Tests must evaluate what they were intended to evaluate.	6. An individual educational plan must be developed for each child.
3. Examiner must be appropriately trained to administer and interpret specific test results.	7. Parents must be involved in discussions of placement and assessment.
4. Placement decisions cannot be made on the basis of any single factor. A multidisciplinary team or group of educational practitioners must make the decision.	

Source: Wodrich, (1997). Children's Psychological Testing.

African American children still remain overrepresented in EMR classes (Gardner & Miranda, 2001).

Social scientists speculate that this practice continues because teacher training programs fail to adequately expose teachers to cultural issues and how those issues impact test performance of African American children; schools are not monitored for their compliance to the federal law; and are not required to demonstrate improvement in tests scores of children placed in EMR classes. (Nelson, 1995)

Teacher Attitudes, Expectations and Teaching Styles. The teacher expectancy theory holds that teachers communicate both subtly and overtly their attitudes and expectations about their students' achievement capabilities. In response, students perform according to the teacher's attitudes and expectations (Rosenthal & Jacobson, 1982). In the specific case of African American children, researchers have observed that very often teacher attitudes and expectations for success are lower for African American students than for White students (Seyfried, 1998).

Beane (1985) found that even when academic performance is similar, teachers view African American students as low achievers and majority students as high achievers. They are critical of their academic work and pessimistic about their prognosis for academic success; they often judge Black students as the least studious and least prepared, and the teachers describe the Black students as talkative, lazy, fun-loving, high strung, and rebellious. In one detailed observation of student-teacher classroom interaction, White students received more praise and encouragement for their classroom performances regardless of the teacher's race than did African American students (Baker, 1999).

Rong (1997) proposes that these teacher attitudes and expectations are caused in part by cultural incongruence: The majority of the teachers are White, female, middle class graduates of teacher training programs. The programs provide little guidance on working with children of color. Therefore, the teachers may have pre-set and sometimes unfavorable notions about the intellectual and academic capabilities of African American children.

In addition to teacher attitudes and expectations, the teaching techniques used in urban school settings fail to prepare and equip African American students with important academic skills and critical learning skills. Carta (1991) found that in a typical day in an inner-city classroom, students are exposed to more audiovisual materials and teacher-directed class discussions than one-on-one teacher interaction and independent seat work. The former requires less active responding from the students, encourages passive attention, and results in lower levels of achievement (Carta, 1991); or what Greenwood, Hart, Walker, & Rishley, (1994) refer to as "developmental retardation." As a consequence of this type of instruction, which fails to challenge and actively engage African American students with the material, students lag behind their peers in suburban schools in their mastery of basic academic skills; and this is reflected in their performance on state and national achievement tests (see Box 5.2).

In terms of specific academic subjects, Strutchens and Silver (2000) found that in the area of math instruction, teachers tend to emphasize reasoning skills in their instruction to White students, whereas teachers tend to use drill-based instruction with their African American students. In terms of assessment, Lubienski (2002) found that African American children are more likely than their White counterparts to receive multiple choice exams, and exams that require fewer computational and reasoning skills.

BOX 5.2

IS THERE AN AFRICAN AMERICAN LEARNING STYLE?

Several social scientists have encouraged educators to tailor their teaching style to the learning and cognitive styles of African American children (Hurley, Boykin & Allen, 2005; Watkins 2002; Willis, 1992). These scholars maintain that the teaching and instructional style used in most elementary schools is an analytical type of style. This type of style involves the use of rules, encourages memory for specific facts, emphasizes the use of logic, and utilizes deductive reasoning. According to Hilliard, this is in contrast to the cognitive style that African American children use to process information. Their style is a relational cognitive style that emphasizes the use of freedom of exploration, memory for the essence of material, and the use of inductive reasoning.

The information presented in the preceding section discusses the major factors that are believed to influence albeit negatively, the academic performance of African American children in the public school system. Other factors such as academic self-confidence, peer influence, and alienation of African American parents from the school system are also linked as well.

Academic Self-Concept and Peer Influence. Some scholars argue that the public school system has created a sense of learned helplessness or a cycle of frustration within African American children and as a result their academic performance is adversely impacted (Graham, 1994). According to Claude Steele (1995), as a consequence of repeated exposure to indifferent and negative treatment from teachers, African American children internalize those experiences, and construct a "mental model." This mental model is easily retrievable even when the stimulus is absent. Steele refers to this as stereotype threat. Any situation can trigger the activation of the mental model, and those experiences become so salient and vivid that the children foreclose on their academic abilities and their academic performance is hampered.

Alternately, Fordham and Ogbu (1986) argue that African American children seek out negative experiences, which affirm their sense of low self esteem, in order to protect their identity or buffer their self-esteem from the indifferent and negative treatment received in school. This is acted out in their resistance or opposition to teachers, or to the authority structure of the school. The peer culture, rather than the school culture, becomes the respected authority figure in the school environment. Peers then, play a profound role in influencing each other's academic achievement. This peer culture provides opportunities, especially for African American boys, to demonstrate competence and to maintain a sense of self-respect (Polite & Davis, 1999).

Alienation of African American Parents From the Educational System. Researchers have long acknowledged that parental support and involvement in the academic lives of their children is a key variable in ensuring the academic success of children (Tucker, Harris, Brady, & Herman, 1996). However, low-income African American parents do not participate at the same level as do middle class parents in the academic lives of their children (Halle, Costes & Mahonney, 1997). Such factors as their single parenthood, their socioeconomic status, and their low educational attainment level have been identified as contributing to their low participation rates (Zionts, Zionts, Harrison, & Bellinger, 2003). Teachers often describe low-income African American parents as uninterested, inaccessible, and difficult to communicate with (Trotman, 2001). Low-income African American parents on the other hand, report feeling unwelcome, alienated, dismissed, and unfairly treated by both teachers and administrators in the public school system. Therefore, they limit their contact with teachers and administrators.

Trotman (2001) offers the following ten suggestions for increasing the involvement of low-income African American parents (Box 5.3).

BOX 5.3

Increasing African American Parental Involvement in Schools

1. Urge parents to remain or become active in their children's educational process.
2. Make sure that each child is properly educated and attends school regularly.
3. Develop a case history of the family in an effort to determine what is hindering their involvement.
4. Establish a rapport with parents.
5. Provide parents with authority.
6. Follow the lead of chapter 1 programs. Implement programs which assist parents in developing their own academic skills.
7. Ask parents about their interest in school.
8. Ask parents who attend meetings to spread the word to other parents.
9. Use parents as teaching partners.
10. Do not judge or criticize parents.

SECTION TWO: SCHOOLS THAT WORK FOR AFRICAN AMERICAN CHILDREN

There are public and private schools located across the United States that are effective in facilitating the academic success of African American children. These schools provide African American children with a solid educational foundation that prepares them for college and later employment opportunities.

The next section of the chapter focuses on discussing the characteristics of both public and private schools that work for African American children.

Public School Models

The concern with the failure of public schools to effectively educate African American children forced scholars to critically examine the structure of the public school system, identify those aspects that were in need of modification, and develop and implement programs or models that were sensitive to African American cultural and historical issues.

These schools follow either James Comer's School Development Program Model, or Ron Edmonds Effective School Model. Examples of these schools were highlighted in the 1988 special issue of the *Journal of Negro Education*. Each school is located in an urban area, where the majority of the families are low income, and the majority of the children are from single-parent family homes. Each of the schools has received both national and local recognition for significantly improving the students' achievement test scores, increasing school attendance, and decreasing disciplinary problems.

Dr. James Comer conceived the idea of the School Development Program (SDP), in 1968, with the conviction that schools located in low-income areas were capable of providing African American students with a quality and a solid education. He believed that public schools could improve academic achievement outcomes for African American children if collaborative relationships were established between administrators, teachers and parents; he also believed that administrators, teachers, and parents, rather than district school boards, should assume the leadership role and determine the structure of key aspects of the school. The core features of the SDP are presented below.

Governance and Management Team. This team is composed of the principal, teachers from each grade level, parents, and members of the mental health team. This team is responsible for implementing academic plans and evaluating curricula, staff development, student achievement, and the general climate of the school. Unlike typical urban public schools, which are under the auspices of school boards, or the principals, the governance and management team, assumes total control over the functioning of the school.

Mental Health Team. The mental health team, according to Comer, is a crucial and important element of the school. In typical urban public schools, there is usually one school psychologist (with a very heavy cases load) assigned to several schools, shouldering the responsibility for working with a number of teachers and students from many school districts. This person is also responsible for assessing and meeting the mental health needs of the students.

In the SDP, this becomes the responsibility of a team of individuals called the mental health team. This team is composed of social workers, psychologists, and teachers who provide counseling and assessment for students, consult with teachers, and offer outreach to the children and their families. In addition, the team is in charge of developing and implementing alternative methods for dealing with behavior problems.

Parent Participation. Parents assume a variety of roles in the SDP model, ranging from being classroom aides and hall monitors to library assistants. Unlike in the typical urban public school setting, parents' participation is actively sought and rewarded.

Staff Development and Training. In the usual urban school setting, the focus of staff development and training is decided by the school administrators or principals. In the SDP model, teachers select the topics as well as the consultants.

How do children who attend schools which employ the SDP model perform? According to Haynes, Comer and Hamilton-Lee (1988), there have been observed changes in both academic achievement and the school climate. Over a four-year period, schools employing the SDP model have experienced significant increases in reading and math scores, exceeding both district and state level performances. Furthermore, these schools have observed a decrease in suspensions and behavioral problems. However, a more recent comprehensive independent evaluation of schools employing the Comer SDP model (Cook, Murphy & Hunt, 2000) found that over a 4-year period, although initial improvements were observed in academic performance, behavior problems, and truancy, these gains faded by the end of a 4-year period.

The late Dr. Ronald Edmonds (1982), who like Dr. Comer held that the urban public school system could be reformed to improve the academic achievement of African American children, developed the Effective Schools Model (ESM). However, unlike the SDP, which provides guidance on implementing structural changes within the school, the ESM is a prescriptive for attitude and behavioral change for principals and teachers who work in low-income urban public school environments. The ESM consists of the following prescriptives.

Principals. The ESM encourages principals to assume the role of the instructional leader of the school. They model for teachers an attitude of genuine concern for the academic performance of all children in the school, and an acceptance of the "cultural background" of the children. In addition to their role as instructional leaders, according to the ESM, principals should have an open door policy for parents, and an egalitarian approach to decision making in the school.

Pedagological Attitudes. The teachers and the principal must embrace similar goals related to students' academic achievement and share similar goals on strategies, techniques, and methods to achieve the students' school success.

Provide a Safe and Community-Like Climate for Learning. The school must visually reflect the attitudes of success embraced by principals and teachers. Student work should be displayed; student academic honors should be acknowledged, and the school environment must be safe and in excellent physical condition.

Professional Staff. Teachers should hold similar expectations for the academic capabilities of all of their students and adopt flexible assessment and instructional techniques. According to the ESM, teachers are "driven by pupil performance," and they should adjust their teaching techniques to maximize student mastery and performance.

Flexible Assessment and Instruction. According to the ESM, assessment should be used for diagnostic and remedial purposes rather than placement purposes. The Harford Heights model uses "continuous student assessment" which involves diagnostic tests, summative tests, and proficiency tests, as well as standardized tests.

Examples of the schools that use the ESM are presented in Box 5.4.

Reform movements such as the ones described above have not proved successful in approving academic performance, especially of African American

---

BOX 5.4

EXAMPLES OF SCHOOLS WHICH USE THE EFFECTIVE SCHOOL MODEL

1. Stowe Middle School is located in a midwestern urban environment with 80% African American enrollment. Achievement test score performance indicates that over a 7-year period 95% of the students were passing all sections of proficiency tests (Young, 1988).
2. Harford Heights is located in an eastern urban environment with 95% African American enrollment. There were overall increases in achievement scores in a 3-year period, as well as an increase in school attendance (Nicholsonne, 1988).
3. Lee Elementary School is located in a midwestern urban environment, with 98% African American enrollment. Test scores have improved an average of 64% since the implementation of the ESM (Hughes, 1988).

---

males. That is, schools that employ models such as the SDP or the ESM have not produced significant and lasting gains in the education of African American students (Pollard & Ajirotutu, 2000). Other efforts have focused on creating schools within the public school system designed specifically for African American students. These schools are called immersion schools. Box 5.5 describes an Immersion School.

Independent Black Schools (IBS)

Independent Black Schools have served a critical role in educating African American children for more than two centuries (Lomotey, 1992). The first

BOX 5.5

WHAT IS AN IMMERSION SCHOOL AND DOES IT WORK?

Immersion schools were developed in the early 1990s with the aim of improving the academic achievement of African American children, especially African American males. The pedagogy is primarily African-centered education, derived from an Afrocentric worldview, that focuses on the ways in which African culture and people of African ancestry have contributed to the world (Leake & Leake, 1992).

In Milwaukee Wisconsin, 5,700 of the African American males enrolled in the city's high schools were performing below average, and nearly 50% of them were dropping out of school. To address the problem, Milwaukee created two schools focusing specifically on the needs of African American males. One school targeted elementary school males and the other school targeted high school students. The schools were designed to meet the academic and social needs of African American males; and assist them in developing social competence, communication skills, as well as problem solving and critical thinking skills.

A mentoring program is a core part of the immersion schools' concept and teachers are required to make 18 home visits per semester.

What does an immersion school look like? The structure of the curricula differs significantly from the typical public school. The focus of the curricula is on the contribution of Africans and African Americans to history. Lessons are designed to highlight African culture and history. Such topics as social studies, language arts, math, and home economics would be introduced in the context of a traditional African marketplace. In contrast to the typical public school, there is more of an emphasis on cooperative learning in immersion schools. Finally, the physical environment of the immersion schools reflects an Afrocentric theme (e.g., maps of Africa displayed throughout the school).

How effective are immersion schools? Pollard & Ajirotutu (2000) evaluated the effectiveness of the Milwaukee African American immersion schools, measuring changes in teacher attitudes as well as changes in student performance, both academic and behavioral. They found that at the end of a 5-year period, the students' achievement performance had increased, where 92% of the third graders were performing at or above the state average on math and reading measures. In addition student suspensions and behavioral problems decreased as well. Teacher attitudes had become more favorable about their work environment, although some attrition had occurred during that time period.

Independent Black School (IBS) was founded by Prince Hall in 1798 as a result of his unsuccessful petitions to the city of Boston to establish a separate tax-supported school for Black children (Ratteray & Shujaa, 1987). The civil rights era produced the second wave of IBS. The Freedom Schools of the South represent an example of this effort. These schools were designed to provide African American children during 6 weeks of the summer with academic curricula that focused on remediation and African American history. Since then IBS have been formed to provide African American children with alternatives to the public school system.

The Independent Black Schools are under the auspices of the Council of Independent Black Institutions (CIBI) founded in 1972. CIBI provides teacher training and conducts annual science competitions for participating schools. There are currently 40 IBSs located throughout the United States. The enrollment ranges from a low of 50 to a high of 200 students going from preschool up to twelfth grade, however the highest concentration is at the elementary level. Each IBS consists of a board of directors responsible for establishing school policy; a parent-teacher organization; and a director, in charge of the administration of the school (Ratteray & Shujaa, 1987). The schools are supported primarily by student tuition.

African American children who attend IBSs come from families with diverse socioeconomic status backgrounds and educational backgrounds. IBSs have become educational choices for some African American parents, who express their concerns about the capability of the public school system to effectively educate their children (Ratteray & Shujaa, 1987).

The academic structure of an IBS is similar to that of the typical public school. However, similar to the immersion school concept, the goal of the IBS is to link African cultural knowledge with traditional subject matter. Such topics as math and science are discussed in terms of their historical and cultural significance. A lesson on the counting system might initially focus on the chronological and historical development of counting systems in Africa. Students are then taught to count in both ancient Egyptian and Yoruba systems (Akoto, 1992).

Integrated within curriculum is an emphasis on the seven principles of Ngusabo (Karenga, 1982). These values are introduced to the students in a variety of ways, including establishing dress codes, writing stories, developing cooperative learning experiences, and celebrating holidays (e.g. Kwanzaa). Finally, the role of teachers in an IBS is perceived to be critical for the students' success. Teachers serve as surrogate parents and role models.

How do children who attend IBSs perform on measures of achievement? Ratteray and Shujaa (1987) found that students attending IBSs performed at or above the national norm on such achievement measures as the Comprehensive Test of Basic Skills, the California Achievement Test, the Iowa Test of Basic Skills, the Metropolitan

Achievement Tests, and the Stanford Achievement Test. Sixty-four percent of the children scored above the norm on reading and 50% of the children scored above the norm on math. Children attending IBSs also have a higher sense of self-worth; they experience positive peer pressure, and are more likely to attend college than students not attending an IBS (Ratteray & Shujaa, 1987).

Essentially, the act serves as a blueprint for change, as well as emphasizes the use of incentives and sanctions to produce improvement in achievement test scores.

Has the achievement gap closed since the implementation of NCLB (see Box 5.6)? The answer to this question depends on the source. In April 2006, the federal government issued the following brief report documenting the improvement of African American children improvement on various achievement measures.

- Reading scores for African American fourth graders have increased.
- The achievement gap between African American and White fourth graders is at an all time low in reading and math.
- Studies by the Council of the Great Schools released in March 2006 showed urban students to be improving in reading and math.

BOX 5.6

NO CHILD LEFT BEHIND AND AFRICAN AMERICAN CHILDREN

In 2002 President George W. Bush signed into law Public Law 107–110, which is known as the No Child Left Behind Act (NCLB). The law is a re-authorization of the Elementary and Secondary Act of 1965. The general thrust of the law is "to close the achievement gap with accountability, flexibility, and choice so that no child is left behind." The NCLB law is a 1425-page document that provides direction and guidance to school administrators, and teachers on four basic reform principles.

1. Strong accountability for results
2. Increased flexibility for local control
3. Expand options for parents
4. Emphasize teaching methods proven to work

A comprehensive study by Sunderman et al. (2004) sheds light on teacher perception and reaction to NCLB. According to the findings, while teachers are generally supportive of the mission to improve the academic achievement of children who are attending low-performing schools, they are uncertain about the capability of the law. The law requires there to be a public identification of underperforming schools and a subsequent implementation of sanctions. Students are also allowed to use school vouchers and options. These three policies are meant to improve outcomes for children attending low-performing schools. Many teachers argue that the consequences of these policies will only serve to undermine teacher confidence, encourage teacher flight from low-performing schools, and encourage parents to remove their children from low-performing schools. Furthermore, the law discourages teaching other subjects and encourages a form of teaching to the tests.

The general dissatisfaction with the law is echoed by Mathis (2005) in his article entitled "Bridging the Achievement Gap: A Bridge Too Far?" He raises the following concerns about the effectiveness of NCLB in producing immediate and long-term improvements in the achievement test performance of African American children:

- To effectively and completely close the achievement gap, the underlying problems in society must be confronted.
- Second, poverty, rather than educational reform, is a larger influence on the variance of improving test scores. Schools with high concentrations of poor and minority students will fail to make adequate yearly progress.
- Third, even successful schools fluctuate in achievement gains.

SECTION THREE: AFRICAN AMERICAN CHILDREN AND EARLY INTERVENTION PROGRAMS

A chapter on education is not complete without a discussion of African American children and early intervention programs.

The momentum established by the *Brown v. Board of Education* decision and the 1964 Civil Rights Act laid the groundwork for the types of educational experiences that African American children would encounter for the next four decades. One outcome of this was the development of compensatory education programs or early intervention programs for poor children. These programs were designed with the goals of enhancing the educational readiness of poor children, providing poor children and their families with access to health care and other social support services. The programs that African American children participate in, or have participated in, are discussed below.

According to data released by the U.S. Census Bureau (2006) the percentage of African American children enrolled in preprimary education (67%) is

morning classes and were visited in their homes weekly by their teachers for 90 minutes. IQ demographic data and teacher ratings were collected at ages 11, 14, 15, 19, and 28. The findings revealed that participants in the preschool intervention program were more successful academically (e.g., fewer grade retentions, higher academic achievement scores, and better high school graduation rates) as well as socially (e.g. fewer arrests and fewer out of wedlock births) than those who did not participate in the intervention program.

Why has this program been so successful? According to the project coordinators, as a result of their participation in the program, the children developed school-readiness skills, which prepared them for successful interactions with teachers and helped them to develop positive attitudes about school. Seitz (1990) believes that the home visitation component of the program was an essential ingredient for the academic and social success of the participants. She speculates that parents gained experience in developing positive and comfortable relationships with teachers and they continued this pattern of interaction with teachers throughout the grade school years. They modeled positive behaviors for their children and indirectly influenced their attitudes about school and their academic success.

The program is no longer in operation, but is often cited in the literature and by politicians as an exemplary intervention program for poor African American children.

The Abecedarian Project

The Abecedarian project began in 1972 as an experimental intervention program. The overall goal was to determine the effectiveness of early intervention on later outcomes for African American children. The basic methodology involved assigning 111 infants to an experimental group or control group. The experimental group received 5 years of educational intervention that involved year-round full-day educational childcare, or preschool, along with nutritional supplements, and social support services for the families. The control group received everything but the educational intervention. The results indicated that at age 15, the experimental group in comparison to the control group performed better academically, and required fewer social or remedial services (Campbell & Ramey, 1994).

What conclusions can be drawn about African American children and early intervention programs? Do early intervention programs prepare African American children to succeed in elementary school? Some scholars would argue no, because there is a great deal of discontinuity between the structure of these early intervention programs and the structure of elementary school.

Even with the implementation of Project Follow Through (an elementary form of Head Start), the elementary school experiences can undo the advantages of a year of Head Start and other early intervention programs (Lee et al., 1990).

Future research about Head Start should attempt to isolate the components of the program that most effectively impact achievement. Given the number of African American children who enroll in Head Start, Head Start can serve as a natural laboratory for developing ways to improve education for African American children overall.

PERSPECTIVES ON EDUCATION AND AFRICAN AMERICAN CHILDREN

According to John Jacobs (1989), "there is a growing number of African American youth who face a perilous economic future because they are not adequately prepared to participate in an economy that is undergoing fundamental structural change." Jacobs, then president of the Urban League, made this statement as part of his commentary on the "state of education and African American youth." Eighteen years later, the academic achievement of African American children remains a pressing concern for educators, social scientists, and politicians.

For the past few decades, a plethora of intervention programs, policies, and reform movements have been designed all with the goals of narrowing the achievement gap between African American children and their counterparts from other racial groups. There has also been an exponential increase in the number of books, pamphlets, and articles written on the issue. Despite this attention, the achievement gap persists. Perhaps, it is time to explore other questions about academic achievement and African American children, and focus on identifying the teaching techniques and strategies that facilitate achievement. Furthermore, research should begin to examine effective approaches to engaging poor and disenfranchised African American parents into the academic lives of their children.

The reform movements have had a questionable impact on the academic achievement of African American students (Pollard & Ajirotutu, 2000).

As Theresa Perry (2003) states, "a problem as complex as eliminating the achievement gap requires effort and ideas from many people." The issue of eliminating the achievement gap as well as the issue of resegregation of American public schools will dominate the focus of discourse, politics and research in the 21st century.

CHAPTER SUMMARY

The chapter begins with a discussion of school desegregation. The landmark case *Brown v. Board of Education* changed the educational process for all children in the United States. There is a growing trend toward resegregation of American public schools.

The chapter continues with a discussion of the plight of African American children in the public school system. It is evident from the available achievement data that African American children continue to lag behind their counterparts from other ethnic groups by an average of 30 points on critical measures of academic achievement. School factors (e.g., teacher perception), self-concept, peer influence, and parental involvement are identified in the chapter as causal factors.

Reform movements in the 1970s and the 1980s produced schools with the primary agenda of educating African American children. Those movements have offered suggestions on restructuring schools and offer prescriptives for attitude and behavioral change for teacher and administrators.

Independent Black Schools (IBS) are alternatives to the public school system for many African American children. In addition to the rigorous education, IBSs provide African American children with information about their cultural heritage. According to recent achievement data, African American children who attend IBSs score at or above the national average on achievement measures.

The chapter concludes with a discussion of African American children and early intervention programs. African American children are more likely than their White counterparts to participate in early intervention programs. However, due to the variability in the academic structure and the focus of those programs, achievement gains are negligible or fade by first grade.

ADDITIONAL READINGS

Desegregation

Beals, M. (1994). *Warriors don't cry: A searing memoir of the battle to integrate Little Rock's Central High School*. New York: Pocket Books

Irons, P. (1994). *Jim Crow's children: The broken promise of the Brown decision*. New York: Penguin Press.

Education

Ladson-Billings, G. (1994). *Successful teachers of African American children*. San Francisco: Jossey-Bass.

Lomotey, K. (1990). *Going to school: The African American experience*. SUNY Press: New York.

Polite, V., & Davis, J. (1999). *African American males in school and society: Practices and policies for effective education*. New York: Columbia University Teachers College Press.

Watkins, A. (2002). Learning styles of African American children: A developmental consideration. *Journal of Black Psychology, 28*, 3–17.

Web Sites on Achievement Issues and African American Children

Closing the Achievement Gap. www.ncrel.org/gap.

National Association for the Education of African American Children with Learning Disabilities. www.aacld.org.

National Council on Educating Black Children. www.ncebc.org.

Schools That Work

Akoto, A. (1992). *Nation building. Theory and practice in Afrikan centered education*. Washington, DC: Pan African World Institute.

Bullard, P., & Taylor, B. (In press). *Keeper's of the dream: The triumph of effective schools*.

Collins, M., & Tamarkin, C. (1990). *Marva Collin's way*. Houghton, Mifflin: Boston.

Videotapes on Education and African American Children

Blackside (producer). (1994). *Eyes on the prize: America's Civil Rights Movement. 1954– 1985*. Television series. Washington, DC: Public Broadcasting Service.

Brokaw, T. (producer). (July 23, 2006). *Separate but unequal: Special report on school desegregation*. Television broadcast. New York: NBC News.

Gunther, N., & Lindstrom, J. (producers/writers). (2003). *A tale of two schools*. Videotape. New York: WETA.

CHAPTER 6

Language and Literacy

OVERVIEW

I can skate better than Louis and i be only eight. If you be goin' real fast, hold it. If it's on trios and you be goin' and you don't go in the ring, you be goin' around it. You be goin' too fast, well, you don't be in the ring. You be outside if you be goin' too fast. That man he'a clip you up. I think they call him Sonny. He real tall. (Excerpt taken from Dillard, *Black English*, 1972).

The dialogue in the excerpt taken from Dillard is an example of a speech pattern commonly referred to as Black Dialect, Black English, Ebonics, or African American Vernacular English (AAVE), spoken by members of the African American community.

For more than four decades, American linguists, educational psychologists, developmental psychologists, journalists, and lawmakers have debated whether AAVE is or should be considered legitimate as a language. Central to this issue is the question of where it began and how it differs from Standard English (SE).

With the advent of desegregation, AAVE became a focus of theoretical discourse and research agendas. This was due in part to teacher perceptions and assessments of language competency of African American children.

It is estimated that approximately 8 million African American students in United States schools speak AAVE (Gadsen & Wagner, 1995). Their comparatively low performances on standardized literacy assessments, as well as their low performance on literacy activities in the classroom, have been attributed to the fact that AAVE interferes with their performance on classroom language and literacy activities.

The focus of this chapter is to discuss the language and literacy issues of African American children.

The chapter is divided into five sections. The first section of the chapter discusses the most recent controversy about AAVE, with a specific focus on

111

the 1996 decision by the Oakland school board to use "African American Language Systems" as a pedagogical tool to remedy the poor performance of African American children on reading proficiency tests and language arts measures.

The second section of the chapter focuses on language learning and African American children, with attention paid to such issues as the link between AAVE and reading, and the contribution of the home environment to the language and literacy performance of African American children. The third section of the chapter focuses on language and literacy issues and AAVE. Section four concludes with a discussion of the intervention programs designed to increase SE proficiency in African American children.

Section five discusses the various approaches designed to help educators distinguish language disorders from AAVE. The chapter closes with a discussion of perspectives on language learning.

SECTION ONE: THE CONTROVERSY

INSIDER'S VOICE: THE OAKLAND SCHOOL
BOARD EBONICS RESOLUTION

Whereas, numerous validated scholarly studies demonstrate that African American students as a part of their culture and history as African peoples possess and utilize a language described in various scholarly approaches as "Ebonics" or "Pan-African-Communication Behaviors" or African Language Systems; and

Whereas, the studies have also demonstrated that African Language Systems have origins in West (African) and Niger Congo languages and are not merely dialects of English; and

Whereas, these studies demonstrate that such West and Niger-Congo African languages have been officially recognized and addressed in the mainstream public educational community as worth of study, understanding, or application of its principals, laws, and structures for the benefit of African American students both in terms of positive appreciation of the language and these students' mastery of English language skills; and

Whereas, such recognition by scholars has given rise over the past 15 years to legislation passed by the State of California recognizing the unique language stature of descendants of slaves, with such legislation being prejudicially and unconstitutionally vetoed repeatedly be various California state governors; and

Whereas, judicial cases in states other than California have recognized the unique language structure of African American pupils, and such recognition by courts has resulted in court mandated educational programs which have substantially benefited African American children in the interest of vindicating their equal protection of the law rights under the Fourteenth Amendment to the U.S. Constitution; and

Whereas, the Federal Bilingual Education Act (20 U.S.C. 1402 et seq.) mandates that local educational agencies "build their capacities to establish, implement and sustain programs of instruction for children and youth of limited English proficiency"; and

Whereas, the interests of the Oakland Unified School District in providing equal opportunities for all of its students dictate limited English proficient educational programs recognizing the English language acquisition and improvement of skills of African American students are as fundamental as is language application of bilingual educational principles for others whose primary languages are other than English; and

Whereas, the standardized tests and grade scores of African American students in reading and language arts skills measuring their application of English skills are substantially below state and national norms and such deficiencies will be remedied by application of a program featuring African Language Systems principles to move students from language patterns they bring to school to English proficiency; and

Whereas, standardized tests and grade scores will be remedied by application of a program with teachers and aides who are certified in the methodology of featuring African Language System principles in instructing African American children both in their primary language and both in English,

Now, therefore, be it resolved that the Board of Education officially recognizes the existence and the cultural and historic bases of West and Niger-Congo African Language Systems and each language as the predominantly primary language of African American children; and

Be it further resolved that the Board of Education hereby adopt the report, recommendations and attached policy statement of the Districts' African American Task force on language stature of African American speech; and

Be it further resolved that the Superintendent in conjunction with her staff shall immediately devise and implement the best possible academic program for imparting instruction to African American students in their primary language for the combined purposes of maintaining the legitimacy and richness of such language to facilitate their acquisition and mastery of English language skills.

(Taken from Perry & Delpit, 1998, pp. 143–147)

The Ebonics Resolution described in the Insider's Voice was adopted in 1996, by the Oakland Unified School District, in Oakland, California, to address the problem of the number of African American students in the school district who were failing academically and performing below the state and national average on standardized achievement tests.

This decision by the Oakland Unified School District proved to be controversial, and ignited debate across the nation among politicians, educators, and scholars who challenged the legitimacy of African American Vernacular English as a language system. Furthermore, the decision rekindled theoretical discussions on the link between "deficient language skills," and the academic failure of African American children (Van Keulen, Weddington, & Debose, 1998).

This national reaction to the Oakland School District's proposal seems puzzling given that for more than 40 years linguists have acknowledged that AAVE is a language system with its own rules for phonetics (the sound system of a language), syntax (grammar), and semantics (meaning attached to words) (Dillard, 1972; Labov, 1972). Box 6.1 describes the major differences between AAVE and SE.

Furthermore, researchers have documented that the use of AAVE varies according to age, region, socioeconomic status, and gender. AAVE is more prominent in the speech patterns of younger children, than in the speech patterns of older children (African American adolescents engage in a form of "code-switching"); certain features are more prominent in the speech patterns of African Americans indigenous to the southern region of the United States; AAVE is used more frequently by African Americans from lower socioeconomic groups, than by African Americans from middle- or upper-class groups; and African American boys, in comparison to African American girls, are more likely to speak AAVE (Feagans & Haskins, 1986). Finally, over time, similar to other languages, AAVE has changed in form and function.

BOX 6.1

MAJOR DIFFERENCES BETWEEN **AAVE** AND **SE**

1. **Phonological differences between AAVE and SE.** Phonology refers to the sound system of a language. Phonics, an aspect of phonology, is an important linguistic acquisition because it assists us in reading and pronouncing unfamiliar words. To understand what is heard and read, information must be translated into words that are recognizable and meaningful.

   In SE, phonics can be classified into the following four categories.

The first category is single consonants sounds, which are all the letters of the alphabet with the exception of the vowel sounds a e i o u.

The second category is consonant clusters, which are defined as consonants that appear as successive letters in a syllable. For example, the following word patterns contain consonant clusters: ACT, ASK, DESK, SUGGEST, TEST, and TOLD. In SE, the most familiar consonant clusters are:

bl cr pl sk sn sw scr br dr gl pr sl sp tr str cl fl gr sc sm st tw spr (Durkin, 1989).

One significant difference between AAVE and SE is this category of consonant clusters, specifically the pronunciation of final consonant clusters. In AAVE, the final clusters are reduced so that the final letter is dropped as in the following word patterns: AX, DES, GHOS, LIS, TES. This is called consonant reduction.

The third category is Consonant Digraph, which is defined as the pronunciation of letters depending on whether they are voiced or voiceless. In SE, a common digraph is "th," which is pronounced in two different ways: in the voiced sound that is heard in such words as "them," "the," "there"; in the voiceless, "th" as heard in such words as "than" and "thirst."

In AAVE, "th" may sound like "d" or "f," depending upon its position in a word. For example, "th" sounds like "d" when the initial "th" sound is voiced (e.g. "this" = "dis"); whereas when the final "th" sound is voiceless, it sounds like "f" as in "with" = "wif"; "both" = "bof"; and "mouth" = "mouf."

The final difference between AAVE and SE is in the pronunciation of the letter "r." In SE, the letter "r" is a sound that is most identified by its use in three common words: "her," "far," and "or." In AAVE, the sound "r" is omitted so that the speaker pronounces such words as "door" as "doe" and "court" as "coat."

2. **Syntactic similarities and differences between AAVE and SE.** Syntax refers to the way that words are combined to produce sentences (Van Keulen et al., 1998). Grammar is an important feature of syntax and is defined as a finite set of rules shared by all the speakers of the language that allow them to generate an infinite set of rules shared by the speakers of that particular language.

The major differences between AAVE and SE occur in the use of verb tense, pluralization, person, number, and possession.

Verb Tense

A verb tense allows the speaker to indicate when behavior has occurred. There are six verb tenses used in SE.

1. Present tense (conjugating the verb "to be", the present tense of the verb is "is").
2. Past tense (the past tense of the verb to be is "was").
3. Future tense (the future tense of the verb to be is "will be").
4. Present perfect tense (the present perfect tense of the verb to be is "has been").
5. Past perfect tense (the past perfect tense of the verb to be is "had been").
6. Future perfect tense (the future perfect tense of the verb to is "will have been").

In AAVE, the verb "to be" takes on many different forms. For example an "s" can be added to the present tense, so that the SE sentence, "I eat" changes into "I eats" in AAVE. AAVE usually makes no differentiation between the verb forms in the past tense, but other words in the sentence indicate that action has been completed (Dandy, 1991).

Other uses of the verb "to be" in AAVE include the following.

The verb can be omitted. When "be" is omitted, the speaker is implying that the condition is temporary. For example, "The coffee cold. He going. We hungry."

The use of "be" can also indicate future time. For example, "The boy be here soon."

Pluralization

Pluralization in AAVE is usually shown once so that nearly all nouns have the same form whether singular or plural. For example, "He go every day." "The man want to run."

Person and Number

Unlike SE, which requires an "s" to be added onto the third person singular present verb form, the third person singular present form in AAVE usually retains the same form in person and number.

Possession

In SE, an "s" is added to the word to show possession. In AAVE, an "s" is often omitted and possession is shown by the proximity in which the owner's name precedes the object. For example, "She over at Mary house."

Been

A final difference is in the use of the verb "been." For instance, "been" can be used to show past action. For example, "He been there before." It can also be used to indicate that an action has been recently completed. For example, "I been had that job."

Finally, "been" can be used to emphasize an action that has already occurred, whether just recently or a long time ago. For example, " I been ready to go." "They been married."

3. **Semantics.** Semantics refers to the meaning that we assign to words. A good example of this would be vocabulary development. There are words that are used by speakers of AAVE to convey information (e.g. *bad* means *good*).

4. **Pragmatics.** This refers to the how language is used or how people interact during communication (i.e., turn taking, topic maintenance, topic termination and non-verbal issues). Speakers of AAVE often engage in the use of a variety of non-verbal behaviors that differ from the behaviors used by SE speakers.

Source: Dandy (1991).

Despite the wealth of empirical information on AAVE, there is little contemporary information available on language learning and African American children. The information that exists is based on findings from research conducted over 30 years ago. This is problematic, given the current national estimates on the number of African American children who experience academic problems in school, perform poorly on standardized tests, and are placed in speech/language remediation classes based on their language proficiency.

As a result of this limited and dated corpus of research, social scientists are ill-equipped to provide educators with valuable information on developing effective pedagogical techniques, and intervention programs for African American children who speak AAVE.

SECTION TWO: LANGUAGE LEARNING AND AFRICAN AMERICAN CHILDREN

Early investigations into the language-learning environment of African American children were primarily conducted by anthropologists and linguists. The primary goals of the research were to document the deficiencies in the language-learning environment of African American children and to connect those deficiencies with their poor academic and literacy performance.

Ward (1986) carried out one of the most comprehensive studies on language learning and African American children. Using an ethnographic methodology, she followed seven southern rural African American families from 1968 to 1969. Through informal interviews and observations of families engaged in their daily routines, she observed that the language interactions of poor African American children differed significantly from that of middle-class White children. Many middle-class White children, throughout the day frequently engaged in language interactions with their parents. During these language interactions, their language was expanded, reinforced, and encouraged. In contrast, the African American children in her study rarely engaged in language interactions with their parents. However, when they did interact with their parents, the adults used language as an administrative function—to give orders and to ask questions. During these interactions, the parent, usually the mother, repeated simplified sentences, and in some cases used verbal elaborations. Most of the language situations in the homes of these children used by adults were addressed to other adults, and the language opportunities for the children were primarily received from peers and siblings.

Yet Ward found that these children developed a rich language pattern as well as a rich vocabulary. She concluded that language acquisition in the homes of rural poor African American children occurred through observations and eavesdropping of adult conversations, and primarily through language interaction with peers and with siblings.

Heath (1989), employing a methodology similar to the Ward study, also found that African American children acquired verbal proficiency from observing adults in conversation. However, she extended her research to explore differences between working-class African American families and middle-class African American families, and was particularly interested in determining how language socialization practices differed within African American families from diverse economic backgrounds. In her observations she noticed that the families differed on five dimensions of language socialization.

Distribution of Critical Functions: Including Primary Language Source. Heath found that in the homes of middle-class African American families, the mothers served as the primary language source and socialization agent for their children. In contrast, in the homes of working-class families, the mothers, in addition to other members of the family, function as language socialization agents for the children.

Type of Talk Addressed to Children and Expectations of Their Roles as Conversationalists. In many middle-class homes, Heath observed that mothers tailored their language to the level of the child and frequently engaged in labeling and naming objects. On the other hand, the mothers in the working-class homes did not simplify language for the child.

Uses of Oral and Written Information. In the homes of middle-class families, uses of oral and written information were frequent and the children in these homes had multiple exposures to oral and written information. However, in the homes of working-class families, access to written information was limited to functional uses and purposes such as writing a grocery list or looking for a telephone number. The primary mode of communication in these homes was the spoken word.

Expectation of Variants of Language to be Learned. Middle-class African American families used SE more frequently than AAVE, and used variants of AAVE depending on the situation or the listener. In contrast, working-class African American families communicated primarily through AAVE. Although the children encountered SE primarily through television and radio, it was not expected that they communicate using SE in their homes.

Judgments of the Competence of Children. Middle-class families placed a priority on providing their children with multiple opportunities for language learning and language interaction (e.g., recounting days' events and talking about future plans). They also saw themselves as the "primary" language teacher for their children. In contrast, working-class families stressed language learning by observation, and the children experienced few "directed" language experiences. These parents did not embrace the belief that they were solely responsible for the language learning of their children.

Feagans (1986) moved in a different direction and explored how poor rural African American children engaged in language experiences with their neighborhood peers and how those language experiences compared with and differed from the neighborhood/peer language experiences of middle-class White children. She discovered that the African American children encountered a variety of language experiences with their neighborhood peers, through dramatic play, storytelling, and engagement in cooperative play. She observed that the use of their language in this environment was much more sophisticated and structured than their language use in the classrooms. In contrast, the middle-class children encountered fewer language opportunities with neighborhood peers. When they did engage in "talk," the conversations focused on issues of play (e.g., playing with Barbie or riding bikes). Thus she concluded that African American children in comparison to their White peers have multiple opportunities for language interactions. However, those opportunities do not seem to be related to their language proficiency in school or the classrooms.

The next wave of research on African American children and language learning occurred during the late 1990s. These studies were motivated in part by the resurgence of interest in exploring the social influences on infant and preschool cognitive development and in part by the realization of the paucity of research on African American children and language socialization.

The overall goals of the research were to examine maternal language use in a structured setting, and to establish how maternal language use predicted infant or preschool language performance. As opposed to examining how one way of language use is better than another, the studies focused simply on how language socialization differs between African American families, White middle-class families, and White working-class families.

The studies for the most part employ quasi-experimental designs and use conventional coding systems to identify certain aspects of maternal language use.

Blake (1994) was specifically interested in exploring whether the form, content, and language use differed between African American infants and White infants. She observed few differences in form and content, but found that that the use of language differed. That is, even at the age of one, African American children—in contrast to White children—learned to use language through their language interactions with their mothers, to convey socio-emotional information (interpersonal roles, appropriate behavior).

Hammer and Weiss (1999, 2002) investigated how maternal language varied according to socioeconomic status. In this study, maternal language was operationalized as communicative acts (statements, directives, questions).

They observed few differences between middle-class African American mothers and working-class African American mothers in their use of communicative acts. However, when these mothers were queried about their beliefs about early language learning, the socioeconomic status differences emerged. Similar to the Heath study, working-class African American mothers in comparison to middle-class African American mothers believed that children learn language via observation and language development occurs naturally; whereas middle-class African American mothers believed that language development occurs in the context of social interaction, through instruction from the mother.

Wallace, Roberts, and Lodder (1998) examined the association between maternal language behaviors and expressive language and receptive language in African American preschool children. They were particularly interested in how that association varied between working-class African American mothers and middle-class African American mothers. The following pattern emerged in their study. Middle-class African American mothers' use of warmth, stimulation, responsiveness, and elaboration was predictive of preschool receptive language scores; whereas, only responsiveness and elaboration were predictive of receptive language for working-class African American mothers. Maternal use of warmth was associated with preschool expressive language scores only for middle-class African American mothers.

What can be concluded about the research on the language learning and African American children?

The research is disjointed, with major gaps in published studies extending for 10 or more years. Therefore, there is no comprehensive and continuous information available on language learning and African American children (unlike the rich body of research available on White children and language learning). In addition, the early research is constrained by its focus on rural and or poor African American children and language learning.

With the exception of the findings of the early ethnographic studies, there seem to be few differences between the language interaction styles of working-class African American mothers, middle-class African American mothers, and White mothers. If these findings are indeed accurate, then it can be assumed that for all children, independent of culture, the early language environment is similar. Therefore, the focus of additional research should be to investigate how, when and why the language differences begin to emerge for African American children.

Few of the studies, with the exception of the Heath research, have focused specifically on AAVE; as a result, little up-to-date information is available on the use of AAVE and language socialization in African American homes.

See Box 6.2 for African American Infants AAVE and Language Development.

BOX 6.2

LANGUAGE ACQUISITION AND AFRICAN AMERICAN CHILDREN

There is evidence which suggests that the emergence of prelinguistic features (e.g., babbling and cooing) and simple sentence constructions (e.g., holophrastic and telegraphic speech) appears around the same age as it does for speakers of SE. However, qualitatively, there is some evidence to suggest that AAVE-speaking infants and toddlers develop more socio-personal function categories, and they tend to express more stative relations about objects in comparison to speakers of SE (Blake, 1994).

Semantic and syntactic differences begin to emerge around age 4 or 5 when the children are producing more complex and structured sentences.

African American children acquire language within the time frame that is similar to speakers of SE.

Semantic categories increase with age. The semantic categories of action and existence are acquired early while the categories of causality and coordination are acquired later.

Pragmatic categories exhibited before 3 years of age include:

a. commenting on the environment (e.g., see doggie).
b. persuading others to do something (e.g., gimme cookie).

> Features of Black Dialect are not prominent before age 3. Features increase as children become older.
>
> There is a great deal of individual variation in the language acquisition for African American children.
>
> *Source: Stockman, 1999.*

Given the paucity of research on normative language learning and African American children, the implicit comparative framework provides little meaningful information on the language socialization of African American children. Clearly, contemporary research is needed in the area of language learning and African American children due to the aforementioned performance issues.

SECTION THREE: LANGUAGE AND LITERACY ISSUES

Language plays a key and critical function in developing, mastering, and sustaining literacy skills (Van Keulen et al., 1998). Knowledge of the meaning of words, the pronunciation of words, and how words fit together to form complex sentences are all linked to literacy proficiency, especially reading proficiency.

As discussed in chapter 3, African American children lag significantly behind their age mates from other ethnic and racial groups on reading achievement measures.

It has been argued that the language skills and language knowledge that some African American children bring to school influences their performance on standardized literacy assessments as well as their performance on literacy activities in the classroom (Scott & Marcus, 2001).

More specifically, social scientists state that African American children, who speak AAVE, have a set of linguistic rules, which interferes with their ability to read and comprehend texts written in SE, to accurately engage in writing tasks, which involve reproducing SE, and to accurately learn to spell SE words.

Investigations for more than two decades focused on testing this "interference hypothesis" with the goals of isolating the specific features of AAVE that might interfere with the reading capabilities of African American children, and subsequently affect their literacy performance.

In a comprehensive review of the interference studies, Schwartz (1982) and Labov (1972) found that the bulk of the studies failed to provide overwhelming evidence in support of the interference hypothesis. Some studies suggested that African American children in comparison to White children experienced difficulty in reading texts written in SE; however, in other studies, there were no measurable differences between the performance of African American children and White children on reading tests written in SE. In addition, Schwartz (1982) and Labov (1972) found that the research differed with respect to reading outcome measure (e.g., reading out loud as opposed to listening comprehension) and age group. Thus, they concluded that it is difficult to provide a definitive statement about the interference of AAVE on the reading performance of African American children. Edwards (1994) concurs and states that the interference studies also have failed to identify such critical issues as how much interference occurs, where it occurs, and whether or not it is significant enough to account for the reading failure of African American children. Therefore Edwards argues that the interference studies provide little credible information linking AAVE and reading failure.

Many researchers have abandoned the interference hypothesis, but there are many who continue to support the belief that AAVE interferes with the reading capabilities of African American children and negatively impacts their literacy performance. This belief is sometimes reflected in the behavior of classroom teachers toward children who speak AAVE, especially those teachers with limited knowledge of AAVE.

In the particular case of reading interactions, knowledge of AAVE not only determines how teachers interact with the children, but also determines the type of guidance, correction, and feedback they provide the children during reading interactions. Teachers with limited knowledge of the features of AAVE, and who view AAVE as a deficient or substandard language, have been observed to provide little or no feedback to the children when they make reading errors and failed to offer suggestions that would help them identify their specific reading errors (Feagans, 1996; Taylor, 1999; Washington & Miller-Jones, 1989). This establishes what McDermott (1977) calls a "communication barrier." Once this "communication barrier" develops children fail to acquire the reading skills needed to decode and comprehend material. Furthermore, they lose their motivation to learn to read, and they withdraw from reading interactions in school as well as at home, and reading becomes an aversive experience for them. The development of reading capabilities is cumulative, and mastering one reading technique is a prerequisite for mastering higher-level reading skills. Once the child has been discouraged and the skill does not develop, a pattern of reading failure has been set in motion (Piestrip, 1973). This can account in part for the poor reading performance of African American children.

On the other hand, when teachers are more knowledgeable about the syntactic and phonological features of AAVE, they provide supportive feedback and reading sustaining behaviors when the children make reading errors. This feedback comes in the form of suggestions on how to decode the information, how to use contextual cues to aid with their reading, and on general reading strategies.

In addition to the school factors just described above, the home environment of African American children, especially those who speak AAVE, has been identified in the social science literature as a major factor contributing to their poor literacy performance. Empirical findings suggest that many poor African American children have few encounters with book-reading activities in their home environment, and even fewer opportunities to observe their parents engaged in book-reading or other literacy behaviors.

In direct observations of African American mothers engaging in book-reading interactions with their children, Anderson-Yokel and Haynes (1994) observed that low-income African American mothers tend not to use reading strategies (e.g., questions) that effectively engage their children in a book-reading interaction.

Recent evidence points to the contrary and indicates that poor African American children do encounter literacy experiences in their homes. However, these experiences are more indirect rather than direct. Two examples of typical literacy experiences of African American children are engaging with oral storytelling (Heath, 1989), and observing parents read newspaper advertisements (Purcell-Gates, 1996). In addition, Pelligrini, Perlmutter, Galda, & Brody (1990) and Harris and Oliver (2002) found that African American mothers do in fact employ strategies that engage their children in a book-reading interaction. Books that are culturally relevant, containing African American characters and themes, are more likely to elicit a variety of book-reading strategies from African American mothers than non-culturally relevant books or picture books.

Nevertheless, scholars maintain that it is the discontinuity between the literacy practices of the home environment and the literacy practices of the school environment that place African American children at a disadvantage in the classroom (Scott & Marcus, 2001). In comparison to their middle-class peers, working-class African American children come to school with little knowledge of book-reading behaviors.

As a consequence, these children are ill equipped to master the language and literacy challenges of their classrooms.

SECTION FOUR: LANGUAGE AND LITERACY INTERVENTION PROGRAMS FOR AFRICAN AMERICAN CHILDREN

For more than four decades, intervention programs have been designed to increase the SE proficiency of African American children who speak AAVE, and increase their reading proficiency and performance on standardized literacy measures. These programs have varied considerably in structure, focus, and measurable outcomes. We begin with a discussion of language intervention programs.

Language Intervention Programs. In 1969, Stewart and Baratz (Stewart, 1969) developed a series of primary readers written in AAVE. They believed that before African American children could master SE, they must first demonstrate proficiency in AAVE and "be provided with the opportunity to read texts consistent with their oral language." However, due to parental and teacher opposition (they believed the children would never learn SE), the program was discontinued, and the effectiveness of the readers was never determined. See examples of tests in Box 6.3.

BOX 6.3

EXAMPLES OF THE TEXTS WRITTEN IN AAVE

Dreamy Mae: A Story in Black Vernacular

This here little sister name Mae was most definitely untogether. I mean, like she didn't act together. She didn't look together. She was just an untogether Sister.

Her teacher was always sounding on her about dreaming in class. I mean like just 'bout every day the teacher would be getting on her case. But it didn't seem to bother her none. She just kept on keeping gon. Like, I guess daydreaming was her groove. And you know what they say: don't knock your Sister's groove. But a whole lotta people did knock it. But like I say, she just kept on keeping on.

One day Mae was talking to herself in the lunchroom. She was having this righteous old conversation with herself. She say, I wanna be a princess with long golden hair. Now can you get ready for that? Long golden hair!

Well, anyway, Mae say if I can't be a princess, I'll settle for some long golden hair. If I could just have me some long golden hair, everything would be all right with me. Lord, if I could just have me some long golden hair.

Directions: Go for what you know about the story "Dreamy Mae." Check out each sentence down below. Circle the letter of the correct answer (a, b, c, or d). There ain't but one right answer to each question, so don't be picking out two.

1. In the beginning of the story, Mae was tripping out on being princess with

    a. dyeing her hair   b. long golden hair
    c. a long dress   d. an Afro

Source: Rickford and Rickford, 1995.

The Bridges Reading Program, initiated in the 1970s by Simpkins et al., was another attempt to use readers written in AAVE. The goals of this program, similar to that of Stewart and Baratz, were to present African American students with narratives written in both AAVE and SE (see examples in Box 6.3). The program was evaluated using a cross-national sample of 7th and 12th grade students. The findings suggested that students participating in Bridges (in comparison to a control group) generally scored higher on some reading comprehension measures, such as the Iowa Test of Basic Skills. Like Stewart and Baratz's readers, the Bridge Reading Program was also met with teacher and parent opposition, and was discontinued.

Current efforts include developing research-based intervention programs using black dialect readers. (See Rickford and Rickford, 1995, in *Linguistics and Education* for an excellent review of those programs).

The Carolina Abecedarian Intervention Project (ABC) was carried out in the 1970s by the Frank Porter Graham Center at the University of North Carolina, and it is the most comprehensive language intervention program developed for African American children to date. The children were involved from preschool until elementary school in a highly structured language curriculum program, which included intensive language interaction between teachers and students (e.g., phonics instruction, reading interactions, and storytelling).

According to the researchers, the ABC children performed better on narrative tasks and were rated higher by teachers on language interaction dimensions in the classroom. However, those differences disappeared by middle school age.

Other language intervention programs have been instructionally based and focused on using specific didactic techniques, which include drill and practice method in phonics, sentence substitution exercises, or emphasis on the development of oral language skills. These programs have produced mixed results in increasing the SE proficiency of African American children.

What works, according to Fogel & Ehri (1998), is an intervention approach, which combines strategy instruction with guided practice and provides feedback on techniques to transform AAVE into SE.

BOX 6.4

USING CALL AND RESPONSE TO FACILITATE LANGUAGE LEARNING
AMONG AFRICAN AMERICAN CHILDREN

Call and Response is an interactional discourse pattern, which helps students who speak AAVE master SE phonology, and syntax. Preliminary results suggest improvements in SE proficiency of children who speak AAVE (see www.cal.org/ericcll for more information).

Literacy Intervention Programs. For more than two decades, literacy intervention programs have been designed to increase the literacy, namely reading proficiency, for poor children in general. Few programs, with the exception of the program highlighted in Box 6.4, are tailored for African American children.

These literacy intervention programs are either school-based, where the children receive additional tutoring in reading and reading support, or an integral part of community outreach organizations (e.g., Boys and Girls Club's "Connecting Through Caring"). These programs typically distribute books and other literacy items to the children.

There are also family-based literacy intervention programs. The goals of these programs are two-fold: (1) to aid parents in improving their literacy skills; and (2) to assist them in learning techniques to engage in literacy activities with their children (see Box 6.5).

Other literacy intervention programs have focused on exclusively on mothers. The goals generally involve teaching mothers how to use certain book reading strategies with their children. Lonigan's and Whitehurst's (1998) Dialogic Reading Training Program and Edwards' (1994) community-based reading program are examples of this effort. Preliminary results suggest that there are immediate improvements in the reading interaction behaviors of these mothers. However, whether or not these improvements translate into increasing reading proficiency for their children has yet to be determined. (See Strickland [2003] for an excellent review of literacy intervention programs for poor children.)

BOX 6.5

URBAN LEAGUE'S NEW INITIATIVE TO INCREASE THE LITERACY RATES AMONG AFRICAN AMERICAN CHILDREN.

The Urban League designed the "Read and Rise Literacy Campaign," in the summer of 2002 to motivate African American parents and caregivers to become active participants in their children's literacy lives. The campaign consists of radio public service announcements, which emphasize the importance of literacy, and parents are offered information on where to acquire a *Read and Rise* literacy packet.

SECTION FIVE: LANGUAGE ASSESSMENT AND AFRICAN AMERICAN CHILDREN: DISTINGUISHING DIALECT FROM A SPEECH LANGUAGE DISORDER

How to distinguish dialect from a speech language disorder for children who speak AAVE has been a perplexing problem for speech language pathologists

encouraging veteran teachers to be open to new approaches to teaching reading to African American children.

The assessment models described in this chapter offer viable alternatives to using traditional language assessments for African American children. Clearly, additional empirical work needs to take place, and training programs should implement steps to adopt these models of assessment.

Given the number of language and literacy intervention programs available for African American students, why haven't we seen a dramatic improvement in their reading achievement scores? Why do the gains fade and fail to translate into achievement in the classroom? What additional research needs to be conducted on the relationship between AAVE and reading achievement?

What should be the core and critical features of teacher training programs? How can teachers incorporate features of AAVE into their teaching?

Should children who speak AAVE be taught to read using Black Dialect readers or readers in SE? What additional considerations need to be made in order to determine the effectiveness of this approach?

CHAPTER SUMMARY

This chapter on language and literacy issues begins with a discussion of the Oakland School district's decision to use AAVE as a teaching tool to improve the language and literacy proficiency of African American children. The chapter continues with a description of the features of AAVE and discussions of the research on the language and literacy learning of African American children. The early studies on language learning and African American children were conducted by linguists and anthropologists, and motivated by the onset of desegregation. The goals of the research were to identify the deficiencies in the language environment of African American children. The second wave of research explored maternal language patterns. Few differences exist between the early language environments of African American infants and White infants.

The types of language and literacy intervention programs available for African American children are also described. Approaches include re-introducing Black Dialect readers into the classroom and targeting literacy efforts to African American parents.

The chapter concludes with a discussion on language assessment and African American children who speak AAVE. New models for language assessment are presented.

ADDITIONAL READINGS

The Controversy

Perry, T., & Delpit, L., (1998). *The real Ebonics debate: Power language and the education of African American students*. Boston: Beacon Press.

Language and Literacy Issues

Paul, D. (2000). *Raising Black children who love reading and writing*. Westport: Bergin & Garvey.

Gunther, N., & Lindstrom, J. (producers/writers). (2003). *A tale of two schools*. Videotape. New York: WETA.

Intervention

Ball, A. F. (1995). Language, learning and linguistic competence of African American children: Torrey revisited. *Linguistics and Education, 7,* 23–46.

Parette, P., Huer, M., & Wyatt, T. (2002). Young African American children with disabilities and augmentative and alternate communication issues. *Early Child Education Journal, 29,* 201–207.

Rickford, J. R., & Rickford, A. E. (1995). Dialect readers revisited. *Linguistics and Education, 7,* 109–126.

Assessment

Craig, H., & Washington, J. (2000). An assessment battery for identifying language impairments in African American children. *Journal of Speech, Language and Hearing Research, 4,* 366–379.

Gopaul-McNicol, S., Reid, G., & Wisdom, C. (1998). The psychoeducational assessment of ebonics speakers: Issues and challenges. *Journal of Negro Education, 67,* 16–23.

Roderkohr, R., & Haynes, W. (2001). Differentiating a dialect from a comparison of two processing tasks and a standardized language test. *Journal of Communication Disorders, 34,* 255–272.

CHAPTER 7

Moral Development

OVERVIEW

Morality is a concept that is of great interest across societies, communities, and families. Despite being a major subject of research in mainstream psychology, relatively little research is devoted to the examination of moral development among African American children. The current chapter provides insight on the relationship between moral development and the African American child. First, we present some of the most prominent and influential theories in moral development. Second, we examine the issue of prosocial behavior and moral reasoning; and third, the connection between morality and Black racial identity. Finally, we investigate moral transgressions particularly in the form of community violence and its impact on African American children.

INSIDER'S VOICE: WHAT IF HEINZ WERE BLACK?

I remember the voices of resistance all through this time. Chalos and Ronnie Blakeney asking what if Heinz were black, what would the judge do then? Wouldn't the story change? Wouldn't the conversation with the judge be different? We all knew that it would. Did we have to not know this? And how could we live, how could we do psychology, how could we talk about morality, knowing what we knew? If we could not act on our knowledge, did we need not to know?

Carol Gilligan, Remembering Larry (Journal of Moral Education, 1998)

The Issues

Many issues need to be considered in the examination of moral development and the African American child. First, the sparse research on African

American children and moral development is mainly because of a cultural deficit perspective (Jagers, 2001). Scholars disagree on where moral decency among African American children derives. Some believe that moral decency is the result of the internalization of mainstream American values and practices (Anderson, 1999; Wilson, 1996). Other scholars purport that moral decency evolves from an African cultural integrity (Oliver, 1989; Ward, 1995).

Second, much of the moral development literature excludes the impact of subculture, gender, and socioeconomic status (Hayes, 1984). Third, relatively little is known about the development of domain distinctions in African American children (Jagers, Bingham, & Hans, 1996). There are numerous studies on the development of domain distinctions among Whites, but relatively little work has been done on children of color. These distinct domains of socialization include moral (rights of self and others), social-conventional (rules of social interactions within particular contexts), personal (actions affecting the self), and prudential (actions which negatively affect the actor). We also need to consider the relationship between covictimization (indirect experience of observing direct acts of violence) and moral development within African American communities. These issues will be discussed throughout the chapter.

SECTION ONE: THEORIES OF MORAL DEVELOPMENT

Moral development is a topic of great interest to societies, communities, and families. Moral development has both intrapersonal and interpersonal dimensions, which are comprised of changes in thoughts, feelings, and behaviors within the standards of right and wrong.

How do children acquire an understanding of right from wrong? Several theories on moral development exist (e.g., Gibbs, 1979; Gilligan, 1982; Kohlberg, 1969; Piaget, 1965; and Turiel, 1983). Historically, the majority of these theories focus upon Eurocentric and male interests.

The viewpoints expressed in the work of prominent morality theorists (i.e., Piaget and Kohlberg) espouse the following premises:

1. Each stage in both Piaget's and Kohlberg's theories is qualitatively different from one another.
2. Development is an invariant sequence. The assumption is that development is a stepwise progression, in which lower stages form the foundation for higher stages.
3. Each stage is a *"structured whole,"* which represents general thought patterns, which are consistently applied across a variety of issues and situational contexts rather than occurring in isolated instances.

4. Stages are universal and apply to individuals throughout the life-span (Gibbs, 1979).
5. Stages are hierarchically integrated. The thought processes which oc-cur at the higher stages of moral development encompass the stages below it (Kohlberg, 1981).
6. The transition between stages can be aided by exposure to enriching experiences (Gibbs, 1979).

Piaget's Theory

Jean Piaget's work remains relevant to contemporary theories of moral devel-opment. In the early 1930s and also in the mid-sixties, Piaget studied 4-to 12-year-old children's thinking about moral issues involving rules in a game of marbles. During the observations, Piaget brought up issues of justice, lies, theft, and punishment. According to his theory of cognitive development, children actively construct an understanding of the world through a series of interaction sequences with the environment. Thus, as a result of being ex-posed to the application of rules in a game of marbles, Piaget concluded that children's understanding of morality is a developmental process that involves two distinct stages: heteronomous morality and autonomous morality.

The first stage, heteronomous morality or moral realism, occurs from 4 to 7 years of age. Children's moral understanding is largely based on strict obedi-ence to rules and authority. According to Piaget, a child's egocentrism (inability to consider the moral perspective of more than one person) is a major factor in this stage. They often assume that their moral feelings are shared by everyone. Children's moral thinking is focused more on the actions rather than the inten-tions of the person committing the act. Furthermore, children assume that all acts will be punished, which is the result of the belief in the notion of immanent justice. In other words, all acts of wrong doing will be punished inevitably.

Another factor in the development of heteronomous moral thinkers is the powerful authority figure. According to Piaget, young children's moral devel-opment is largely based on a vertically structured relationship they have with adults or authority figures. Children's belief in heteronomous morality is a re-sult of feeling powerless in the face of "authoritarian" adults. To heteronomous thinkers, the rules made by all-powerful authority figures are unchangeable, require strict adherence, and any violation of them lets down important people in the child's social world.

Children's strict adherence to heteronomous thinking can be problematic in their interactions with peers. From 7 to 10 years of age, children wobble between the first and second stages of moral development. As children encounter situations with peers where heteronomous thinking is problematic; they are afforded the opportunity to critically evaluate the rules of the situation, and apply them based upon mutual cooperation. According to Piaget, these experiences allow children to process information in more advanced ways, thus they allow for more advanced moral thinking and behavior.

Children from age 10 and up demonstrate autonomous morality. A child's increasing sense of reciprocity is a major factor in the development of autonomous morality. Moral autonomists appreciate the perspective of others, thus one's intentions rather than just one's actions are taken into account in moral transgressions. Another factor in the development of autonomous morality is the social structure of the peer group. In contrast to the vertically structured relationship between parent-child, the horizontally structured social relationships among peers allow for give-and-take, and mutually agreed upon negotiations and resolutions which are more likely to advance moral reasoning.

Kohlberg's Theory: The Ethic of Justice

In the late 1960s, Lawrence Kohlberg expanded upon Piaget's work on moral development. Kohlberg's (1969) well-referenced model has laid down the foundation for much research on the study of morality. Like Piaget, he purported that the interaction between children's thinking and experiences with moral concepts, such as justice, human welfare, and rights, result in the advancement of moral reasoning. Unlike Piaget, he proposed that moral development extends beyond childhood, and it is a longer and more gradual process.

In his book *Essays on Moral Development*, Kohlberg (1981) identified six stages of moral reasoning categorized within three levels—preconventional, conventional, and postconventional morality (see Table 7.1). In the Preconventional Level, good and bad are based on external rewards and punishments. The Preconventional Level begins with Stage 1 *Heteronomous Morality* (ages 5 to 7 years), where children's moral actions are based on physical consequences, namely the avoidance of punishment. Stage 2 (*Instrumental Purpose and Exchange*) occurs between the ages of 8 and 12 years, where children feel free to explore their own interests while letting others do the same. What is right involves an equal exchange or an agreement. In the Conventional Level, individuals have internalized a certain set of standards, but they are externally generated (based on others). In Stage 3 (*Mutual Interpersonal Expectations, Good Relations*) adolescents (ages 13 to 16 years) make every effort to fit in by conforming to the stereotypical standard that is set forth by people close to them (such as the family and the local community). *Social Systems and Conscience Maintenance* occurs in Stage 4 (ages 16 years and higher). Individuals in this stage value the need to maintain the social

TABLE 7.1   Kohlberg's Ethic of Justice Theory of Moral Development

Stage	Characteristics
Level I—Preconventional level (no internalization)	
Stage 1—Obedience and punishment orientation (heteronomous morality)	Moral decisions are based on avoidance of punishment and fear of authority figures.
Stage 2—Instrumental purpose and exchange	Moral actions are based on one's own needs, and what is right involves an instrumental exchange of services.
Level II—Conventional level (intermediate internalization)	
Stage 3—Mutual interpersonal expectations, good relations	Individuals value trust and loyalty. Moral behavior is focused on desire to appear as a good person in one's own eyes and the eyes of others.
Stage 4—Social systems and conscience maintenance	Morality is based upon the rules of the social order, law, and society.
Level III—Postconventional level (full internalization)	
Stage 5—Prior rights and social contract	Understanding that values and rules are relative to one's group, and certain rights and principles should transcend the law.
Stage 6—Universal ethical principles	Individuals develop a sense of morality which is based on universal human rights, and is grounded on individual consciousness rather than law.

order, and it marks a shift in conforming to the standards of the local norms to that of the larger social system (society). In Kohlberg's third level, Postconventional Morality, the individual explores multiple moral paths and chooses the one that best suits his or her own needs. Stage 5 (*Prior Rights and Social Contract*) typically occurs in adulthood. Reasoning is based on principles which are graded on rules and norms which serve to protect fundamental human rights and values. Finally, in Stage 6 (*Universal Ethical Principles*) the highest stage of Kohlberg's theory, moral thinking involves the universal application of respect and dignity to all individuals regardless of law or other social conventions.

Criticisms of Piaget's and Kohlberg's Theories

Generally, Piaget and Kohlberg's theories have sparked much debate and condemnation (Lapsley, 2005). Critics of these theories often note several weaknesses: (1) the assessment of moral reasoning; (2) the focus on male norms and the principle of justice; and (3) the exclusion of culture, social class, and family in moral development.

Limitation 1: Assessment of Moral Reasoning. Rest (1979) argues that moral development should be measured using multiple methods, rather than a unitary technique (i.e., a series of hypothetical moral dilemmas). Walker, deVries, and Trevethan (1987) also note that Kohlberg's hypothetical moral dilemmas lack external validity (see example below). The hypothetical scenarios used in Kohlberg's research do not adequately represent the moral situations that many children and adolescents encounter in everyday experiences. They also note the value of having participants recount moral quandaries from their own experiences. This method of having participants talk about their own experiences may provide essential information about each moral stage, but it also provides examples of how people utilize different ways of processing moral predicaments.

Here is an example of a moral dilemma proposed by Kohlberg:

Heinz Steals the Drug

In Europe, a woman was near death from a special kind of cancer. There was one drug that the doctors thought might save her. It was a form of radium that a druggist in the same town had recently discovered. The drug was expensive to make, but the druggist was charging ten times what the drug cost him to make. He paid $200 for the radium and charged $2,000 for a small dose of the drug. The sick woman's husband, Heinz, went to everyone he knew to borrow the money, but he could only get together about $1,000 which is half of what it cost. He told the druggist that his wife was dying and asked him to sell it cheaper or let him pay later. But the druggist said: "No, I discovered the drug and I'm going to make money from it." So Heinz got desperate and broke into the man's store to steal the drug for his wife. Should the husband have done that?

Limitation 2: The Roles of Gender and the Principle of Care. Carol Gilligan's book *In a Different Voice: Psychological Theory and Women's Development* (1982) argues that Kohlberg's theory is biased against females, and his theory puts abstract principles of *justice* and *equality* in the place of the morality of *care perspective*. As a result, women's moral judgments appear to be less sophisticated than those of men. She asserts that this may be due to the fact that Kohlberg used only male participants in the majority of his research, and thus these responses made up his theory. (See Table 7.2 for additional information on Gilligan's Morality of Care Theory).

Limitation 3: Culture, Social Class, and Family Influences. Other criticisms of Kohlberg's and Piaget's theories of moral development involve the absence of culture. Piaget and Kohlberg emphasized universals in moral development, thus there has not been much work on the influence of cultural context (Hayes, 1984). Many argue that the emphasis has been based on Western civilizations. Moral judgments of individuals from non-industrialized and non-western societies tend to be less advanced when Kohlberg's scoring system is used. However, cultural morals such as communal equity and collective happiness which are valued in some collectivists societies are not adequately measured by Kohlberg's scoring system. As a result, the cultural universality of Kohlberg's theory is questioned.

In a comparison of urban males in the United States, Taiwan, and Mexico, Kohlberg (1981) found that middle-class children progressed at faster and farther rates in moral development than lower-class children. Social class differences can be attributed to differences in moral judgments using Rest's Defining Issues Test (DIT) of Moral Development. If the sequence of development is relatively stable, the rate of development may be influenced by social class (Ostrovsky, Parr, & Gradel, 1992). This issue warrants further examination.

Kohlberg argues that the stages of moral development are not products of socialization. Therefore, family practices do not provide opportunities to systematically teach new structures of moral reasoning. Advances in moral development are generated from children's own thinking about moral problems. Kohlberg does note that children's peer relations provide social experiences to promote their moral advancement by stimulating their mental processes. Many developmentalists agree with Piaget and Kohlberg's view on the importance of peer relationships in morality, but the role the family plays in the development of moral reasoning is questioned and challenged in current research.

Gilligan's Theory: The Ethic of Care

Carol Gilligan (1982) criticized Kohlberg for his view that the highest moral judgments rest in principles of justice. Gilligan's work showed that women reason in a voice that relies on a care perspective, which is a moral perspective that emphasizes interconnectedness and communication with others. Gilligan (1982) categorized three levels of moral reasoning—caring for self, caring for others, and caring for both self and others, with transitions between levels 1 and 2, and 2 and 3 (see Table 7.2). In the Caring for Self (Preconventional Level), morality is viewed as standards set forth by society, and a person's own needs come first. In the Caring for Others (Conventional Level), individuals have internalized stereotypical societal standards in which the self must be sacrificed for others. In Gilligan's third level, Caring for Both Self and Others (Postconventional Level), care becomes a universal duty to the individual and to others.

TABLE 7.2   Gilligan's Ethic of Care Theory of Moral Development

Level	Characteristics
Level 1—Preconventional: Caring for self (ethic of survival)	Concern only with self, needs and survival; morality imposed by society.
Level 1.5—Transition from survival to conventional responsibility and goodness	Integration of responsibility and care; responsibility as basis for balance between self and others.
Level 2—Conventional: Caring for others (ethic of conventional goodness)	Adopt societal values; social participation involving care for the dependent and unequal.
Level 2.5—Transition from conventional goodness to reflective care	Ponders the expense one pays for protecting and caring for others; shift from self-sacrifice to truth and honesty.
Level 3—Postconventional: Caring for both self and others (ethic of care)	Self-chosen responsibility to care for self and others; balance achieved between selfishness and selflessness.

Gibbs's Sociomoral Reasoning Model

Gibbs, Basinger, and Fuller (1992) criticized Kohlberg's postconventional morality level because they view stages 5 and 6 as moral philosophies rather than moral reasoning. The last two stages of Kohlberg's theory are rarely reached (Snarey, 1994). As a result, Gibbs et al. developed a model of moral development, which consists of four stages that range from immature morality (self-centered) to moral maturation (interpersonal and societal centered). Stage 1 (Unilateral and Physicalistic reasoning) emphasizes physical or concrete places and events as the basis for moral judgments. Stage 2 (Exchanging and Instrumental reasoning) encompasses psychological self-perspectives (or self-interests). In Stage 3 (Mutual and Prosocial reasoning), the individual's sense of morality is preoccupied with interpersonal relationships and expectations. Finally, the most advanced moral reasoning stage (Systemic and Standard) occurs when one's moral base is centered on the maintenance of basic human rights and values for others in their social system.

Theorists such as Piaget, Kohlberg, Gibbs, and Gilligan have taken a constructivist approach to morality and suggest that moral advancement is based on cognitive maturation and occurs in universal stages and that are born out of principles based on ethics of care and justice. Cultural theorists believe that moral reasoning is culturally based (Shweder & Borne, 1984). Western versus non-western cultures have different moral orientations (that is, individualistic versus collectivist, respectively). Children adopt an understanding of self and a sense of morality from participating in their culture (Shweder, Mahapatra, & Miller, 1987).

Despite the increase in literature on cultural variations in moral development, a relatively small amount of scholarship examines moral development among African American children.

Humphries' Culture and Empathy Model

Humphries, Parker, and Jagers (2000) examined the moral reasoning of urban fifth-and eighth-grade African American children. Specifically, their model explores the relationship among gender, empathy, and cultural orientation (i.e., communalism over competitive individualism) with moral development. They suggest that African American children's cultural commitment to communalism would advance the development of a morality of care. Figure 7.1 outlines Humphries et al's. (2000) model of moral reasoning. The model proposes that cultural orientation is relevant to the development of moral reasoning. Empathy can be viewed as a mediator between communalism and sociomoral reasoning among African American children. Furthermore, the model highlights that older African American children will display greater moral maturity than younger African Americans.

Woods and Jagers (2003) investigated the role of communal orientation in the moral reasoning of 13- and 14-year-old African American adolescents. Their findings support the notion that Afrocultural values such as affect, religion, and communalism positively predict moral reasoning among African American children. Furthermore, their work proposes a negative relationship between Anglocultural values (such as individualism, material well-being, and competition) and moral reasoning among African Americans.

Turiel's Domain Theory: Moral Rules and Social Conventions

In contrast to the traditional cognitive developmental stage theories and cultural psychological morality models, domain theory draws a distinction between moral reasoning and social convention. *Moral rules* involve the intrinsic consequences of actions for the rights and welfare of others (Jagers, Bingham, & Hans, 1996). Moral prescriptions are widely accepted interpersonal responsibilities that are not accepted by social consensus (Turiel, 1998, 2002). *Social conventions* are rules created to maintain the social system. The rules are arbitrary and regulate behaviors within certain situational contexts.

According to domain theorists, such as Nucci (2001), Smetana (1995), and Turiel (1998), children function within a series of parallel developmental frameworks or domains (e.g., moral, conventional, and personal). In this

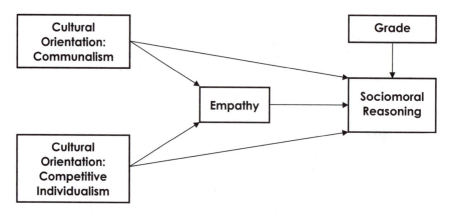

FIGURE 7.1   Cultural and empathy model for moral reasoning.
(Adapted from Humphries et al., 2000).

model, children "develop multiple forms of social reasoning that simultane-
ously include concerns with rights and justice *and* tradition and authority"
(Neff & Helwig, 2002, p. 1430). Due to the complexity of the larger society
in which children exist, they are required to retrieve and process information
from more than one domain. The resulting action depends on many factors,
such as the particular situation, how the situation is interpreted, and the manner in which the conflicting frameworks are coordinated (Turiel, 2002). Furthermore, this theory allows for more inconsistency in reasoning judgments
of children across contexts. This inconsistency is perceived as normative and
commonplace (Neff & Helwig, 2002), as opposed to Kohlberg's theory.

A substantial amount of research has examined the development of domain
distinctions in middle-class European Americans. However, relatively little
work, besides Jagers, Bingham, and Hans (1996), has focused on domain
development among African American or lower-class children in the United
States.

SECTION TWO: PROSOCIAL BEHAVIOR
AND AFRICAN AMERICAN CHILDREN

The small amount of research that has examined moral development of African American children has been built upon a cultural deficit perspective (Jagers,
2001). Considerable negative media attention and research has been devoted
to negative outcomes among African American children, especially those from
poor and urban environments. Relatively little focus has been given to prosocial
behaviors and attitudes of African American youth (McMahon, Wernsman, &

Parnes, 2006; Woods & Jagers, 2003). The development and factors related to the concept of prosocial behavior in African American children merits attention.

Prosocial behavior is any voluntary behavior intended to benefit another person with the expectation of gaining something in return. Developmental and cognitive theorists purport positive relationships between cognitive and emotional processing abilities and prosocial behavior. This progression is likely due to the changes in social contexts and the role of empathy interpersonal relationships (McMahon, Wernsman, & Parnes, 2006). There is debate on whether empathy is an essential ingredient for prosocial behavior (Miller, Bernzweig, Eisenberg, & Fabes, 1991, Roberts & Strayer, 1996;); however, few studies have examined this issue. Besides empathy, there are other factors that are known to influence prosocial behavior in children. Even though the amount of research on African American children in this area is notably sparse, it is important to consider the possible influence of these factors in this population.

Possible Factors Influencing Prosocial Behavior in African American Children

Many factors have been shown to influence and predict the amount, type, quality, and success of prosocial behavior in which a child engages (Eisenberg & Fabes, 1998). A few of these factors such as family, socioeconomic status, age, sex, and race will be discussed in the subsequent sections.

Family

In a meta-analysis of prosocial behavior, family factors accounted for one-half of the variance in children's prosocial behaviors (Eisenberg & Fabes, 1998). If empathy is viewed as a necessary component to prosocial behavior then it is reasonable to speculate that children from homes with multiple siblings and single parents may experience more open communication with family members. Thus, this open discussion about emotion may facilitate the development of empathy and prosocial behavior (Rehberg & Richman, 1989; Zahn-Waxler, Radke-Yarrow, & King, 1979). Due to the changing demographics of the African American family, this idea is worth further examination.

The type of parenting style also may influence a child's prosocial behavior. MacDonald and Parke (1984) posit that White families who adopt authoritarian and permissive parenting styles are linked to a lower degree of prosocial behavior and more negative peer experiences (Miller et al., 1991); however, an increase of prosocial behavior is evident among authoritative families. In addition, males raised in authoritarian families are inclined to be more prosocial than males from authoritative or permissive families (Miller et al., 1991).

Socioeconomic Status

In Western cultures, such as in the United States, prosocial behaviors are desired and expected at some level from everyone. However, the level of expectation may vary from individual to individual depending on a many factors (e.g., cultural orientation, gender, age, and socioeconomic status). Investigations on the role of socioeconomic status (SES) in children's prosocial judgments and behavior are scant, especially among African American youth. Based on a sample of high and low SES Brazilian children, Eisenberg, Zhou, and Koller (2001) theorize that more advantaged social classes may value an autonomous and individualistic cultural orientation than those from more disadvantaged groups, who place more value on communalism. African American children have a stronger sense of communal orientation over an individualistic or minority orientation (Jagers & Mock, 1993). Eisenberg et al. (2001) purport that children from low SES backgrounds are expected to engage in more authority-based (preconventional) reasoning if their cultural orientation is more communal than children from higher social classes. As a result, children from lower SES classes may not appear as advanced on measures of moral and prosocial reasoning due to the inherent cultural and class biases of the assessments. These issues can readily be applied to samples of African American children.

Another issue related to lower social class that is worth consideration is one's amount of exposure to others in need of assistance (Eisenberg et al., 2001). It is plausible that constant exposure to distress may be related to a more advanced or abstract type of moral reasoning in children from disadvantaged social classes (Eisenberg et al., 2001). These ideas are exploratory and research is needed to validate these propositions.

Age, Sex, and Race

Research posits a positive correlation between age and prosocial behaviors (see Eisenberg & Fabes, 1998, for a review). This trend appears to stabilize in early adolescence. However, there are other factors in addition to age that influence a child's willingness to act prosocially. Children are influenced by the age and gender of the target, the type of prosocial behavior, the type of assessment used, and the presence of an observer (Eisenberg & Fabes, 1998). Young children are likely to be more prosocial with children similar to themselves, at least in terms of gender and social experience.

Socialization may account for gender differences in prosocial behavior. Overall, children behave in ways that are consistent with gender-role stereotypes (Miller et al., 1991). Society expects girls to assist, console, and teach others, as opposed to boys, who are socialized towards independence

(Eisenberg & Fabes, 1998). Conversely, noticeable gender differences have not emerged in other studies on rates of prosocial behavior (Eagley & Crowley, 1986; Eisenberg & Mussen, 1989). Furthermore, gender distinctions in prosocial behavior are based largely upon White participants.

White children engage in prosocial acts at higher rates with other White children, rather than with African American children (Zinser, Rich, & Bailey, 1981). Some believe that this may be due to a preference for same-race over cross-race peers (Graham & Cohen, 1997; Graham, Cohen, Zbikowski, & Secrist, 1998), and more positive beliefs about same-race peers (Aboud, 1988). However, Zimmerman and Levy (2000) found that younger White preschool children were more likely to report that they would act prosocially towards African American children than older White preschoolers. Racial socialization may account for prosocial behavior among African American children. Children may behave in ways that are consistent with racial and gender stereotypes. The influence of race on moral development among African American participants warrants attention.

Morality and Racial Identity Development

Schools and educational curriculums across the country have implemented "character education" programs as a way to increase moral behavior. Ward (1995) asserts that in order to increase moral behavior, it is best to examine it in connection to racial identity development. The association of prosocial behavior to Black racial identity in African American children has been examined in a few studies.

Theorists such as Cross, Helms, Parham, and Thomas developed *Nigrescence* models to explain the development of ethnic identity in African Americans. Nigrescence refers to the process by which African Americans learn to understand or identify with their Blackness. The model contains five stages which African Americans must move through to achieve healthy identity development. According to Helms (1990) the stages of Black racial identity progress as follows:

1. *Pre-encounter*—an anti-Black attitude and endorsement of the White cultural perspective. In this stage individuals work to eliminate the perceived social stigma of being African American.
2. *Dissonance or Encounter*—the individual experiences either a positive or a negative encounter which is so highly salient that it becomes a motivating factor in challenging previously held anti-Black cultural beliefs. This encounter prompts a move towards a Black racial identity.

3. *Immersion-Emersion*—the individual excitedly adopts a new Black racial identity, while disparaging and withdrawing from other racial and cultural groups. During the second phase of this stage (emersion), the individual's sense of excitement reaches a point of balance.

4. *Internalization*—all of previous stages are resolved and a new healthy Black racial identity is internalized. Individuals become more secure and flexible in their thinking and worldview.

5. *Internalization-Commitment*—a person not only has a solid sense of his or her own racial identity, but they are also committed to helping others (within and outside of their racial group) find a solid sense of identity.

Moreland and Leach (2001) suggest that moral development and racial identity development have common characteristics. The two constructs can be related to traditional morality stage theorists (see Table 7.3). First, preconventional morality (Stage 1) and pre-encounter racial identity are cognitive representations external to oneself. In the second stage of preconventional morality and the encounter stage of racial identity, awareness of the self or sense of individualism begins to materialize. Third, conventional morality (Stages 3 and 4) and immersion-émersion racial identity draw attention to a newly formed identity and connection to the community. The final theme draws a connection between postconventional morality (Stages 5 and 6) and internalization of racial identity. The common element here is that the individual has become more accepting of others and has adopted an appreciation for universal rights.

TABLE 7.3 Moreland and Leach's Common Themes Between Moral Development and Racial Identity Theories

Construct	Moral development	Racial identity
Cognitive development	Comprehension	Cognitive style
Ego development	Self-concept	Self-actualization, self-esteem
Education level	Linear progression	Linear level progression
	Level	**Status**
External self	Preconventional	Pre-encounter
Self-awareness	Preconventional (stage 2)	Encounter
Shared community	Conventional	Immersion-emersion
Objectivity/openness to others	Postconventional	Internalization

Source: *Journal of Black Psychology,* 27(3), 2001, p. 258.

SECTION THREE: MORAL DEVELOPMENT
AND COMMUNITY VIOLENCE

Numerous research studies show that many African American children from low-income, urban environments are much more likely to experience violence in their communities than African Americans or White children who reside in less violent areas (Bowen & Bowen, 1999). Approximately 50%–95% of African American children living in inner cities have been victimized directly or have indirectly witnessed (covictimized) violence in their community (Belgrave & Allison, 2006; Myers & Thompson, 2000). Bell and Jenkins (1993) as well as Campbell and Schwartz (1996) report that low income, urban African American youth have witnessed shootings (57%–70%), stabbings (55%), and murder (22%–50%). Unfortunately, not only are some low-income, urban youth witnesses to and victims of violent crime, but many are perpetrators of it. The United States Department of Justice Statistics (2006) report that Blacks (55.7%) comprised a majority of the violent felons under age 18 between 1990 and 2002 (see Figure 7.2).

Exposure to community violence may have a significant impact on children's cognitive sense of morality (i.e., sense of justice and empathy) and on the behavioral outcomes of their moral development (Kuther & Wallace, 2003). Also, it is important to understand African American's attitudes and beliefs about such violence. One perspective of this issue is illuminated by Elijah Anderson, a sociologist, from the University of Pennsylvania (see Insider's Voice).

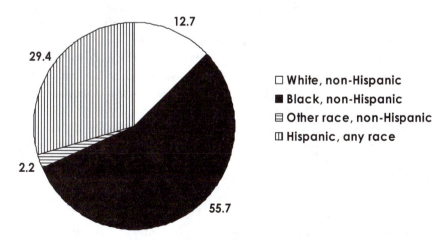

FIGURE 7.2   Race distribution of violent felons in the 75 largest U.S. counties, who were under 18 years old at date of arrest, 1990–2002 (Adapted from U.S. Dept. of Justice, 2006).

INSIDER'S VOICE: DISSECTING THE 'CODE OF THE STREET'
FROM THE *PHILADELPHIA ENQUIRER* (JULY 2006)

Of all the problems besetting the poor inner-city black community, none is more pressing than that of interpersonal violence and aggression. It wreaks havoc daily with the lives of community residents and increasingly spills over into downtown and residential middle-class areas.

Muggings, burglaries, carjackings, and drug-related shootings, all of which may leave their victims or innocent bystanders dead, are now common enough to concern all urban and many suburban residents. The inclination to violence springs from the circumstances of life among the ghetto poor—the lack of jobs that pay a living wage, the stigma of race, the fallout from rampant drug use and drug-trafficking, and the resulting alienation and lack of hope for the future.

As the Philadelphia region deindustrializes and globalizes, great numbers of inner-city poor people fail to cope with these changes. The result is concentrated and racialized urban poverty with a structural cast. A certain lawlessness prevails in these neighborhoods, but when residents summon the police, they often arrive late or are felt to abuse the very people who called them.

The community feels unprotected and alienated from the police and the justice system, their faith in the civil law undermined by the lawlessness they witness in their communities daily. Out of self-defense, the community adopts the principles of "street justice"—"an eye for and eye, a tooth for a tooth"—and a retaliation dynamic becomes common. In these circumstances, reputation, or "street credibility," becomes ever more coveted—if not for deterrence, then for self-respect—and becomes a precious coin traded for a sense of security in the 'hood.

Simply living in such an environment places young people at special risk of falling victim to aggressive behavior. Although there are often forces in the community which can counteract the negative influences—by far the most powerful being a strong, loving, "decent" (as inner-city residents put it) family committed to middle-class values—the despair is pervasive enough to have spawned an oppositional culture. It is the culture of "the streets," whose norms are often consciously opposed to those of mainstream society.

These two orientations—decent and street—socially organize the community, and their co-existence has important consequences for residents, particularly children growing up in the inner city. Above all, this environment means that even youngsters whose home lives reflect mainstream values—and the majority of homes in the community do—must be able to handle themselves in a street-oriented environment.

This is because the street culture has evolved what may be called a code of the streets, which amounts to a set of informal rules governing interpersonal public behavior, including violence. The rules prescribe both a proper comportment and a proper way to respond if challenged. They regulate the use of violence and so allow those who are inclined to aggression to precipitate violent encounters in an approved way.

The rules have been established and are enforced mainly by the street-oriented, but on the streets the distinction between street and decent is often irrelevant; everybody knows that if the rules are violated, there are penalties. Knowledge of the code is thus largely defensive; it is literally necessary for operating in public. Therefore, even though families with a decency orientation are usually opposed to the rules of the code, they often reluctantly encourage their children's familiarity with it to enable them to negotiate the inner-city environment.

At the heart of the code is the issue of respect—loosely defined as being treated "right," or granted the deference one deserves. However, in the troublesome public environment of the inner city, as people increasingly feel buffeted by forces beyond their control, what one deserves in the way of respect becomes more and more problematic and uncertain. This in turn further opens the issue of respect to sometimes intense interpersonal negotiation.

In the street culture, especially among young people, respect is viewed as almost an external entity that is hard-won but easily lost, and so must constantly be guarded. The rules of the code, in fact, provide a framework for negotiating respect.

The person whose very appearance—including his clothing, demeanor and way of moving—deters transgressions feels that he possesses, and may be considered by others to possess, a measure of respect. With the right amount of respect, for instance, he can avoid "being bothered" in public. If he is bothered, not only may he be in physical danger but he has been disgraced or "dissed" (disrespected). Many of the forms that dissing can take might seem petty to middle-class people (maintaining eye contact for too long, for example), but to those invested in the street code, these actions become serious indications of the other person's intentions.

Consequently, such people become very sensitive to advances and slights, which could well serve as warnings of imminent physical confrontation.

This hard reality can be traced to the profound sense of alienation from mainstream society and institutions felt by many poor inner-city black people, particularly the young. The code of the street is actually a cultural adaptation to a profound lack of faith in the police and the judicial system. The police are most often seen as representing the dominant white society and not caring to protect inner-city residents. When called they may not respond, which is one reason many residents feel they must be prepared to take extraordinary measures to defend themselves and their loved ones against those who are inclined to aggression.

Lack of police accountability has in fact been incorporated into the status system: the person who is believed capable of "taking care of himself" is accorded a certain deference, which translates into a sense of physical and psychological control. The street code emerges where the influence of the police ends and personal responsibility for one's safety is felt to begin. Exacerbated by the proliferation of drugs and easy access to guns, this volatile situation results in the ability of the street-oriented minority (or those who effectively "go for bad") to dominate the public spaces.

Especially among young people, this reality encourages a relentless campaign for "street cred" that ironically is undermined by success in school and the accumulation of other conventional forms of human capital. Additionally, this campaign for street cred, based on a reputation for so many victorious fights to one's credit, results in a proliferation of police contacts and records for too many young males that virtually renders too many of them unemployable.

The inner-city economy at "ground zero" depends on three interrelated sources: low-wage jobs, welfare payments and the idiosyncratic, irregular underground economy. Capital circulates between and among these elements, and when any one of which proves unproductive, people are encouraged to rely on the remaining ones. Hence, despite a real scarcity of economic resources in the inner-city poor community, to make ends meet, many people often engage in numerous everyday exchanges—bartering, lending, as well as illegal enterprises such as the drug trade—that are carried on without the benefit of civil law, with a "street justice" filling the void.

The drug trade is stratified by "top dogs," "middle dogs," and "low dogs." But to work in the drug trade, one must have a firearm, often obtained illegally, in order to deter "stick up" boys and others with whom beefs develop. Because of the relentless campaign for street credibility, beefs quickly result in gun play.

As this cycle plays itself out, employers are encouraged to further discriminate against black males, further exacerbating their employability while fueling the cycle of joblessness, alienation, violence, and early death.

Elijah Anderson (2006). Dissecting the "code of the street," an excerpt from the book, Code of the street: Decency, violence, and moral life of the inner city. Philadelphia Enquirer, July 27, 2006. Reprinted by permission of author.

Even though it is assumed that there is a clear connection between moral development and exposure to community violence there is paucity of research in this area (Kuther & Wallace, 2003). Ward (1988) examined reactions the reactions from urban youth to perceived violence in the home, school, and community; and Fields, as cited in Kuther and Wallace (2003), analyzed children's moral orientations from politically violent situations (e.g., war). Early and middle-adolescents from violent areas engaged in retribution and lower levels of moral reasoning than children from nonviolent areas.

Despite the scant literature on the influence of covictimization on moral development there are suggestions as to how one must go about developing interventions and theoretical models with African American youth. Garbarino (1991, 1993) recommends that research on the implications of covictimization for moral development among African American children include the linkage of multiple causal factors with both positive and negative developmental outcomes. Second, we must incorporate and appreciate the participants' cultural norms (Kuther & Wallace, 2003). As far as future research on moral development and community violence, it is necessary to examine the singular and interactive effects of the cognitive, social, and emotional domains. Furthermore, it is important to consider the influence of family and community contexts on the socialization of morality among African American children.

It must be emphasized that not all children from economically deprived environments are negatively affected by or are perpetrators of violence. Many African American youth are protected by resilient characteristics such as supportive families, high self-regard, and cultural identity (Belgrave & Allison, 2006). As a consequence, these children are likely to have more adaptive moral standards, which serve to effectively regulate their emotional processing and perspective taking abilities (Kliewer, Cunningham, Diehl, Parish, Walker, Atiyeh et al., 2004). An example of a program aimed to reduce community violence and promote resilience by creating a supportive neighborhood network was created by Rosario Ceballo (see Box 7.1 for details).

BOX 7.1

Violence Intervention Program

The Neighborhood Club: A Supportive Intervention Group for Children Exposed to Urban Violence

By Rosario Ceballo

Many children residing in impoverished neighborhoods are bombarded by incidents of violence and their aftermath. Consequently, rates of exposure to community violence are exceptionally high for many poor, urban children (Bell & Jenkins, 1991; Fitzpatrick, 1993; Gladstein, Rusonis, & Heald, 1992; Lorion & Saltzman, 1993). For example, among 170 fifth and sixth graders in a metropolitan school system, over 80% reported regularly hearing the sounds of gunfire in their neighborhoods, and one in every six children

environment; 3) assisting children in developing safety skills for dealing with chronic environmental violence; 4) teaching children about the process of grief and mourning; and 5) minimizing the influence of PTSD symptoms on educational tasks and other daily life events. The group is not intended to provide children with individual psychotherapy. Thus, children are not asked to speak directly about trauma-related incidents in their past. Group leaders make every effort to assure that discussions about neighborhood violence occur in displacement, one step removed from the personal experience. For example, the group will discuss what "most children" are likely to feel in dangerous situations and will normalize the fact that "most children and even adults are scared by people with guns."

Ten Neighborhood Clubs have been conducted at three public and charter schools located in poor, high-crime neighborhoods in Detroit. In 1995, the number of FBI Part I Crimes (murder, rape, robbery, assault, breaking and entering, larceny, auto theft, and arson) in one of the neighborhood's police precincts reached a total of 3,741 (Detroit Police Department, 1995). Children were selected to participate in the groups by their school principals and teachers, based on knowledge of the children's family backgrounds, their exposure to violence, and an understanding of the general aims of the group. The children ranged in age from 9 to 12 years, and there were roughly equal numbers of boys and girls. Their racial backgrounds included Caucasians, African Americans, and Latino/as, with the largest concentration of Latino/a children being of Mexican-American descent. Additionally, Spanish-speaking children participated in Neighborhood Clubs with bilingual graduate student leaders, who translated information as needed.

Club Themes

Titles and topics of the weekly group sessions are: 1) Introductions, 2) So Many Feelings, 3) Neighborhood Drawings, 4) Skits and Safety Plans, 5) When Somebody Dies..., 6) Gangs in the Neighborhood, 7) Newspaper Review, and 8) Goodbye Party. While group facilitators are guided by a detailed manual outlining all Neighborhood Club sessions and activities, what follows here will be a brief synopsis of each session, with special attention given to clinically relevant material from the group experiences.

Introductions

The group leaders open the first session by introducing themselves to the children and explaining the purpose of the group: to provide a safe place for them to talk about their neighborhoods and the different kinds of things— both good and scary—that can happen there. It is important not to focus solely on negative neighborhood events, since people can demonstrate remarkable signs of strength and resilience in even the most desperate situations. Thus, no neighborhood or community is "all bad." Early in this session, the children's assistance is elicited in establishing group rules. (In several groups, the children insisted that the rules should include no guns or knives. The facilitators complied and wrote a "no weapons" rule on the board, accompanying other rules that one might more typically expect from fourth and fifth graders.) Additionally, the group leaders explain and discuss a confidentiality or privacy rule. During this initial session, the children also make collages that describe themselves, which they then use when introducing themselves to the rest of the group.

As soon as the purpose of the Neighborhood Club is explained, the children often begin spontaneously sharing stories about their encounters with violence. In one group, a child said he had seen a stabbing, another child started to describe a drive-by shooting, and a third announced that his neighbor had been attacked. Having received permission to talk about their experiences with violence, the children seized the opportunity, and it felt to the group leaders as if a floodgate had opened. The clinical challenge at this point was to encourage the children's enthusiasm for sharing and discussing such events while also moving this discussion into displacement. Although many of the children in these groups were eager to discuss their experiences with violence, it is important for the overall functioning of the group to discuss such issues in displacement because other group members may not be ready to confront traumatic material so directly.

So Many Feelings

In the second session, the main group activity is to play a "feelings" game in which one child makes a face to illustrate a feeling, while the rest of the group guesses what feeling the child is acting out. Invariably, the children enjoy and become deeply engaged in this activity, which helps them identify, name, and express emotions while also creating a sense of group cohesion. The group facilitators use this session to normalize a broad spectrum of feelings and to discuss how to manage difficult feelings such as anger and fear. The group may discuss strategies for coping with angry feelings that are hard to control, outlets such as hitting a pillow, talking with a friend, or taking deep breaths and slowly counting to ten.

Neighborhood Drawings

The primary goal for the third session is fostering discussion about the positive and violent aspects of children's neighborhoods within the context of a safe and supportive group atmosphere. Additional goals include normalizing children's feelings regarding violent incidents and helping them develop strategies for coping with strong and frightening feelings. Drawing is the main activity here, in large part because children's drawings may "initiate the therapeutic process of countering the passive, helpless stance of the traumatized victim" (Eth & Pynoos, 1985, p. 289). During this session, each child is asked to make two drawings, one depicting "things that they like about their neighborhood" and the other, on a separate sheet of paper, "things that they don't like." During this time, the group leaders have an opportunity to circulate among the children and talk to them about their drawings one-on-one. Next, the children collectively work on two large, mural-like drawings on poster board, again one of "the best things" and the other of "the worst things in neighborhoods," with each child asked to contribute something to both drawings.

When the group drawings are finished, the facilitators lead a discussion in which each child is encouraged to describe and explain what they drew as a contribution to the mural. In depicting the "best things," children typically draw attractive houses, flowers, trees, smiling people, schools, churches, and pets. The group leaders then encourage the children to talk about positive experiences and the strengths that they gain from such things and people. It is critical to approach this work with an openness and respect for cultural differences and idiosyncratic community norms. For example, a girl in one group drew a cemetery to represent the "best things." The leaders, somewhat puzzled and concerned, talked with her to ensure that she had properly understood the instructions. Afterward, one of the teachers noted that many families in this girl's neighborhood identify the cemetery as a peaceful haven, one of the few spots in which they can find grass, trees, and solitude.

To represent "worst things," the children in these groups have drawn—in astonishing detail—shootings, robberies, bleeding people, graffiti, drug deals, and abandoned houses. While the children may express some initial nervousness, they quickly become eager to "let go" of the sights and sounds of violence. In one drawing, a child filled the page with a gun, a knife, garbage, and stray dogs. Another child drew her house and wrote, "I hate everything [in my neighborhood] but not my house or my backyard." In this case, the group facilitators empathized with the girl's distress at living in a neighborhood with so few positive attributes, while they also supported the enormous importance of having a safe and loving home.

Drawings provide an inroad, a starting place, for children to begin a discussion of things that they may have no words to express. The drawings, coupled with the response of caring and empathic adults who can tolerate the fear evoked by violence, produce a cathartic effect for many of the children.

Skits and Safety Plans

The fourth session takes an extremely concrete and practical approach to the environmental dangers and challenges facing poor, inner-city children. The overall purpose of this session is prevention; specific goals include teaching children safety skills and helping them restore a sense of control over aspects of their lives and environments.

The group leaders begin this session by asking the children what kinds of things they can do to feel safe in their neighborhoods. Their lists usually include things like avoiding unsafe areas, never walking alone, dropping to the ground if they hear gunfire, and having more than one way or one route to get home. In one of the groups, a boy suggested that pretending to have a gun could be another strategy. The group facilitators replied that, while they understood his desire to feel as safe as possible, there were lots of reasons why carrying weapons was a bad idea in the long run. They stressed that violence is never a good strategy, that violence always leads to more violence.

The children are then divided into three groups, each of which is assigned a specific scenario, for example: "During lunch time, you and your friends find out that one of the kids in your class brought a knife to school. What does your group of friends do about this?" Answers to the questions are acted out in skits, and many props are provided for the children (e.g., wallet, leather jacket, baseball cap), making this a particularly popular activity. The facilitators assist each group in designing and practicing their skit; the groups take turns performing; and the facilitators subsequently lead discussions that include consideration of other things the children could have done in the given situation.

When Somebody Dies...

The fifth session tackles the difficult subjects of death and mourning. Since inner-city children often are close to the victims of violence, the need to assist them with the process of grief and mourning is especially salient (Osofsky, Wewers, Hann, & Fick, 1993). Many of the children in these groups know people in gangs, often older siblings or extended family members, and many have known someone who has died violently.

This session begins by asking the children to define "violence." Sometimes the group debates the answers, arguing, for example, about whether yelling can be categorized as violent. Group leaders turn to the subject of dying by noting that people die for many reasons, but sometimes people die as the result of a violent event. Initially, the facilitators must address children's questions and concerns about what happens when someone dies, correcting misconceptions and offering accurate information that is respectful of different cultural beliefs and practices.

Specific strategies for grief and mourning are then addressed in displacement: one of the group leaders reads aloud from a book in which the death of a person or a pet occurs. Subsequent discussion centers on ways in which the book's protagonist can be made to feel better about his or her grief. For example, the character can remember the dog on special days, keep a photograph of the animal in a wallet, talk to someone about feeling sad and lonely, or share things with the dog by writing it a letter. Next, the children are asked to suggest special things that can be placed in a "memory box" (a nicely decorated shoe box) to help the storybook character remember his or her dog. The children typically come up with a long and creative list of objects that can be put in the memory box. Moreover, some children adapt these strategies and apply them to other painful situations. In one group, a number of members with absent fathers talked poignantly about what they could put in a memory box to remember their missing parent.

Gangs in the Neighborhood

The central focus of the sixth session is on preventing children's involvement with gang activities. The session tends to elicit children's personal stories about their encounters with gangs. One boy, for example, revealed that his older brother was a gang member who had been shot. In another group, a girl mentioned that she had been attacked by a gang member. This led another child to fabricate a more elaborate, frightening, and somewhat unbelievable story about a gang-related encounter. One advantage of dealing with such stories via displacement is that the facilitators do not have to worry about delineating truth from fiction. They deal with the underlying fears and emotional conflicts created by such events—real or imagined—as they may apply to all of us.

At the outset of this session, the children are encouraged to discuss forthrightly the pros and cons of belonging to a gang. When the children in one group talked about how gangs may have started, one boy suggested that, "It was because somebody was lonely and they wanted to feel tough, so he got a group of people who were lonely too and formed a gang." While the groups never discuss local gang signs, colors, or territories, the group leaders do provide children with general information about street gangs. For example, the children are told that when you join a gang, you are typically "beaten up" or "jumped" as part of your initiation.

The children are also asked to draw up a list of reasons why it is never smart to join a gang. These lists typically include reasons such as: gang members lie about loyalty and friendship; the first thing gang members do is beat you up; gang membership will bring you lots of enemies; most gang members get in trouble with the police or go to jail; you could get blamed for something other gang members did; you might get killed in gang fights; and gang members won't let you leave when you want to.

Specific goals for this session include 1) highlighting why the disadvantages of joining a gang outweigh the benefits, and 2) teaching children safety skills that are particularly relevant to gang activity. The children are asked to act out specific things that they can do when approached by gang members, with the group leaders playing the part of recruiting gang members, e.g., proposing that a child run a drug-related errand. Each child has the opportunity to role-play the implementation of one of four strategies: 1) stomping his or her foot firmly, saying "no" loudly, and running away; 2) "faking out" the gang members by promising to help them tomorrow, but saying that, "I have to go home, now"— and then, of course, never returning; 3) giving the gang members anything they ask for, because one's own health and safety are most important; and 4) acting "crazy" or "sick enough to vomit" so that the gang members will become un- comfortable and leave the child alone. In discussing each of these approaches, the facilitators repeatedly stress that all the children have the know-how and the ability to make smart choices. The children so greatly enjoy "standing their ground" with gang members that they often ask to repeat these exercises over and over.

The Newspaper Review

The seventh session addresses many issues related to the end of a thera- peutic experience. Goals at this stage include reviewing material that has been covered in previous meetings, discussing the many feelings associated with endings and separations, and creating a tangible final product: a news- paper that provides each child with a memory of the group—a technique that Kalter, Pickar, and Lesowitz (1984) reported having successfully used as a concluding activity with children participating in divorce groups.

During this session, group members work in pairs to produce the news- paper. With assistance from the group leaders, the children write stories about their Neighborhood Club activities, interview other group members, write or dictate responses for an advice column about neighborhood prob- lems, and draw funny pictures or cartoons. They typically approach these tasks with vigor, excitement, and a unified sense of team effort.

Goodbye Party

In the last session, the group celebrates by holding a party at which the group leaders, in conjunction with the school principal or a teacher, give each child a diploma and a copy of the final, printed newspaper. The purpose of this last session is to celebrate the children's accomplishments in the group and to mark the ending with an opportunity to say their good-byes to the group leaders.

Theoretical Considerations

A conceptual framework based on the resiliency literature provides one theoretical underpinning for the approach taken in this intervention. A great deal of research has explored the identification of factors that allow certain children to excel despite overwhelming odds. Two dimensions of resilient functioning are particularly pertinent to the Neighborhood Club groups: 1) actively trying to cope with stress, as opposed to more passively reacting to it; and 2) having an open, supportive educational climate that encourages constructive coping with problems (Garbarino & Kostelny, 1994; Garbarino, Kostelny, & Dubrow, 1991). Accordingly, the Neighborhood Club specifically and directly encourages children to cope actively with the stress of environmental danger and insecurity. In the groups, children plan and practice concrete strategies for protecting themselves in the community, and discuss various means of coping with the emotional difficulty of experiencing violence. Further, because this intervention takes place in the children's school, it thereby fosters an open and supportive school climate in which teachers and other school personnel are willing to talk about community violence.

The Neighborhood Club additionally relies on empowerment theory—with roots in both feminist theory and community psychology—and the belief that affirming a client's own abilities and self-determination will improve that individual's quality of life. Moreover, many studies indicate that a sense of personal control is associated with greater ability to cope with illness and other life stressors (Peterson & Bossio, 1991). Since we cannot change the random, unpredictable nature of urban violence, the Neighborhood Club emphasizes factors and choices that children can control in order to bolster their safety. Group facilitators strive for a delicate balance between acknowledging the profound sense of dread and vulnerability that frequent, random violence engenders and bolstering children's sense of mastery and control over their environments.

In addressing the needs of an impoverished, at-risk population of children, this intervention intertwines the unique approaches of two rather different clinical orientations. An emphasis on emotional expression and the uncovering of underlying intrapsychic motives and conflicts sits at the core of psychodynamic theory. The children in the Neighborhood Clubs are eager to discuss their emotional reactions to violence. They have described rage-filled wishes to seek revenge for a prior wrong—and they usually understand that their reaction is fueled by the need to feel strong and powerful, like the gang members in their neighborhoods.

Given the real and imminent dangers facing these children, it would be remiss to exclude the provision of concrete and practical strategies that can bolster their safety. In seeking to attain its goals, the present intervention relies on many techniques used in cognitive behavioral therapies, such as role-play, stress management skills, and activity planning. This merger of theoretical approaches may well provide the best "defense" for children facing the formidable threats of community violence.

Conclusion

A study designed to contrast intervention groups with matched control groups on pre- and post-test measures is a necessary step in empirically evaluating this program. While this is not available at present, anecdotal evidence from teachers and parents does support the utility of the Neighborhood Club groups. Teachers have reported that the groups have had a calming effect on their most troubled students. And, both teachers and parents have reported that children are more willing to talk about problems and concerns following group participation.

The Neighborhood Clubs help children feel less isolated in their exposure to urban violence, provide empathic connections to peers who share similar thoughts and feelings, empower children by building a sense of control over certain aspects of their lives, and teach concrete coping strategies and safety skills. This intervention model has several implications for individual psychotherapy. The specific activities and clinical approaches proposed may be thoughtfully transferred and reshaped by clinicians working with inner-city children in other settings. As clinicians and researchers, we must not allow the enormity of the problem to silence our response; the alternative is to relinquish hope and responsibility for those who are the least powerful and in the greatest need—poor children who cannot dodge or escape the onslaught of violence permeating their communities.

PERSPECTIVES ON AFRICAN AMERICAN CHILDREN AND MORAL DEVELOPMENT

We believe that prospective investigations of moral development among African American children should focus on diverse factors such as age, socioeconomic status, family and community structures, media, and racial identity. It is important that we begin to view African American children from a prosocial behavioral perspective rather than from a cultural deficit viewpoint. This is particularly significant for African American youth because of the barrage of stereotypic and negative media attention targeted at them. The impact of the media, such as TV, film, music, magazines, and other information technologies (e.g., computers, video games, the Internet) on African American children and moral development is warranted.

Future research on moral development should utilize more valid research designs with African American children. For example, the use of moral dilemmas that are sensitive to the cultural-contextual nuances of the sample may enhance the internal and external validity of the assessment or study. Furthermore, future studies should include longitudinal designs. Such designs will be beneficial in examining the long term effects of various characteristics on moral reasoning and behaviors.

Finally, there is a need to further examine the relationship between cultural orientation and moral reasoning on African American children. A better understanding of the cultural orientation of African American youth may minimize adults' misunderstandings about the moral behavior and attitudes of some African American youth; and, it may be useful in the development of more socially desirable conflict resolution skills for many children. Thus, such newly acquired social-cognitive competence may prove useful in self- and relationship-development with family, teachers, and peers.

CHAPTER SUMMARY

This chapter focuses on moral development and the African American child. The chapter starts with a discussion of the major moral development theories, that is, Piaget's theory and Kohlberg's Ethic of Justice Theory. A critical analysis of the utility of these theories with African American children is explored. A discussion of the biases and limitations inherent in stage theories of morality is offered, as well as an examination of some methodological weaknesses of traditional morality assessments. The Ethics of Care Theory by Gilligan, Gibb's Sociomoral Reasoning, Humphries' Cultural and Empathy Model, and Turiel's Domain Theory are described in subsequent sections of this chapter.

Parts two and three of the chapter focus on the relationship of moral development on prosocial behavior and Black racial identity, respectively. The similarities between moral development theories; and the nigrescence and Black Racial Identity models are discussed. The concluding section of the chapter examines the impact of community violence on African American youth's sense of moral reasoning. The need for more research on this topic is stressed, and recommendations on creating culturally sensitive models of community violence and morality are illustrated.

ADDITIONAL READINGS

Anderson, E. (1999). *Code of the street: Decency, violence, and the moral life of the inner city.* New York: W. W. Norton & Company.

Bowen, N. K., & Bowen, G. L. (1999). Effects of crime and violence in neighborhoods and schools on the school behavior and performance of adolescents. *Journal of Adolescent Research, 14*(3), 319–342.

Garbarino, J., Kostelny, K., & Dubrow, N. (1991). What children can tell us about living in danger. *American Psychologist, 46,* 376–383.

Graham, J. A., Cohen, R., Zbikowski, S., & Secrist, M. (1998). A longitudinal investigation of race and sex as factors in children's friendship choices. *Child Study Journal, 28,* 245–266.

CHAPTER 8

Social Contexts in the Lives of African American Children: Family and Peers

OVERVIEW

This chapter examines the African American child in social contexts, such as the family and peers. Over the last several decades American families have experienced many demographic changes. The landscape for the typical middle-class American family has shifted from a nuclear two-parent household to an increase in single-parent families (particularly female-headed households), and grandparent-headed households. These demographic trends have unduly affected African American families, and they have important implications for African American children's socialization within family and peer contexts.

In this chapter, we describe several models which guide family research and note some demographic changes involving African American families. We review some of the demographic trends affecting the African American family structure, such as single-mother, single-father, and grandparent-headed households as well as African American foster families. Furthermore, the social world of African American peers is another focus in this chapter. In particular, children's peer relationships and friendships with same- and other-race peers are discussed.

Issues

Today, family researchers are much more responsive to the dearth of research on children within the African American family. Due to this increased awareness, research in this area is much more sensitive to African American communities. Historically, a number of issues have plagued this line of research. As previously mentioned in a number of chapters of this text, one major concern is that the limited scholarship on African American families mainly emanates from a deficit perspective. Once again, the White American family standard was (and to a certain extent continues) to be used as a basis of comparison for the family lives of African American children. As a result much of the published work emphasized dysfunctional rather than positive characteristics of African American families. Fortunately, much of the new scholarship in this area emphasizes the strengths within African American families.

Second, several methodological issues negatively effect the research on African Americans. Design limitations may indirectly create a negative image of African Americans (Littlejohn-Blake & Darling, 1993). Murry, Smith and Hill (2001) note that race and ethnicity are often confounded with socioeconomic assessments and community of residence. Thus, it is difficult to tease apart the authentic effects of culture and ethnicity.

Other methodological constraints include sampling issues and the underutilization of qualitative research designs (Littlejohn-Blake & Darling, 1993). For a better understanding of the African American child within a family context, it is important that participants are recruited from a variety of socioeconomic, residential, and age levels. These recruiting efforts will represent a more balanced or less skewed understanding of child development within an array of African American structures. It is also important to use designs that are better suited to uncover the rich nuances of the African American family. One cannot deny the significance of quantitative designs, but they only provide a limited glimpse into the social, emotional, and cognitive aspects of African American family life. On the other hand, qualitative research designs may provide much needed insight into the family lives of African American children. It is important to note that both designs are subject to misinterpretation, but published work on the family based in each method provides a more thorough understanding and a greater appreciation of the diversity within and across African American families.

INSIDER'S VOICE: THE NEGRO AMERICAN FAMILY

Within the family, each new generation of young males learn the appropriate nurturing behavior and superimpose upon their biologically given maleness this learned parental role. When the family breaks down . . . this delicate line of transmission is broken. Men may flounder badly in these periods, during which the primary unit may again become mother and child, the biologically given, and the special conditions under which man has held his social traditions in trust are violated and distorted.

Daniel Patrick Moynihan, The Negro American Family: The Case for National Action (1965).

BOX 8.1

THE MOYNIHAN REPORT

In 1965, Daniel Patrick Moynihan (assistant secretary at the United States Department of Labor) published a report called *The Negro American Family: The Case for National Action*. The report was a piece of research based on the work of the renowned sociologist, E. F. Frazier. The report described the ongoing disintegration of the African American family. It emphasized the weakened role of African American men and stressed the need that public policies be designed to strengthen the economic role for African American males.

The report raised questions about the ability of the African American family to continue its function as a positive socialization agent of future generations. Moynihan asserted that the problems in the African American family impinged on the entire nation. Thus, he reported that the United States was threatened by the cycle of social deterioration among American Blacks which contributed to illegitimacy, welfare dependency, crime, and poor education.

According to Battle and Coates (2004), Moynihan's report created a stir among social scientists and led to three assumptions in research conducted on African American families from 1965 to 1995. The first assumption was that African American children brought up by two-parent families headed by males are better off than children from a single-parent household. Second, African American single mothers are unskilled at parenting and are especially ill-equipped to take care of boys, which place them at a disadvantage. Finally, African American single-headed families are culturally deviant, and this pathology creates negative aspirations and distorted social roles for their children (Moynihan, 1965).

SECTION ONE: MODELS OF THE AFRICAN AMERICAN FAMILY

The scholarship on African American families has endured many permutations over the past 50 years (Harry, Klingner, & Hart, 2005). It is not our intent to provide a detailed historical analysis of African American family life. In this section, we present some of the paradigms that have shaped this research over time.

Pathological Model

The *pathological* (or *culturally deviant*) model mainly focuses on the negative characteristics of the African American family and ascribes many of these problems to inherent deficiencies (Barnes, 2001). This view emerged partly because of the highly controversial report by D. P. Moynihan (1965; see Box 8.1), which purported that matriarchal African American families deterred healthy masculinity for male children due to a lack of exposure to positive role models (Battle & Coates, 2004). Still others believe that pathology in the African American family is the result of the historical impact of racism and poverty, but more importantly, they purport that distinct cultural values and behaviors are the main causes of socioeconomic deprivation and family dysfunction (Anderson, 1999; Fine, Schwebel, & James-Myers, 1987; and Moynihan, 1965).

According to Barnes (2001), the pathological model espouses the following five assumptions:

1. A comparative analysis between African Americans and Whites in social, economic, and political development;
2. White family norms are universal and should be used as a standard of comparison for African American families;
3. Minimize the positive implications of African American family life;
4. Negatively represent the culture and life within African American communities;
5. Suggest that some African American cultural values be modified to match traditionally White values (Fine et al., 1987).

Furthermore, White and Parham (1990) cite a couple of shortcomings with the pathological model. First, the proponents of this model fail to examine the notion that an African American single parent can serve as an appropriate role model for both male and female children. Second, some researchers have inflexible views of what constitutes a family; thus, their writings perpetuate a myopic view of the African American family (White & Parham, 1990).

Cultural Equivalent Model

The cultural equivalent view of African American family life deemphasizes any negative characteristics and draws focus to the commonalities they share with White families after controlling for social class distinctions (Allen, 1978; Fine et al., 1987; Scanzoni, 1971). The African American family is viewed as adaptive as long as it conforms to the White middle-class standard of family life. Even though this type of standard is used to evaluate the functioning of African American families, followers of this approach often use it to focus on strengths rather than dysfunction (Bryan & Coleman, 1988).

Researchers (such as Barnes, 2001; Billingsley, 1992; Fine et al., 1987; Littlejohn-Blake & Darling, 1993) propose several strengths in the African

American family life. Children in African American homes as compared to some children from traditional middle-class White homes often witness more equality and gender role flexibility between African American parents, strong kinship networks, a strong sense of pride, a model of an unwavering work ethic, and an emphasis on achievement. According to Fine et al. (1987), African American families headed by a single mother are more effective than single-mother White families. In addition, it appears that the notion of illegitimacy may be more negative for White than African Americans families.

An additional strength among children in African American families includes a highly internalized sense of spirituality or religious affiliation, (Billingsley, 1992; Littlejohn-Black & Darling, 1993). African American children are socialized to use their spiritual beliefs as a mechanism for survival, thus this spiritual system becomes a foundation for inner strength (Boyd-Franklin, 1989).

Children from African American families often witness strong kinship patterns in their families. These strong ties emphasize collective survival and moral support in dealing with the daily hassles of life (Fine et al., 1987; White & Parham, 1990). The members of this strong kinship network often do not live in the same household. They function as a minicommunity in which any relative is readily available in a time of need. Also, African American children often witness informal adoptions in their families. Many African American families take care of their relatives' or friends' children (temporarily or permanently) when their parents are unable to care for them. Thus, African American children witness the flexibility and power of social-familial networks that have been a part of many African American families throughout history.

Some believe that African American and White families hold similar ideals, but the difference lies in ability to access these values in an American society. African American children are socialized to develop a dual identity. One identity manages the values of the dominant culture, while the other juggles the demands of what it means to be an African American (Burgest & Goosby, 1985). As a result, African Americans and Whites may take different paths to accomplish these goals. In conclusion, many of the negative characteristics evidenced in some African American families may be a direct response to the uphill battle to access these goals.

Emergent Model

This model does not have a great deal of empirical support, but it has received much attention theoretically and conceptually (Barnes, 2001). Unlike the pathological and cultural equivalent models, the *emergent model* emphasizes the underlying cultural connections between African American and African culture. McAdoo (1988) posits that though there may be few "direct one-to-one carryovers" from Africa, there is nonetheless much continuity in family traditions. West African cultural values such as interconnectedness, collective responsibility, language, support, religion, and caretaking responsibilities for children continue to extend to African American families today (Barnes, 2001; Sudarkasa, 1997; White & Parham, 1990). It is also important to note that African American families are more rooted in *consanguinal* (blood) rather than *conjugal* (marriage) bonds than White families (Sudarkasa, 1997).

Ecology Models of the Family

Today, many researchers approach the study of the family from a *systems approach* (see Kreppner & Lerner, 1989). The systems perspective of human development examines the interaction of individuals within and between families and social environment, and assesses their influence on individual development and family functioning. The ecological paradigm posited by Bronfenbrenner (1986) can be useful to examine the impact of the environment on African American child development.

A systems approach to understanding families has several guiding principles, which are helpful in understanding their functional and interactive components (see Connard & Novick, 1996; Kreppner & Lerner, 1989). Some of these principles are described in the next section.

Guiding Principles of Family Systems Theory

Equifinity. Unlike the pathological and cultural equivalent models, this principle posits that there are many routes to healthy development. Two children may experience the same event, but their reactions may take different forms.

Interdependence. One part of the system cannot be understood in isolation from the other parts. African American children cannot be understood outside the context of their families. In this research bi-directional interactions within that child's family and between the family and its social environment are considered.

Subsystems. Each family is comprised of several parts or systems (such as parent-child, spousal, and sibling). The relationship between and across the subsystems are examined for potential influences on child development.

Circularity. There is constant change as children develop. As African American children develop they are likely to experience issues which are different from other races. This principle examines the constant change in individual family members. It also focuses on how this individual change influences the family system as a whole.

TABLE 8.1.   Bronfenbrenner's Ecology of the Family as a Context for Human Development

Type of ecological model	Family environmental contexts
Mesosystem	• Ecology and family genetics • Genetics-environment interaction in family processes • Family and the hospital • Family and day care • Family and the peer group • Family and school
Exosystem	• Family and work • Parental employment and family life • Maternal employment and the family • Parental support networks • Family and the community
Chronosystem	• Range of topics (such as divorce, poverty, education, single-parent, etc.)

External Systems Affecting the Family

According to Bronfenbrenner (1986) ecological research paradigms can be examined as three external environmental models which affect the family: (1) Mesosystem models, (2) Exosystem models, and (3) Chronosystem models.

The *Mesosystem* models examine the relationships between the principal settings in African American child interacts. The *Exosystem* models refer to the settings in which children rarely enter, such as a parent's workplace or social networks; however, these settings indirectly affect child development.

Finally, *Chronosystem* models represent how time and chronological age within and across individuals and environments influence human development. Table 8.1 lists some common ecological models related to the family and the types of environments worth examination within each system (see Bronfenbrenner (1986) for additional information).

SECTION TWO: AFRICAN AMERICAN FAMILY STRUCTURE AND CHILD DEVELOPMENT

All parents are faced with the task of raising their children to function competently in society; however, for African American parents this task is often confounded by discrimination or racism. The African American family structure has shifted from two-parent households in the 1960s to single-female-headed households today. Barnes (2001) proposed three basic family structures for African Americans: nuclear, single-parent, and augmented. These family types will be discussed in the subsequent sections.

Nuclear Family

A *nuclear* family consists of a father, mother, and children. Today 7.5% of African American children under the age of 18 live in a two-parent married couple household (U.S. Census Bureau, 2004). For the past century marriage behavior in the United States has changed dramatically. In the 1950s there were small differences between African American and White American marital patterns. However, from the 1960s to the present, African American children's home lives have shifted from a majority being raised in a nuclear family to a new majority of being raised by a single parent.

Research on economically stable nuclear African American families is limited. Being raised in a nuclear family can have many potential advantages for African American children, as long as there is low conflict among the parents. Conflict is what typically undermines children's development (Hetherington, 1999). Two-parent families often have more financial and emotional resources, and time for their children (Seccombe, 2000). African American children learn gender role flexibility, as African American nuclear families are generally egalitarian in role division (Jackson, 1993; Staples, 1986); but the traditional gender-role divisions are prevalent as well (Brewer, 1988). Children living with two married parents have more daily interactions, such as eating meals together and talking or playing, than those living with unmarried parents. Other aspects of children's lives appear to be affected more by the number of parents available than by parents' marital status.

Unfortunately, an African American child being raised by two parents in the home does not always equate to economic prosperity (see Table 8.2 for poverty statistics). Many African American children are poor because of the prevalence of poverty in their households and communities. The poverty experienced by many African American children is the result of the complex interaction between politics, culture, economics, race, gender, and social class (Brewer, 1988). Unfortunately, we know very little about the influence of economic pressures on the development of African American children in nuclear families (Conger et al. 2002), as the majority of research has focused on single-parent African American families.

TABLE 8.2.   Poverty Rates (Percent Below Poverty Level) in 1999 for Children Under 18 Years by Race and Hispanic Origin and Living Arrangements

Race and Hispanic origin	Living in married-couple family group	Living in mother-only family group	Living in father-only family group	Living with neither parent
Non-Hispanic White	4.7	28.1	14.1	18.45
Black or African American	11.4	47.4	27.5	38.8
American Indian and Alaskan Native	18.5	50.0	32.8	38.3
Asian	11.3	31.4	17.4	19.5
Native Hawaiian and other Pacific Islander	15.5	39.6	22.8	26.8
Two or more races	10.6	37.9	21.6	25.3
Hispanic (of any race)	19.5	47.2	27.8	31.1

(Adapted from the U.S. Census Bureau, 2004).

The *family stress model* was originally based on economically disadvantaged White families in the rural Midwest (see Conger, Rueter, & Conger, 2000; Conger, Rueter, & Elder, 1999). Conger and colleagues (2002) extend this model out of a need to examine the influence of economic stressors on child development in two-parent African American households. As depicted in Figure 8.1, the model focuses on the mediated relationships among negative financial and economic pressures, caregivers' relationships and moods, parental involvement, and child adjustment.

The model posits that the amount of economic pressure within the family is related to two aspects of financial hardships (i.e., low family per capita income and negative financial events). These dimensions of hardship are hypothesized to indirectly influence the families in terms of emotions, behaviors, and relationships (Conger et al., 2002).

Even though a high number of African American children live in poverty, it is important to note that a large number of children live in economically stable two-parent homes. The number of highly educated, upwardly mobile African American families is the highest it has been than in any other period in U.S. history. According to the United States Census Bureau (2003a), 52% of African American couples earned at or above $50,000. Future research needs

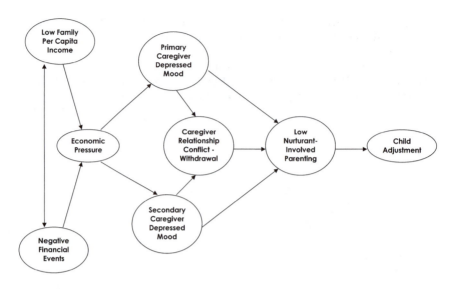

FIGURE 8.1   Family stress model.
Source: (Conger et al., 2002).

to focus on the economic diversity of African American families rather than dwell on economically disadvantaged households.

African American Single-Parent Families

According to the U.S. Census Bureau (2004) a single parent consists of a male or female parent who is not currently living with a spouse. Single parents may be married (not living with their spouse), widowed, or never married. The number of single parents and their children is increasing rapidly. There are conflicting perspectives as to what type of family living arrangements are best for children. As stated earlier in this chapter, it was common for research to view the single-parent household from a pathological perspective; however, today the single-parent family structure provides a viable option to the nuclear family. The majority of the research literature is on single mothers rather than single fathers. Children raised in single-parent living arrangements may have more additional stresses than children from nuclear homes, but nonetheless the majority of them find socially appropriate ways to adapt and flourish. The following sections will briefly examine African American families headed by single mothers and single fathers.

The number of single-mother households has increased dramatically over the past 40 years. According to the U.S. Census Bureau (2003b) and the Children's Defense Fund (2005) the number of African American children under the age of 18 years living with a single mother and a single cohabiting mother was 48% and

TABLE 8.3   Percent of Children Under 18 Years With Single Parents and Cohabiting Parents

Race and Hispanic origin	Living with a single mother	Living with a single father	Living with a single cohabiting mother	Living with a single cohabiting father
All children	23	5	11	33
Non-Hispanic White	16	4	14	29
Black	48	5	6	30
Asian and Pacific Islander	13	2	11	40
Hispanic (of any race)	25	5	12	46

(Adapted from the U.S. Census Bureau, 2003).

6%, respectively (see Table 8.3). Regardless of race, children living in mother-only family groups experience the highest rates of poverty (see Table 8.2).

There are many reasons why African American female households with minor age children have higher poverty rates than White female households with minor children. This chapter will not focus on the reasons why this may be, but a large part of it involves the economic deterioration of a segment of the African American community and the contextual stressors on these families (see Taylor, Tucker, Chatters, & Jayakody, 1997, for additional explanations).

Studies on African American children from two-parent homes compared to homes headed by single mothers show many differences, such as social difficulties and school dropout rates (McLanahan, 1985). On average, by 16 years of age, there is an increased risk of sexual activity (Hogan & Kitagawa, 1985), teenage pregnancy, and less representation in the labor force among daughters from African American female-headed homes regardless of social class. These trends merit further examination, as the female-headed household structure is more common and has become more acceptable over the past 20 years.

African American single, father-headed homes are not as prevalent as their female counterparts, but the numbers are increasing. Approximately 5% of African American children live with a single-parent father and another 30% live with a single-cohabiting father (U.S. Census Bureau, 2003b). Many of the single, non-cohabiting fathers are single parents mainly because of divorce and out-of-wedlock births. A high percentage (27.5%) of African American children who reside with a single father also experience poverty (U.S. Census

Bureau, 2004). Economic hardship among single fathers examined in conjunction with the number of children in financially strained single-female African American headed households illustrates the high numbers of economically deprived African American youth.

Over the past 15 years, the role of the African American father has garnered much interest among social scientists. Despite the negative image portrayed in the television media of the African American father as uninvolved and absent in the lives of his children, the recent literature research does not support this image. Numerous studies from the fields of psychology and sociology highlight positive dimensions of African American fatherhood. Many African American fathers provide a sense of stability, academic achievement, and a nurturing environment for their children (Smith, Krohn, Chu, & Best, 2005).

Being a single parent requires a lot of hard work and commitment. African American single mothers and fathers need to establish strong supportive networks with friends or in their communities. Children living with a single parent often find that their parents are more respectful and value their individual viewpoints to various situations. Single parents, especially single-father households, often show an increased commitment to daily care, education, and moral development (Allen & Doherty, 1996).

Augmented Families

Augmented families is defined as families in which other relatives or unrelated friends reside in the home and care for the children (Barnes, 2001; White & Parham, 1990). While there are many conceptualizations of augmented families, we will focus on two types: grandparents as head of the household; and African Americans in foster care.

Children live with grandparents for many reasons. Grandparents serve as a source of child care and family assistance. The reverse is also true, where the elder may live with a child and grandchildren because they require support (U.S. Census Bureau, 2003b). The majority of households where a grandparent lives with children under the age of 18 are households in which the primary householder is the grandparent, while a smaller percent of grandparents live in someone's else's household (typically their children). The U.S. Census (2003b) reports that 9% of African American children are more likely to reside with a grandparent compared to Hispanic, non-Hispanic White, and Asian/Pacific Islander children (6%, 4%, and 3%, respectively). Also, compared to other groups, African American children are much more likely to reside with a grandmother, rather than both grandparents.

Grandparents who are the primary householder (that is, the caretaker of both the parents and grandchildren) often assist young mothers in child rearing; thus, they serve as *coparents* for their grandchildren. This multigenerational assistance may seem to have many advantages such as increased financial resources and closer kinship bonds, but some research has shown that it may be less than ideal. Stevens (1984) reports that a grandmother's attempts to coparent may be viewed as unwanted and seen as criticism. Some possible consequences of this assistance may cause many young parents to feel criticized and depressed (Kalil, Spencer, Spieker, & Gilchrist, 1998), and they may disengage from their parents and children in an attempt to regain a sense of privacy.

These data indicate that children who reside with their grandparents without a parent are often at a financial disadvantage. Many of these families have economic constraints, which force them to live without healthcare and insurance; thus, many grandparent-headed householders find it difficult to raise their grandchildren without some form of public assistance.

Many grandparents parent their grandchildren full time. This often is due to a particularly disruptive circumstance in the parents' lives, such as mental, drug, or emotional problems, HIV/AIDS, or incarceration (Dressel & Barnhill, 1994; Jendrek, 1994; Joslin & Brouard, 1995; Joslin & Harrison, 1998). The problems faced by the parents negatively impact family relations among grandparents, parents, and grandchildren. Many African American grandparents take on this responsibility as a way to keep the family together, as many children in situations such as this are sent to live in foster care (Terling-Watt, 2001). Kelly and Damato (1995) report that grandchildren often have a difficult time adjusting to the living situation with a grandparent due to issues such as (1) confusion about appropriate role models, (2) differences in ages, (3) children's limited comprehension of circumstances about the living arrangement, (4) lack of clear parameters surrounding parental visits, and (5) undue attachment to grandparents. These stressors may increase the risk of depression and poor health in grandparents (Fuller-Thompson & Minkler, 2000) and their grandchildren.

In September 2004, the number of children in foster care has increased to 517,000 (Adoption and Foster Care Analysis and Reporting System [AFCARS], 2006), as compared to 560,000 in 1998 (Adoption and Foster Care Analysis and Reporting System [AFCARS], 2000). In 2004, 34% of children in the child welfare system were African American compared to 40% White (non-Hispanic), and 18% Hispanic. Approximately 283,000 children exited the foster care system in 2004; the majority of children were White, non-Hispanic (45%), 29% were African American, and 17% were Hispanic.

African American children are more likely to live with non-biological care-givers more than other racial and ethnic groups in the United States. There is not much research available on foster care in the United States, mainly due to a lack of high quality data collection across many communities. It has been reported that African American children are three times more likely to have been in foster care (Belgrave & Allison, 2006). African American children are likely to remain in foster care and are placed in multiple homes due to longer stays in the welfare system, and they are often put in foster care as a result of parental neglect (Taylor, Jackson, & Chatters, 1997).

In summary, the family helps shape the child's cognitive, emotional, and social development (Barker & Hill, 1996). Regardless of the family structure, parents strive to orient their children with a sense of motivation and direc-tion in order to function effectively in society. As shown in Figure 8.2, some children raised in dysfunctional homes may display an array of negative emo-tional, behavioral, and social maladjustments (Barker, 1991). It is important that parents provide an adequate amount of nurture, structure, and socializa-tion to African American children in a manner that ensures a strong sense of self, racial identification, and perseverance in order to achieve educational and economic success (Barker & Hill, 1996; Frabutt, Walker, & MacKinnon-Lewis, 2002).

SECTION THREE: THE PEER GROUP

A substantial amount of research has shown that strong kinship bonds may be a buffer to stress and may elevate psychological heath (House, Umberson, & Landis, 1988). This section of the text examines the important roles of two additional social contexts—peers and friendships—in the lives of African American children. Over the years, there has been a steady increase in re-search on peer relationships and friendships among children. A much smaller literature has investigated peer relationships and friendships among African American children (Graham & Cohen, 1997; Graham, Cohen, Zbikowski, & Secrist,1998).

African American Children's Peer Relationships

Peer relationships are commonly examined as (1) *group evaluations*, a uni-lateral and group-oriented summary of a child's liking of each individual in a particular setting, and (2) *friendships*, unique, dyadic relationships (Bu-kowski & Hoza, 1989). In general, peer relationships can provide social and emotional support (Berndt & Perry, 1986), assist in children's developing

Family Functioning Behaviors

	Healthy Families	Troubled Families
Nurture	Strong personality/ ego development	Weak ego state
	Secure	Fearful; inadequate; needy
	Affection/belonging	Sociopathic/psychopathic
	Accessible	Personality disorder
	Limit setting	Confused; intrusive
	Autonomy valued, encouraged, respected	Loss of self identity
	Supportive	Loss of self-esteem
	Clear, open expression of feelings	Abandonment; rejection; denial of emotions
	Strong boundaries	Chaos, vague and poorly defined boundaries
	Understanding	Lack roots; attachments
	Security	Marked absence of leadership
	Leadership	Poor socialization; poor survival skills
	Self determination	
Structure	Strong coalition	Weak coalition (dominance versus submissiveness)
	Rational problem solving	Internal conflict; lacks direction and decision making
	Input accepted (negotiation and problem solving)	
	Assigned task performance	Unable to perform and carry out tasks
	Creates social reality	Confused; inconsistent
	Open communication	Contradictory messages
	Clarifying	
	Clear role expectations	Lacks gender identity
	Unified; collaborative	Insufficient survival skills
	Identity	Confused self-concept; poor group identity
	Cultural heritage	Oppressed; confused loyalty; cultural incompetence
	Autonomy	Dependent; self-deprecating
Enculturation/ socialization	Self-reliant	Lack of focus; dependence among family members
	Liberated	Deprecated character; maladaptive behaviors; self-defeating behaviors
	Awareness and appreciation of lifestyle, values, and pluralism	Lacks understanding of socialization processes; political/ economic oppression

FIGURE 8.2.   Barker and Hill's family functioning behaviors.
Source: (*Journal of Black Studies, 27(1),* 1996, p. 82).

self-awareness (Sullivan, 1953), and help build a solid foundation for developing and practicing social and cognitive skills (see Asher & Coie, 1990; Berndt & Ladd, 1989; Hartup, 1983, 1989; Piaget, 1932).

Research examining race awareness has shown that significant differences exist between African American and White children regarding racial attitudes or preferences. These disparities have been tested in psychological and educational research over the past 60 years using line drawings, dolls, and photographs (Clark & Clark, 1939, 1947; Morland, 1966; Radke, Sutherland, & Rosenberg, 1950). Regardless of race, children displayed an increasing awareness of racial differences starting at 3 years of age (Clark & Clark, 1939; 1947). Powell (1985) found that African American children often expressed a strong pro-White bias *and* a highly favorable self-concept. It is important to note that this research documents stereotypical beliefs of children and may not reflect behaviors and attitudes in actual relationships.

Children's sociometric ratings and nominations have shown that same-race and same-sex biases against peers have changed over the years. African American children exhibit an increasing racial bias with age; that is, older African American children often rate children same-race peers higher than younger African American children (Singleton & Asher, 1979).

African American Children's Friendships

Unlike peer relationships which are based on group evaluations, children's friendships are characterized as mutual, dyadic relationships (Graham & Cohen, 1997; 1998). Friendships provide a base to practice social skills; they allow an individual to socially compare to others and to themselves; and they promote a feeling of group belonging, instrumental support, and emotional intimacy (Rubin, 1980; Way, 1996).

The *similarity-attraction hypothesis* posits that interpersonal attraction is largely driven by similarities (actual or perceived) between individuals (Aboud & Mendelson, 1996). These commonalities (such as demographic variables, behaviors, attitudes, self-concept, etc.) assist in creating a close bond between individuals by a) validating one's own attitudes and behaviors as well as b) providing contexts to exercise enjoyable activities (Graham & Cohen, 1998). For African American children, this similarity is a main function in friendship selection through childhood and adolescence.

Race is strongly linked with measures of children's friendships within a classroom context. Among elementary school-aged children same-race friendships are to a great extent more numerous than other-race friendships (Graham & Cohen, 1997; Hartup, 1983). African American children were less inclined to choose White classmates for best friends as they grew older; however, they still maintained a greater affability toward African American peers and other-race peers than did White children (Graham & Cohen, 1997; Hallinan & Teixeira, 1987). This cordiality may partly be due to the amount of opportunity children have for other-race versus same-race interactions (Hallinan & Smith, 1985; Hallinan & Teixeira, 1987; Kistner, Metzler, Gatlin, & Risi, 1994).

There are notable differences between gender and age in friendships. Girls' friendship networks are more exclusive and intimate than boys' (Eder & Hallinan, 1978). Their relationships often vary in their styles of influence (Serbin, Sprafkin, Elman, & Doyle, 1984), activities, language styles (Maltz & Borker, 1983), and types of play (Maccoby, 1988; 1990). In terms of age,

African American adolescent males often develop a *bravado* identity (also known as hypermasculine). Cunningham and Meunier (2004) report that a hypermasculine persona can serve as a protective mechanism for many males in high-risk environments. This reactive attitude may be a way of dealing with discomfort among peers, and it may also be linked to a lack of exposure to positive role models. Belgrave and Allison (2006) recommend that prevention efforts and interventions should focus on creating positive relationships among African American males. They also recommend that interventions for African American females' friendships focus on reducing *relational aggression* (attempt to harm another through social manipulation/ ostracism) and enhancing mutual cooperation, problem solving, and life skills (see Belgrave, 2002; Belgrave et al., 2004).

PERSPECTIVES ON AFRICAN AMERICAN CHILDREN AND SOCIAL CONTEXTS

Future research on the social development of African American children within social contexts should examine the diversity of complex relationships of African Americans within families and peer groups. In order to accomplish this task, some of the methodological limitations which have plagued past research in this area should be addressed. First, researchers need to be careful to eliminate confounds among race, ethnicity, socioeconomic assessments, and community of residence. For a better understanding of the African American child within a family context, it is important that participants are recruited from a variety of socioeconomic, residential, and age levels. Second, it will be useful to use a mix of quantitative and qualitative research designs. Such designs may be better suited to uncover the rich nuances of the African American family.

More specifically, future developmental scholarship should focus on stable African American couples, the elderly, and a single-parent family (mothers or fathers) structure to parenting processes and child developmental outcomes among African Americans of varying socioeconomic statues. Future research should also focus on the processes and outcomes of parents' involvement in school activities (such as homework), and provide suggestions for school practices to enhance the effectiveness of parental involvement in the educational setting of African American children.

The field will benefit from a more extensive analysis of the social relationships of African American children (e.g., peers, siblings, friendships, and teachers) particularly in terms of the quality, structure, behavioral, and affective dimensions. Finally, the role of family variables in child resiliency and adaptation within samples of African American children needs further exploration.

CHAPTER SUMMARY

This chapter focuses on social contexts in the life of the African American child. The chapter starts with a discussion of some of the issues that are faced by many researchers in child and family studies. Section one presents some of the leading conceptual models used to examine African American families, including the pathological, cultural equivalent, emergent, and ecological systems. The next section explores African American family structures and child development. Specifically, we discuss three family types: (1) nuclear, (2) single-parent, and (3) augmented. We highlight the demographic shifts in the nuclear family structure, and discuss the characteristics of children raised in this family configuration. A critical analysis of the family stress model by Conger and colleagues (2002) is explored with African American nuclear families. We focus on single-headed households, as well. The number of single family households provides a sounding board for discussion about how African American children fare in homes headed by single mothers, as well as single fathers. In the subsection on augmented families, we provide a glimpse of the impact of African children being raised by grandparents or who are a part of the foster care system. The final section of the chapter aims to reveal the importance of social contexts in the lives of African American children, notably peer relationships and friendships.

ADDITIONAL READINGS

Family Structure

Alexander, R., & Curtis, C. (1996). A review of empirical research involving the transracial adoption of African American children. *Journal of Black Psychology*, 22, 223–235.

Clark, K. (2003). *Black fathers: A call for healing*. Doubleday: New York.

Theoretical Models and African American Families in General

Cheatham, H., & Stewart, J. (1990). *Black families*. Somerset, NJ: Transaction Publishers.

Hill, S. (1998). *African American children: Socialization and development in families*. Thousand Oaks, CA: Sage Publications.

White, J. L., & Parham, T. A. (1990). *The psychology of blacks: An African American perspective.* Englewood Cliffs, NJ: Prentice-Hall.

Video

Bailen, G. (producer). (2000). *Granparents raising grandchildren.* Video. Available from Fanlight Productions, 4196 Washington Street, Suite 2, Boston, MA 02131.

CHAPTER 9

Epilogue: Where Do We Go From Here?

No society can survive without children. The rhetoric that holds children to be our greatest national resource is true, but the reality is that we do little to demonstrate any conviction of its truth.

Shelia B. Kamerman (1980)

As we begin the new millennium, and a new political era, the statement by Dr. Kamerman is resoundingly accurate, especially when we consider the status of African American children in the 21st century.

To improve the quality of life for African American children in the 21st century, the following six issues must be addressed empirically.

POVERTY

Statistically, African American children are more likely than their counterparts from other racial groups to reside in poor homes. In the middle of the 20th century poor African American single mothers headed those homes; today, grandparents maintain them. It is well documented in the empirical literature that poverty produces a host of negative biological, cognitive, and psychosocial outcomes. Subsequent research is needed to help identify the internal, situational and external factors that prevent African American families from successfully transitioning out of poverty. It may be that the "transition pathways" are different for poor African American families, and the structure of "welfare to work" programs fail to consider those differences.

CULTURAL DIVERSITY WITHIN THE AFRICAN AMERICAN POPULATION

The unprecedented growth of African American children in 1995, in part to due the aforementioned immigration factors, suggests that the African American population is becoming diverse with respect to culture. This implies that the African American culture is not monolithic and awareness of the multiplicity of backgrounds that constitute the African American culture merits consideration in future research in the 21st century.

FAMILY CONSTELLATION

The family constellation of African American children is ever changing. For example, the number of African American children remaining in the foster care system is a disturbing one. They are essentially abandoned and neglected by the welfare system. As a result, some African American children experience lifelong challenges. Fundamental questions must be asked about African American children and foster care. For example, are efforts made to reunify them with their parents or families, after intervention has been conducted? Is kinship foster care a viable alternative? Finally, the problems inherent in the welfare system that contribute to the abandonment and neglect of African American children should be identified.

Researchers should also began to investigate the adjustment and quality of life of African American children residing in father-headed households, given the prominence that African American fathers are playing in the lives of their children.

Ruiz (1998) suggests that given the increase in the number of African American children residing in grandparent-maintained homes, and the economic challenges present in those homes, research should be devoted to exploring the following questions. (1) What is the impact of primary caregiving on the health and well-being of African American grandmothers? (2) Are there rural-urban differences in caregiving? (3) What are the sources and types of social support received by grandparent caregivers? (4) Which group of factors produces the most favorable outcomes for African American children residing in grandparent-maintained homes?

Finally, the number of African American children living in middle-class homes has increased in the last three decades. Such questions as do their psychosocial functioning, their academic experiences, and their mental health issues differ from those of their low-income counterparts remain unanswered.

HEALTH CARE

Improving access to health care for poor children in general and poor African American children in particular has been a public health agenda item for more than 30 years. Outreach initiatives have been implemented at the national, state, and community levels to improve health care in the African American community. However, the initiatives have been minimally effective. Therefore, a re-evaluation of the structure of outreach methods must be conducted. What barriers continue to exist for African American children and their families? And why do these barriers persist? Are there more effective outreach models that take into account cultural, political, and historical issues for African-children and their families?

EDUCATION

Is the public school system providing African American children with a solid educational foundation? African American children still lag behind their peers from other racial groups on critical measures of achievement, and that gap has persisted for more than 30 years. Interventions, reforms, and legislation have been proposed in various forms for several decades. And the question "How do we close the achievement gap?" has been a popular topic for social scientists. Perhaps the new question should be how do we **assist** African American children in developing academic skills? Investigators should identify the teaching formats (e.g., styles, structure) that consistently facilitate their academic achievement.

VIOLENCE

African American children are more likely to witness violence and be victimized by violence than their counterparts from other racial groups. Thus exposure to violence has become a part of the developmental process for some African American children.

Furthermore, African American children are more likely than their counterparts from other racial groups to be incarcerated in correctional facilities. They make up 46% of the juveniles in those facilities (U.S. Justice Department's Office of Juvenile Justice and Delinquency Prevention, 2006). Violence prevention and intervention programs abound. Yet, violence in the lives of African American children persists. What are the critical ingredients for a successful program? What type of intervention models need to be implemented?

What contextual, environmental, and individual factors must be considered in developing effective violence intervention programs for African American children?

In summary, the six issues identified above represent a sampling of the challenges facing African American children in the 21st century. However, addressing those issues is a first step.

References

Aboud, F. (1988). *Children and prejudice*. Oxford: Basil Blackwell.

Aboud, F. E., & Mendelson, M. J. (1996). Determinants of friendship selection and quality: Developmental perspectives. In W. M. Bukowski, A. F. Newcomb, & W. W. Hartup (Eds.), *The company they keep: Friendship in childhood and adolescence* (pp. 87–112). New York: Cambridge University Press.

Adoption and Foster Care Analysis and Reporting System. (2000). *Adoption and Foster Care Analysis and Reporting System (AFCARS) data submitted for the FY 1998, 10/1/97 through 9/30/1998*. Retrieved September 26, 2006, from http://www.acf. hhs.gov/programs/cb/stats_research/afcars/tar/report3.pdf.

Adoption and Foster Care Analysis and Reporting System. (2006). *Adoption and Foster Care Analysis and Reporting System (AFCARS) data submitted for the FY 2004, 10/1/03 through 9/30/2004*. Retrieved September 26, 2006, from http://www.acf. hhs.gov/programs/cb/stats_research/afcars/tar/report11.pdf.

Akoto, A. (1992). *Nation building. Theory and practice in Afrikan centered education*. Pan African-World Institute.

Allen, L., & Majidi-Ahi, S. (1998). African American children. In J. T. Gibbs, & L. N. Huang (Eds.), *Children of color:Psychological intervention with culturally diverse youth* (pp. 143–170). San Francisco: Jossey Bass.

Allen, W. D., & Doherty, W. J. (1996). The responsibilities of fatherhood as perceived by African American teenage fathers. *Families in Society, 77*, 142–155.

Allen, W. R. (1978). The search for applicable theories of black family life. *Journal of Marriage and the Family, 40*, 117–130.

Alloy, L. B., Abramson, L. Y., Raniere, D., & Dyller, I. M. (1999). Research methods in adult psychopathology. In P. C. Kendall, J. N. Butcher, & G. N. Holmbeck (Eds.), *Handbook of research methods in clinical psychology* (2nd ed., pp. 466–498). New York: Wiley.

American Psychiatric Association. (2000). *Diagnostic and statistical manual* (4th ed.). Washington, DC: American Psychiatric Association.

American Lung Association. (2004). Retrieved from www.lungusa.org.

Anderson, E. (1999a). *Code of the street: Decency, violence, and the moral life of the inner city*. New York: W. W. Norton & Company.

Anderson, E. (1999b). Code of the streets. In C. A. Gallagher (Ed.), *Rethinking the color line: Readings in race and ethnicity*. CA: Mayfield Publishing Company.

Anderson-Yokel, J., & Haynes, W. (1994). Joint picture book reading strategies in working class African American and White mother-toddler dyads, *Journal of Speech, Language, and Hearing Research, 37*, 583–593.

Anggold, A., Erkanli, A., Farmer, E., Fairbank, J., Burns, B., Keeler, G., et al. (2002). Psychiatric disorders, impairment, and service use in rural African American and White youth. *Archives of General Psychiatry, 59,* 893–904.

Angle, C. (1993). Childhood lead poisoning and its treatment. *American Behavioral Pharmacology Toxicology, 32,* 409–434.

Armstrong, D., Lemanek, K., Pegelow, C., Gonzalez, J., & Martinez, A. (1993). Impact of lifestyle disruption on parent and child coping, knowledge, and parental discipline in children with sickle cell anemia. *Children's Health Care, 22,* 189–203.

Asher, S. R., & Coie, J. D. (Eds.). (1990). *Peer rejection in childhood.* Cambridge: Cambridge University Press.

Astley, S., & Clarren, S. (2000). Diagnosing the full spectrum of fetal alcohol exposed individuals: Introducing the 4 digit diagnostic code, *Alcohol and Alcoholism, 35,* 400–410.

Avruch, S., & Cackley, A. (1995). Savings achieved by WIC benefits to women prenatally. *Public Health Reports, 110,* 27–34.

Baker, J. (1999). Teacher-student interaction in urban at-risk classrooms: Differential behavior, relationship quality, and satisfaction with school. *The Elementary School Journal, 100,* 57–69.

Baltes, P., & Nesselroade, J. (1979). History and rationale of longitudinal research. In J. Nesselroade & P. Baltes (Eds.), *Longitudinal research in the study of behavior and development* (pp. 1–39). New York: Academic Press.

Banks, W. C. (1976). White-preference in Blacks: A paradigm in search of a phenomenon. *Psychological Bulletin, 83,* 1179–1186.

Bankston, C., & Caldas, S. (1996). Majority African American schools and social injustice: The influence of de facto segregation on academic achievement. *Social Forces, 75(2),* 535–555.

Barbarin, O. (1993). Coping and resilience: Exploring the inner lives of African American children. *Journal of Black Psychology, 19,* 478–492.

Barker, N. (1991). Working with abused children. *Journal of Child and Youth Care, 6(3),* 1–18.

Barker, N. C., & Hill, J. (1996). Restructuring African American families in the 1990's. *Journal of Black Studies, 27(1),* 77–93.

Barnes, S. L. (2001). Stressors and strengths: A theoretical and practical examination of nuclear, single parents and augmented African American families. *Families in Society: The Journal of Contemporary Human Services, 82,* 449–460.

Barnett, W. (1993). Benefit cost analysis of preschool education: Findings from a 25 year follow-up. *American Journal of Orthopsychiatry, 63,* 500–508.

Battle, D. (1997). Language and communication disorders in culturally and linguistically diverse children. In D. K. Bernstein & E. Tiegerman-Farber (Eds.), *Language and communication disorders in children.* Needham Heights, MA: Allyn & Bacon.

Battle, J., & Coates, D. L. (2004). Father-only and mother-only, single-parent family status of black girls and achievement in grade twelve and two-years post high school. *Journal of Negro Education, 73(4),* 392–407.

Battle, R. S., Cummings, G. L., Barker, J. C., & Krasnovsky, F. M. (1995). Accessing an understudied population in behavioral HIV/AIDS research: Low income African American women. *Journal of Health and Social Policy, 7*, 1–18.

Beane, D. (1985). *Mathematics and science: Critical filters for the future of minority students*. Washington, DC: The Mid-Atlantic Center for Race Equity, The American University Press.

Belgrave, F. Z., & Allison, K. W. (2006). *African American psychology: From Africa to America*. Thousand Oaks, CA: Sage Publications.

Belgrave, F. Z. (2002). Relational theory and cultural enhancement interventions for African American adolescent girls. *Public Health Reports, 117(Suppl. 1)*, 76–81.

Belgrave, F. Z., Reed, M. C., Plybon, L. E., Butler, D. S., Allison, K. W., & Davis, T. (2004). The impact of a culturally enhanced drug prevention program on drug and alcohol refusal efficacy among urban African American girls. *Journal of Drug Education, 34(3)*, 267–279.

Bell, C. C., & Jenkins, E. J. (1993). Community violence and children on Chicago's Southside. *Psychiatry, 56(1)*, 46–54.

Berndt, T. J., & Perry, T. B. (1986). Children's perceptions of friendships as supportive relationships. *Developmental Psychology, 22*, 640–648.

Betancourt, H., & Lopez, S. R. (1993). The study of culture, ethnicity, and race in American psychology. *American Psychologist, 48*, 629–637.

Betancourt, J., Green, A., Carillo, J., & Ananaeh-Firempong, O. (2003). Defining cultural competence: A practical framework for addressing racial/ethnic disparities in health and health care. *Public Health Reports, 118*, 293–302.

Bidaunt-Russel, M., Valla, J., Thomas, J., Bergeron, L., & Lawson, E. (1998). Reliability of the Terry: A mental health cartoon-like screener for African American children. *Child Psychiatry and Human Development, 28*, 249–263.

Billingsley, A. (1992). *Climbing Jacob's ladder: The enduring legacy of African American families*. New York: Touchstone Books.

Blake, I. (1994). Language development and socialization in young African American children. In P. Greenfieled, & R. Cocking, (Eds.), *Cross cultural roots of minority child development* (pp.167–195). Hillsdale, NJ: Lawrence Erlbaum Associates.

Bowen, N. K., & Bowen, G. L. (1999). Effects of crime and violence in neighborhoods and schools on the school behavior and performance of adolescents. *Journal of Adolescent Research, 14(3)*, 319–342.

Boyd-Franklin, N. (1989). *Black families in therapy*. New York: Guilford Press.

Boykin, W. (1986). Triple quandary and the schooling of Afro American children. In N. Nesser (Ed.), *The school achievement of minority children: New perspectives* (pp. 57–92). Hillsdale, NJ: Lawrence Erlbaum Associates.

Brems, C. (2004). *A comprehensive guide to child psychotherapy*. Long Grove, IL: Waveland Press.

Brewer, R. M. (1988). Black women in poverty: Some comments on female-headed families. *Signs, 13(2)*, 331–339.

Bronfenbrenner, U. (1979). *The ecology of human development*. Cambridge, MA: Harvard University Press.

Bronfenbrenner, U. (1986). Ecology of the family as a context for human development: Research perspectives. *Developmental Psychology, 22,* 723–742.

Brooks-Gunn, J., & Markman, L. (2005). The contribution of parenting to ethnic and racial gaps in school readiness. *Future of Children, 15,* 139–165.

Brown v. Board of Educ., 347 U.S. 483 (1954).

Brown, F. (1994). Brown and educational policy: Making at 40. *Journal of Negro Education, 63,* 336–348.

Brown, S. (1989). *Prenatal care: Reaching mothers, reaching infants.* Washington, DC: National Academy Press.

Bruckman, M., & Blanton, P. (2003). Welfare to work single mothers' perspectives on parent involvement in Head Start: Implications for parent-teacher collaboration. *Early Childhood Education Journal, 30,* 145–150.

Bruno, J., & Doscher, L., (1981). Contribution to the harms of racial isolation: Analysis of a quest for teacher transfer in a large urban school district. *Educational Administration Quarterly, 17,* 93–108.

Bryant, B. L., & Coleman, M. (1988). The black family as portrayed in introductory marriage and family textbooks. *Family Relations, 37,* 255–259.

Bryson, Y. (2006). HIV-! Transmission: Recent advances and therapeutic interventions, *AIDS, 10,* 33–42.

Buescher, P., Horton, S., Devaney, B., Roholt, S., Lenihan, A., Whitmire, J., et al. (2003). Differences in health services between white and African American children enrolled in Medicaid in North Carolina. *Maternal Child Health Journal, 7,* 45–52.

Bukowski, W. M., & Hoza, B. (1989). Popularity and friendship: Issues in theory, measurement, and outcome. In T. J. Berndt & G. W. Ladd (Eds.), *Peer relationships in child development* (pp. 15–46). New York: Wiley.

Burden, M., Jacobsen, S., Soko, R., & Jacobsen, J. (2005). Effects of prenatal alcohol exposure on attention and working memory at 7.5 years of age. *Alcoholism, Clinical and Experimental Research, 29,* 443–452.

Burgest, M.D.R., & Goosby, M. (1985). Games in black male/female relationships. *Journal of Black Studies, 15(3),* 277–290.

Burton, L. (1992). Black grandparents rearing children of drug addicted parents: Stressors, outcomes and social service needs. *The Gerontologist, 36,* 744–751.

Campbell, C., & Schwartz, D. F. (1996). Prevalence and impact of exposure to interpersonal violence among suburban and middle school students. *Pediatrics, 98,* 396–403.

Campbell, F., & Ramey, C. (1994). Effects of early intervention on intellectual and academic achievement: A follow-up study of children from low income families. *Child Development, 2,* 684–698.

Caplan, N., & Nelson, S. D. (1973). On being useful: The nature and consequences of psychological research on social problems. *American Psychologist, 28,* 199–211.

Carta, J. (1991). Education for young children in inner-city classrooms. *American Behavioral Scientists, 34,* 440–453.

Caughy, M., Randolph, S., O'Campo, P., & Nickerson, K. (2002). The Africentric home environment inventory: An observational measure of the racial socialization features of the home environment for African American preschool children. *Journal of Black Psychology, 28,* 37–52.

Cellano, M., Geller, R., Phillips, K, & Ziman, R. (1998). Treatment adherence among low income children with asthma. *Journal of Pediatric Psychology, 23,* 345–349.

Center on Budget and Policy Priorities, 2000. Retrieved from www.cbpp.org.

Centers for Disease Control and Prevention, National Center for Health Statistics, 2006. Retrieved from www.cdc.org.

Chasnoff, I., Griffith, D., Freier, C., & Murray, J. (1992). Cocaine/polydrug use in pregnancy: Two-year follow-up. *Pediatrics, 89,* 284–289.

Child Trends Data Bank. (2004). Retrieved from www.childtrends.org.

Children's Defense Fund. (2005). *The state of America's children.* Washington, DC: Children's Defense Fund.

Chiodo, L., Jacobson, S., & Jacobson, J. (2004). Neurodevelopmental effects of postnatal lead exposure at very low levels. *Neurotoxicology and Teratology, 26,* 359–371.

Christian, M., & Barbarin, O. (2001). Cultural resources and psychological adjustment of African American children: Effects of spirituality and racial attribution, *Journal of Black Psychology, 27,* 43–63.

Cicchetti, D., & Garmezy, N. (1993). Perspectives and promises in the study of resilience. *Development and Psychopathology, 5,* 741–762.

Clark, K. B., & Clark, M. K. (1939). The development of consciousness of self and the emergence of racial identity in Negro preschool children. *Journal of Social Psychology, 10,* 591–599.

Clark, K. B., & Clark, M. K. (1940). Skin color as a factor in racial identification of Negro preschool children. *Journal of Social Psychology, SPSS Bulletin, 11,* 156–169.

Clark, K. B., & Clark, M. K. (1947). Racial identification and preference in Negro children. In T. M. Newcomb & E. L. Hartley (Eds.), *Readings in social psychology* (pp. 169–178). New York: Holt.

Cole, M., Cole, S., & Lightfoot, C. (2005). *The development of children* (5th ed.). New York: Worth Publishers.

Coles, C., Platzman, K., Smith, I., & James, M. (1992). Effects of cocaine and alcohol use in pregnancy on neonatal growth and neurobehavior status. *Neurotoxicology & Teratology, 14,* 23–33.

Coll, C. G., Lamberty, G., Jenkins, R., McAdoo, H. P., Crnic, K., Wasik, B. H., et al. (1996). An integrative model for the study of developmental competencies in minority children. *Child Development, 67,* 1891–1914.

Comer, J. P. (1995). *School power: Implications of an intervention project.* New York: Free Press.

Comer, J. P. (1998, November). Educating poor minority children. *Scientific American, 259,* 42–48.

Conger, K. J., Rueter, M. A., & Conger, R. D. (2000). The role of economic pressure in the lives of parents and their adolescents: The family stress model. In L. J. Crockett & R. J. Sibereisen (Eds.), *Negotiating adolescence in times of social change* (pp. 201–223). Cambridge, England: Cambridge University Press.

Conger, R. D., Rueter, M. A., & Elder, G. H., Jr. (1999). Couple resilience to economic pressure. *Journal of Personality and Social Psychology, 76,* 54–71.

Conger, R. D., Wallace, E. W., Sun, Y., Simons, R. L., McLoyd, V., & Brody, G. H. (2002). Economic pressure in African American families: A replication and extension of the family stress model. *Developmental Psychology, 38(2),* 179–193.

Congressional Black Caucus Foundation Health Organization. (2004). Retrieved from www.cbcfnc.org

Connard, C., & Novick, R. (1996). *The ecology of the family: A background paper for a family-centered approach to education and social service delivery.* Retrieved September 23, 2006, from http://www.nwrel.org/cfc/publications/ecology2.html.

Cook, T., Murphy, R., & Hunt, D. (2000). Comer's school development program in Chicago: A theory-based evaluation. *American Educational Research Journal, 37,* 535–597.

Copeland, V. (2005). African-Americans: Disparities in health care access and utilization. *Health & Social Work, 30,* 265–270.

Cornbleth, C., & Korth, W. (1980). Teacher perceptions and teacher student interaction in integrated classrooms. *Journal of Experimental Education, 48,* 259–263.

Coscia, J., Ris, D., & Succop, P., & Dietrich, K. (2003). Cognitive development of lead exposed children from ages 6 to 15 years: An application of growth curve analysis. *Child Neuropsychological, 9,* 10–21.

Costello, E., Angold, A., Burns, B., Stangl, D., Tweed, D., Erkanli, A., et al. (1996). The Great Smokey Mountain study of youth: Goals, designs, methods and prevalence of DSM-IIIR disorders. *Archives of General Psychiatry, 53,* 1290–1136.

Craig, H., & Washington, J. (2000). An assessment battery for identifying language impairments in African American children. *Journal of Speech, Language and Hearing Research., 4,* 366–379.

Cross, W. (1991). *Shades of Black.* Philadelphia: Temple University Press

Cunningham, M., & Meunier, L. N. (2004). The influence of peer experiences on bravado attitudes among African American males. In N. Way & J. Chu (Eds.), *Adolescent boys in context: Exploring diverse cultures of boyhood* (pp. 219–234). New York: New York University Press.

Curie, J., & Thomas, D. (2000). School quality and the longer-term effects of Head Start. *The Journal of Human Resources, 34,* 756–774.

Dandy, E. (1991). *Black communication: Breaking down the barriers.* Chicago: African American Images.

Daniel, J., & Daniel, J. (1999). African American childrearing: The context of a hot stove. In T. Socha & R. Diggs (Eds.), *Communication, race and family: Exploring communication in Black, White, and biracial families* (pp. 25–43). Miahwah, NJ: LEA.

Davey, B., Harrell, K., Stewart, J., & King, D. (2004). Body weight status, dietary habits, and physical activity levels of middle school aged children in rural Mississippi. *Southern Medical Journal, 97,* 571–577.

Davidoff, M., Petrini, J., Damus, K., Russell, R., & Mattison, D. (2002). Neural tube defect-specific infant mortality in the United States. *Teratology, 66,* 12–22.

Davis, R. (1989). Teenage pregnancy: A theoretical analysis of a social problem. *Adolescence, 24,* 19–28.

Davis, S., & Ford, M. (2004). A conceptual model of barriers to mental health services among African Americans. *African American Research Perspectives, 10,* 44–54.

Dentler, R. (1991). School desegregation since Gunnar Myrdal's American dilemma. In C. Willie, A. Garibaldi, & W. Reid (Eds.), *The education of African Americans* (pp. 28–50).

Devaney, B. (1992, September). *Very low birthweight among Medicaid newborns in five states: The effects of prenatal WIC participation.* Alexandria, Virginia: U.S. Department of Agriculture.

Dietrich, K., Berger, O., & Succop, P. (1993). Lead exposure and the motor developmental status of urban six year old children in the Cincinnati Prospective Study. *Pediatrics, 91,* 301–307.

Dillard, J. (1972). *Black english.* New York: Vintage Books.

Dilworth-Bart, J., & Moore, C. (2006). Mercy mercy me: Social injustice and the prevention of environmental pollutant exposures among ethnic minority and poor children. *Child Development, 77,* 247–265

Dressel, P. L., & Barnhill, S. K. (1994). Reframing gerontological thought and practice: The case of grandmothers with daughters in prison. *Gerontologist, 34,* 685–691.

Dumas, J. E., Rollock, D., Prinz, R. J., Hops, H., & Blechman, E.A. (1999). Cultural sensitivity: Problems and solutions in applied and preventive intervention. *Applied and Preventive Psychology, 8,* 175–196.

Duncan, G., & Magnuson, K. (2005). Can family socioeconomic resources account for racial and ethnic test score gaps? *Future of Children, 15,* 35–54.

Dutton, S., Singer, J., & Devlin, A. (1998). Racial identity of children in integrated, predominantly White and Black schools. *Journal of Social Psychology, 136,* 41–53.

Eder, D., & Hallinan, M. T. (1978). Sex differences in children's friendships. *American Sociological Review, 43,* 237–250.

Edmonds, R. (1982). Program of school improvement: An overview. *Educational Leadership, 39,* 4–14.

Edwards, P. (1993). Before and after school desegregation: African American parents' involvement in schools, *Educational Policy, 7,* 340–369.

Edwards, P. (1994). Responses of teachers and African American mothers to book reading intervention programs. In Dickinson, (Ed.), *Bridges to literacy: Children families and schools* (pp. 175–208). Cambridge, MA: Blackwell Publishers.

Eisenberg, N., & Fabes, R. A. (1998). Prosocial behavior and development. In B. Damon (Ed.), *Handbook of child psychology* (pp. 701–778). New York: Academic Press.

Eisenberg, N., & Mussen, P. H. (1989). *The roots of prosocial behavior in children.* New York: Wiley.

Eisenberg, N., Zhou, Q., & Koller, S. (2001). Brazilian adolescents' prosocial moral judgment and behavior: Relations to sympathy, perspective taking, gender-role orientation, and demographic characteristics. *Child Development, 72(2),* 518–534.

Ellwood, C., & Crane, J. (1990). Family change among Black Americans: What do we know? *Journal of Economic Perspectives, 14,* 65–84.

Environmental Protection Agency. (2005). Retrieved from www.epa.gov.

Feagans, L. (1996). *Children's talk in communities and classrooms.* Cambridge, MA: Blackwell Publishers.

Feagans, L., & Haskins, R. (1986). Neighborhood dialogues of Black and White 5 year olds. *Journal of Applied Developmental Psychology, 7,* 701–708.

Fife, B. (1992). *Desegregation in American Schools: Comprehensive intervention strategies.* New York: Praeger.

Fine, M., Schwebel, A., & James-Myers, L. (1987). Family stability in Black families: Values underlying three different perspectives. *Journal of Comparative Family Studies, 18,* 1–23.

Fiscella, K. (2003). Racial disparity in infant and maternal mortality: Confluence of infection, and microvascular dysfunction. *Maternal and Child Health Journal, 2,* 45–43.

Fitzgibbon, M. (2005). Two year follow-up results for hip-hop to health jr.: A randomized controlled trial for overweight prevention in minority children. *Journal of Pediatrics, 146,* 618–25.

Fogel, H., & Ehri, L. (1998). Teaching elementary students who speak black English vernacular to write in Standard English: Effects of dialect transformation practice. *Contemporary Educational Psychology, 25,* 212–235.

Fordham, S., & Ogbu, J. (1986). Black students' school success: Coping with the "burden of acting White." *Urban Review, 18,* 176–206.

Frabutt, J., Walker, A. M., & MacKinnon-Lewis, C. (2002). Racial socialization messages and the quality of mother/child interactions in African American families. *Journal of Early Adolescence, 22(2),* 200–217.

Friedman, D., Cohen, B., & Mahan, C. (1993). Maternal ethnicity and birth weight among blacks. *Ethnic Discourse, 3,* 255–269

Fuller-Thomson, E., & Minkler, M. (2000). The mental and physical health of grandmothers who are raising their grandchildren. *Journal of Mental Health and Aging, 6,* 311–323.

Gadsen, V., Smith, R., & Jordan, W. (1996). The promise of desegregation: Tendering expectation and reality in achieving quality schooling. *Urban Education, 31,* 381–402.

Gadsen, V., & Wagner, D. (1995). *Literacy among African American youth: Issues in learning, teaching and schooling.* Creskill, NJ: Hampton Publishing.

Gall, J., Gall, M., & Borg, W. (2005). *Applying educational research: A practical guide* (5th ed.). Boston, MA: Pearson Education.

Galloway, S., & Harwood-Nuss, A. (1988). Sickle-cell anemia: A review. *The Journal of Emergency Medicine, 6,* 213–226

Garabaldi, A. (1997). Four decades of progress and decline: An assessment of African American educational attainment. *Journal of Negro Education, 66,* 1–12

Garabaldi, A., & Bartley, M. (1989). Black school pushouts and drop outs: Strategies for reduction. In W. Smith & E. Chunn (Eds.), *Black education: A quest for equity and excellence* (pp. 227–235). New Brunswick, NJ: Transaction Publishers.

Garbarino, J. (1993). Children's response to community violence: What do we know? *Infant Mental Health Journal, 14,* 103–115.

Garbarino, J., Kostelny, K., & Dubrow, N. (1991). What children can tell us about living in danger. *American Psychologist, 46,* 376–383.

Gardner, R., & Miranda, A. (2001). Improving outcomes for urban African American students. *The Journal of Negro Education, 70,* 255–263.

Garmezy, N. (1983). Resiliency and vulnerability to adverse developmental outcomes associated with poverty. *American Behavioral Scientist, 34,* 416–430.

Germonious, A., & Bound, J. (1990). Black/White differences in women's reproductive-related health status: Evidence from vital statistics. *Demography, 27,* 457–466.

Geronimous, A. (1996). Black/White differences in the relationship of maternal age to birth weight: A population-based test of the weathering hypothesis. *Social Science Medicine, 42,* 589–597.

Gibbs, J. C. (1979). Kohlberg's moral stage theory: A Piagetian revision. *Human Development, 22,* 89–112.

Gibbs, J. C., Basinger, K.S., & Fuller, D. (1992). *Moral maturity: Measuring the development of sociomoral reflection.* Hillsdale, NJ: Lawrence Erlbaum.

Gill, K., Thompson, R., Keith, B., Tot-Faucette, M., Noll, S., & Kinney, T. R. (1993). Sickle cell disease pain in children and adolescents: Change in pain frequency and coping strategies overtime. *Journal of Pediatric Psychology, 18,* 621–637.

Gilligan, C. (1982). *In a different voice: Psychological theory of women's development.* Cambridge, MA: Harvard University Press.

Gilligan, C. (1998). Remembering Larry. *Journal of Moral Education, 27,* 125–140.

Goldenberg, R., Patterson, E., & Freese, M. (1992). Maternal demographic, situation and psychosocial factors and their relationship to enrollment in prenatal care: A review of the literature. *Women & Health, 19,* 133–151.

Gopaul-McNicol, S. (1988). Racial identification and racial preference of Black preschool children in New York and Trinidad. *Journal of Black Psychology, 14,* 65–68.

Gopaul-McNicol, S., Reid, G., & Wisdom, C. (1998). The psychoeducational assessment of Ebonics speakers: Issues and challenges. *Journal of Negro Education 67,* 16–23.

Gopaul-McNicol, S., & Thomas-Presswood, T. (1998). *Working with linguistically and culturally different children: Innovative clinical and educational application approach.* Boston: Allyn & Bacon.

Gould, J., & LeRoy, S. (1988). Socioeconomic status and low birth weight: A racial comparison. *Pediatrics, 82,* 896–904.

Grady, P. (2005). Socioeconomic status, health status and pregnancy. *American Journal of Obstetrics and Gynecology, 192,* 51–52.

Graham, J. A., & Cohen, R. (1997). Race and sex as factors in children's sociometric ratings and friendship choices. *Social Development, 6,* 355–372.

Graham, J. A., Cohen, R., Zbikowski, S., & Secrist, M. (1998). A longitudinal investigation of race and sex as factors in children's friendship choices. *Child Study Journal, 28,* 245–266.

Graham, S. (1992). "Most of the subjects were white and middle class": Trends in published research on African Americans in selected APA journals, 1970–1989. *American Psychologist, 47,* 629–639.

Graham, S. (1994). Motivation in African Americans. *Review of Educational Research, 64,* 55–117.

Graue, M. E., & Walsh, D. J. (1998). *Studying children in context.* Thousand Oaks, CA: Sage Publications.

Graziano, W., Varca, P., & Levy, J. (1982). Race of examiner effects and the validity of intelligence tests. *Review of Educational Research, 52,* 469–498.

Greenfield, P. M., & Cocking, R. R. (1994). *Cross-cultural roots of minority child development.* Hillsdale, NJ: Lawrence Erlbaum Associates.

Greenwood, C., Hart, Walker, D., & Rishley, T. (1994). The opportunity to respond and academic performance revisited: A behavioral theory of developmental retardation and its prevention, In R. Gardner, D. Sainte, J. Cooper, T. Heron, W. Heward, J. Eshleman, et al. (Eds.), *Behavior analysis in education: Focus on measurably superior instruction* (pp. 213–224). Pacific Grove, CA: Brooks/Cole.

Hall, W. S. (1974). Research in the black community: Child development. In J. Chunn (Ed.), *The survival of black children and youth.* Washington, DC: Nuclassics & Science Publishing.

Halle, T., Costes, B., & Mahonney, J. (1997). Family influences in school achievement in low-income African American children. *Journal of Educational Psychology, 89,* 527–537.

Hallinan, M. T., & Smith, S. S. (1985). The effects of classroom racial composition on students' interracial friendliness. *Social Psychology Quarterly, 48,* 3–16.

Hallinan, M. T., & Teixeira, R. A. (1987). Opportunities and constraints: Black-white differences in the formation of interracial friendships. *Child Development, 58,* 1358–1371.

Hammer, C. (2001). Come sit down and let mama read: Book reading between African American mothers and their infants. In J. Harris, A. Kamhi, & K. Pollock (Eds.), *Literacy in African-American communities* (pp. 21–44). Hillsdale, NJ: Erlbaum.

Hammer, C., & Weiss, A. (1999). Guiding language development: How African American mothers and their infants structure play interactions. *Journal of Speech, Language, and Hearing, 42,* 1219–1233.

Hammer, C., & Weiss, A., (2000). African American Mothers' views of their infants' language development language-learning environment. *American Journal of Speech Language Pathology, 9,* 126–140.

Harris, Y. R., & Oliver, G. J. (2002, August). *An investigation of the structure and content of oral narratives produced by African American mothers and their preschool children.* Paper presented at the International Conference for the Study of Behavioral Development, Ontario, Canada.

Harry, B., & Anderson, M. (1994). The disproportionate placement of African American males in special education programs: A critique of the process. *Journal of Negro Education, 63,* 602–619.

Harry, B., Klinger, J., & Hart, J. (2005). African American families under fire: Ethnographic views of family strength. *Remediation and Special Education, 26,* 101–112.

Hartup, W. W. (1983). Peer relations. In E. M. Hetherington (Ed.), P. H. Mussen (Series Ed.), *Handbook of child psychology, vol. 4: Socialization, personality, and social development* (pp. 103–196). New York: Wiley.

Hartup, W. W. (1989). Behavioral manifestations of children's friendships. In T. J. Berndt & G. W. Ladd (Eds.), *Peer relationships in child development* (pp. 46–70). New York: Wiley.

Hayes, E. (1981). *Busing and desegregation: The real truth.* Springfield, MA: Thomas.

Hayes, E. D. (1984). Moral judgment among Black adolescents and White adolescents from different socioeconomic levels. *Journal of Negro Education, 53*(4), 418–423.

Haynes, N., Comer, J., & Hamilton-Lee, M. (1988). The School Development Program: A model for school improvement. *Journal of Negro Education, 57,* 11–21.

Health United States and Healthy. (2000). *People review.* Hyattsville, MD: U.S. Department of Health and Human Services, Centers for Disease Control, National Center for Health Statistics.

Heath, S. (1989). Language socialization. In D. Slaughter (Ed.), *New Directions for Child Development, 42,* 29–41 San Francisco: Jossey Bass.

Helms, J. (Ed.). (1990). *Black and White racial identity: Theory, research, and practice.* Westport, CT: Greenwood Press.

Hernstein, R., & Murray, C. (1994). *The bell curve: Intelligence and class structure in American life.* New York: The Free Press.

Hetherington, E. M. (1999). Should we stay together for the sake of the children? In E. Mavis Hetherington (Ed.), *Coping with divorce, single parenting and remarriage: A risk and resiliency perspective* (pp. 93–117). Mahwah, NJ: Lawrence Erlbaum.

Hilliard, A. (1976). *Alternatives to IQ testing: An approach to the identification of gifted minority children* (final report). San Francisco: San Francisco State University. (ERIC Document Reproduction Service No. ED147009).

Hines-Martin, V., Malone, M., Kim, S., & Brown-Piper, A. (2003). Barriers to mental health access in African American population. *Issues in Mental Health Nursing, 24,* 237–265.

Hogan, D., & Lichter, D. (1995). Children and youth living arrangements and welfare. *Child Today, 36,* 9–13.

Hogan, D. P., & Kitagawa, E. M. (1985). The impact of social status, family structure, and neighborhood on the fertility of black adolescents. *American Journal of Sociology, 90,* 825–855.

Horn, I., & Beal, A. (2004). Child health disparities: Framing a research agenda. *Ambulatory Pediatrics, 4,* 269–275.

Horowitz, E. (1939). Racial aspects of self-identification in nursery school children. *The Journal of Psychology, 7,* 91–99.

House, J. S., Umberson, D., & Landis, K.R. (1988). Structures and processes of social support. *Annual Review of Sociology, 2,* 293–318.

Howard, A., & Scott, R. A. (1981). The study of minority groups in complex societies. In R. H. Munroe, R. L. Monroe, & B. Whiting (Eds.), *Handbook of cross-cultural human development* (pp. 113–152). New York: Garland.

Kreppner, K., & Lerner, R. (1989). Family systems and the life span development: Issues and perspectives. In K. Kreppner, & R. Lerner (Eds.), *Family systems and life-span development* (pp. 1–13). Hillsdale, NJ: Lawrence Erlbaum.

Kumanyika, S., & Grier, S. (2006). Targeting interventions for ethnic minority and low-income populations. *Future of Children, 16,* 187–207.

Kuther, T. L., & Wallace, S. A. (2003). Community violence and sociomoral development: An African American cultural perspective. *American Journal of Orthopsychiatry, 73(2),* 177–189.

Labov, W. (1972). *Language in the inner city.* Philadelphia: University of Pennsylvania Press.

Landry, K., & Smith, T. (1998). Neurocognitive effects of HIV infection on young children: Implications for assessment, *Topics in Early Childhood Special Education, 18,* 160–168.

Lapsley, D. K. (2005). Moral stage theory. In M. Killen & J. Smetana (Eds.), *Handbook of moral development* (pp. 37–66). Mahwah, NJ: Lawrence Erlbaum.

Larry P. et al. v. Wilson Riles, Superintendent of Public Instruction for the State of California et al., No C-71-2270 (N.D. Cal. 1979).

Leake, D., & Leake, B. (1992). Islands of hope: Milwaukee's African American immersion schools. *Journal of Negro Education, 61,* 24–29.

Lee, V., Brooks-Gunn, J., Schnur, E., & Liaw, F. (1990). Are Head Start effects sustained? A longitudinal follow-up comparisons of disadvantaged children attending Head Start, no preschool, and other preschool programs. *Child Development, 61,* 495–507.

Lerner, R. M. (1984). *On the nature of human plasticity.* New York: Cambridge University Press.

Levine, B. (1992, February 16). Insider's Voice—Infant Mortality. *LA Times,* p. A1.

Lia-Hoagberg, B. (1990). Barriers and motivators to prenatal care among low-income women. *Social Science Medicine, 30,* 487–495.

Liaw, F., & Brooks-Gunn, J. (1994). Cumulative risks and low birth weight children's cognitive and behavioral development. *Journal of Clinical Child Psychology, 23,* 360–372.

Liberman, E., Ryan, K., Manson, R., & Schoenbaum, S. (1987). Risk factors accounting for racial differences in the rate of premature birth. *The New England Journal of Medicine, 17,* 743–748.

Lin-Fu, J.(1979). What price shall we pay for lead poisoning in children. *Child Today, 36,* 9–13.

Littlejohn-Blake, S., & Darling, C. O. (1993) Understanding the strengths of African American families. *Journal of Black Studies, 23,* 460–471.

Lomotey, K. (1992). Independent Black Institutions: African centered education models, *Journal of Negro Education, 61,* 455–462.

Lonigan, C., & Whitehurst, G. (1998). Relative efficacy of parent and teacher involvement in a shared reading intervention for preschool children from low income backgrounds. *Early Childhood Research Quarterly, 32,* 263–290.

Lubienski, S. (2002). A closer look at Black-White mathematics gaps: Intersections of race and SES in NAEP Achievement and Instructional Practices Data. *The Journal of Negro Education, 71,* 269–287.

Lukens, J. (1981). Sickle cell disease. *Disease Month, 27,* 1–56.

Maccoby, E. E. (1988). Sex as a social category. *Developmental Psychology, 24,* 755–765.

Maccoby, E. E. (1990). Sex and relationships: A developmental account. *American Psychologist, 45,* 513–520.

MacDonald, K., & Parke, R. D. (1984). Bridging the gap: Parent-child play interaction and peer interactive competence. *Child Development, 55,* 1265–1277.

Macmillian, D., Hendrick, I., & Watkins, A. (1988). Impact of Diana, Larry P., and PL 94-142 on minority students. *Exceptional Children, 54,* 426–432.

Magnuson, K., & Waldfogel, J. (2005). Early childhood care and education: Effects on ethnic and racial gaps in school readiness. *Future of Children, 15,* 169–198.

Mahard, R., & Crain, R. (1983). Research on minority achievement in desegregated schools. In C. Rossell & W. Hawley (Eds.), *The consequences of school desegregation* (pp. 103–125). Philadelphia: Temple University.

Maltz, D. N., & Borker, R. A. (1983). A cultural approach to male-female miscommunication. In J. A. Gumperz (Ed.), *Language and social identity* (pp. 195–216). New York: Cambridge University Press.

Marshall, S. (1994). Ethnic socialization of African-American children: Implications for parenting, identity development, and academic achievement. *Journal of Youth and Adolescence, 24,* 377–396.

Mathis, W. (2005). Bridging the achievement gap: A bridge too far? *Phi Delta Kappa, 86,* 590–593.

McAdoo, H. (1992). Upward mobility and parenting in middle income Black families. In A. K. Burlew, W. Banks, H. McAdoo, & D. Azibo (Eds.), *African American psychology. Theory research and practice* (pp. 63–85) Newbury Park: Sage Publications

McAdoo, H. P. (1997). *Black families* (3rd ed.). Thousand Oaks, CA: Sage Publications.

McAdoo, J. (1988). Modification of racial attitudes and preferences in young children. In H. P. McAdoo (Ed.), *Black families* (3rd edition). Thousand Oaks, CA: Sage Publications.

McDermott, P. (1977). Social relations as a context for learning. *Harvard Educational Review, 47,* 198–213.

McEwen, M., Johnson, P., Neatherlin, J., Millard, W., & Lawrence, G. (1998). School based management of chronic asthma among inner city African American school children in Dallas Texas. *Journal of School Health, 68,* 197–200.

McLanahan, S. S. (1985). Family structure and the reproduction of poverty. *American Journal of Sociology, 90,* 873–901.

McLoyd, V. C. (2004). Linking race and ethnicity to culture: Steps along the road from inference to hypothesis testing. *Human Development, 47,* 185–191.

McLoyd, V. C. (1991). What is the study of African American children the study of? The conduct, publication, and changing nature of research on African American children. In R. L. Jones (Ed.), *Black psychology* (3rd ed., pp. 419–440). Berkeley: Cobb & Henry.

McLoyd, V. C. (1998). Changing demographics in the American population: Implications for research on minority children and adolescents. In V. C. McLoyd & L. Steinberg (Eds.), *Studying minority adolescents: Conceptual, methodological, and theoretical issues* (pp. 3–28). Mahway, NJ: Erlbaum.

McLoyd, V. C., & Randolph, S. M. (1984). The conduct and publication of research on Afro American children. *Human Development, 27,* 65–75.

McLoyd, V. C., & Randolph, S. M. (1985). Secular trends in the study of Afro American children: A review of *Child Development, 1936–1980. Monographs of the Society for Research in Child Development, 50,* 78–92.

McMahon, S. D., Wernsman, M. A., & Parnes, A. L. (2006). Understanding prosocial behavior: The impact of empathy and gender among African American adolescents. *Journal of Adolescent Health, 39,* 135 -137.

McRoy, R., Oglesby, Z., & Grape, H. (1997). Achieving same race adoptive placements for African American children: Culturally sensitive practice approaches. *Child Welfare, 76,* 85–104.

Mikhail, B. (2000). Prenatal care utilization among low-income African American women. *Journal of Community Health Nursing, 17,* 235–246.

Miller, P. A., Bernzweig, J., Eisenberg, N., & Fabes, R. A. (1991). The development and socialization of prosocial behavior. In R. Hinde & J. Groebel (Eds.), *Cooperation and prosocial behavior* (pp. 54–77). New York: Cambridge University Press.

Miller, S. A. (1998). *Developmental research methods* (2nd ed.). Upper Saddle, NJ: Prentice Hall.

Milloy, C. (1994, July 17). Motherly advice on lead and children. *Washington Post,* p. B6.

Moreland, C., & Leach, M. M. (2001). The relationship between Black racial identity and moral development. *Journal of Black Psychology, 27(3),* 255–271.

Morland, J. K. (1966). A comparison of race awareness in northern and southern children. *American Journal of Orthopsychiatry, 36,* 22–31.

Moynihan, D. P. (1965). *The Negro American family: The case for national action.* U.S. Department of Labor. Retrieved September 23, 2006 from http://www.children. smartlibrary.org/NewInterface/segment.cfm?segment = 1806.

Multiethnic Placement Act of 1994, P.L. 103–382, 108 Sta. 4057.

Murray, J., & Bernfield, M. (1998). The differential effect of prenatal care on the incidence of low birth weight among blacks and whites in prepaid health care plan. *The New England Journal of Medicine, 319,* 1385–1391.

Murray, V. M., Smith, E., & Hill, N. (2000). Race, ethnicity, and culture in studies of families in context. *Journal of Marriage and the Family, 63,* 911–914.

Mushak, P., & Crocetti, A (1989). Determination of numbers of lead exposed American children as a function of lead source: Integrated Summary of a report to the U.S. Congress on childhood lead poisoning. *Environmental Research, 50,* 11–36.

Myers, H. F., Rana, P. G., & Harris, M. (1979). *Black child development in America, 1927–1977.* Westport, CT: Greenwood.

Myers, M. A., & Thompson, V. L. (2000). The impact of violence exposure on African American youth in context. *Youth and Society, 32,* 253–267.

National Assessment of Educational Progress. (2006). Retrieved from www.nces.gov/nationsreportcard/.

Nagayama Hall, G. C. (2001). Psychotherapy research with ethnic minorities: Empirical, ethical, and conceptual issues. *Journal of Consulting and Clinical Psychology, 69,* 502–510.

National Asthma Association. (2004). Retrieved from www.lungusa.org

National Center for Environmental Health (2006). Retrieved from www.cdc.gov/nceh.

National Center for Health Statistics. (2003). Health, United States, 2003. Hyattsville, MD: Public Health Service. Retrieved from www.nces.edu.gov.

Needleman, H., & Bellinger, D. (1991). The health effects of low level exposure to lead. *Annual Review of Public Health, 12,* 111–140.

Needleman, H., Gunnoe, C., Leviton, A., Reed, R., Perersie, H., Maher, C., et al. (1979). Deficits in psychologic and classroom performance of children with elevated dentine levels. *The New England Journal of Medicine, 300,* 689–695.

Neff, K. D., & Helwig, C. C. (2002). A constructivist approach to understanding the development of reasoning about rights and authority within cultural contexts. *Cognitive Development, 17,* 1429–1450.

Neighbors, H. (1997). The (mis) diagnosis of mental disorders in African Americans. *African American Research Perspectives, 3(1),* 1–11

Nelson-Le Gall, S., & Glor-Scheib, S. (1985). Help-seeking behavior in elementary classrooms: An observational study. *Contemporary Educational Psychology, 10,* 58–71.

New rules for moms and dads. (1999, June). *Ebony, 54(8),* 72–80.

Nicholsonne, M. (1988). Strides toward excellence: The Harford Heights model. *Journal of Negro Education, 57,* 282–291.

Nucci, L. P. (2001). *Education in the moral domain.* New York: Cambridge University Press.

O'Hare, W., Pollard, K., Mann, T., & Kent, M. (1991). African-Americans in the 1990's. *Population Bulletin, 46,* 1–40.

Oakes, J. (1995). Two cities' tracking and within school segregation. *Teachers College Record, 96,* 681–690.

Office of Minority and Women's Health. (2006). Retrieved from www.bphc.hrsa.dhhs.gov/omwh.

Ogbu, J. U. (1974). Origins of human competence: A cultural ecological perspective. *Child Development, 61,* 311–346.

Ogbu, J. U. (1992). Understanding cultural diversity and learning. *Educational Research, 21,* 5–14.

Oliver, W. (1989). Black males and social problems: Prevention through Afrocentric socialization. *Journal of Black Studies, 20,* 15–39.

Ostrovsky, M., Parr, G., & Gradel, A. (1992). Promoting moral development through social interest in children and adolescents. *Individual Psychology, 48(2),* 218–225.

Oyemade, U., & Rosser, P. (1980). Development in Black children. *Advances in Behavioral Pediatrics, 1,* 153–179.

Pagnini, D., & Reichman, N. (2000). Psychosocial factors and the timing of prenatal care among women in New Jersey's Health Start Program. *Family Planning Perspectives, 32,* 56–64.

Parker, W. (2003). Black-white infant mortality disparity in the United States: A social litmus test. *Public Health Reports, 118,* 336–337

Pelligrini, A., Perlmutter, J., Galda, L., & Brody, G. (1990). Joint reading between Black Head Start children and their mothers. *Child Development, 61,* 443–453.

Perloff, R. (2006). Communication and health care disparities. *American Behavioral Scientists, 49,* 755–759.

Perry, T., Steele, C., & Hilliard, A. (2003). *Young gifted and black: Promoting high achievement among African American students.* Boston, MA: Beacon Press.

Perry, T., & Delpit. L. (1998). The Oakland ebonics resolution. In T. Perry & L. Delpit (Eds.), *The real ebonics debate.* (pp. 143–147). Boston: Beacon.

Pestronk, R., & Franks, M. (2003). A partnership to reduce African American infant mortality in Genese County, Michigan. *Public Health Reports, 118,* 324–335.

Peters, M. (1988). Racial socialization of young Black children. In H. P. McAdoo & J. L. McAdoo (Eds.), *Black children: Social, educational and parental environments* (pp.159–173). Beverly Hills, CA: Sage Publications.

Peterson, J., Sterling, Y., & Stout, J. (2002). Explanatory models of asthma from African American caregivers of children with asthma. *Journal of Asthma, 39,* 577–590.

Petrini, J., Damus, K., Russell, R., Poschman, K., Davidoff, M., & Mattison, D. (2002). Contribution of birth defects to infant mortality in the United States. *Teratology, 66,* 3–6.

Piaget, J. (1932). *The moral judgment of the child.* London: Routledge and Keagen Paul.

Piaget, J. (1965). *The moral judgment of the child.* New York: Free Press.

Pickren, W., & Tomes, H. (2002). The legacy of Kenneth B. Clark to the APA. *American Psychologist, 57,* 51–59.

Piestrip, A. M. (1973). Black dialect inference and accommodation of reading instructions in first grade. *Monographs of Language Behavior Research Laboratory,* (No. 4).

Polite, V., & Davis, J. (1999). *African American males in school and society: Practices and policies for effective education.* New York: Columbia University Teachers College Press.

Pollack, H., Kuchik, Cowan, L., & Hacimamutoglu, S. (1996). Neurodevelopment, growth and viral load in HIV infected infants. *Brain Behavior and Immunity, 10,* 298–312.

Pollard, D. (1989). Against the odds: A profile of academic achievers from the urban underclass. *Journal of Negro Education, 58,* 297–304.

Pollard, D., & Ajirotutu, C. (2000). *African-centered schooling in theory and practice.* Westport CT: Bergin & Garvey.

Powars, D. (2001). Hydroxyurea in very young children with sickle cell is not a cure all. *Journal of Pediatrics, 139,* 763–764.

Powell, G. J. (1985). Self-concepts among Afro-American students in racially isolated minority schools: Some regional differences. *Journal of the American Academy of Child Psychiatry, 24,* 142–149.

Powell-Hopson, D., & Hopson, D. (1988). Implications of doll color preference among Black preschool children and white preschool children. *Journal of Black Psychology, 14,* 57–41.

Prasse, D., & Reschly, D. (1986). Larry P: A case of segregation, testing or program efficiency. *Exceptional Children, 52,* 333–346.

Purcell-Gates, V. (1996). Stories, coupons, and the *TV Guide*: Relationships between home literacy. experiences and emergent literacy knowledge. *Reading Research Quarterly, 31,* 406–428.

Pursley-Crotteau, S. (2001). Perinatal crack users becoming temperant: The social psychological processes. *Health Care for Women International, 22,* 49–66.

Radke, M., Sutherland, J., & Rosenberg, P. (1950). Racial attitudes of children. *Sociometry, 13,* 154–171.

Ratteray, J., & Shujaa, M. (1987). *Dare to choose: Parental choice at independent neighborhood schools.* Washington, DC: Institute for Independent Education.

Reeb, K., Graham, A., Zyzanski, S., & Kitson, G. (1987). Predicting low birthweight and complicated labor in urban black women: A biopsychological perspective. *Social Science Medicine, 25,* 1321–1327.

Rehberg, H. R., & Richman, C. L. (1989). Prosocial behaviour in preschool children: A look at the interaction of race, gender, and family composition. *International Journal of Behavioral Development, 12(3),* 385–401.

Reschly, D. (1980). *Nonbiased assessment.* Des Moines, IA: State of Iowa, Department of Public Instruction.

Rest, J. (1979). *Development in judging moral issues.* Minneapolis: University of Minnesota Press.

Rickford, J., & Rickford, A. (1995). Dialect readers revisited. *Linguistics and Education, 7,* 107–128.

Roberts, D. (2002). *Shattered bonds: The color of child welfare.* New York: Basic Books.

Roberts, W., & Strayer, J. (1996). Empathy, emotional expressiveness, and prosocial behavior. *Child Development, 67,* 449–470.

Rochelle, A. (1994, September 1) Two Georgia boys may be proof of sickle cell anemia cure. *Atlanta Constitution,* p. A1.

Rong, X. (1997). Effects of race and gender on teachers' perception of the social behavior of elementary students. *Urban Education, 31,* 261–290.

Rosenberg, K., Desai, R., & Kan, J. (2002). Why do foreign born blacks have lower infant mortality rates than native born blacks? New directions in African American infant mortality research. *Journal of the National Medical Association, 94,* 770–778.

Rosenthal, R., & Jacobsen, L. (1992). *Pygmalion in the classroom: Teacher expectation and pupils' intellectual development.* New York: Irvington.

Ross, M., & Aday, L. (2006). Stress and coping in African American grandparents who are raising their grandchildren. *Journal of Family Issues, 27,* 912–932.

Rubin, Z. (1980). *Children's friendships.* Cambridge, MA: Harvard University.

Ruiz, D. (1998). Intergenerational households maintained by African American grandmothers: New roles and challenges for the 21st Century. *African American Research Perspectives,* 57–68.

Russo, C., Harris, J., & Sandridge, R. (1994). *Brown v. Board of Education* at 40: A legal history of educational opportunities in American public education. *Journal of Negro Education, 63,* 297–309.

Ryan, L., Ehrlich, S., & Finnegan, L. (1987). Cocaine abuse in pregnancy: Effects on the fetus and newborn. *Neurotoxicology and Teratology, 9,* 295–299.

Sameroff, A., Seifer, R., Baldwin, A. & Baldwin, C. (1993). Stability of intelligence from preschool to adolescence. The influence of social and family risks factors. *Child Development, 64,* 80–97.

Sanchez, W. (1995). Working with diverse learners and school staff in a multicultural society. Greensboro, NC: Eric Clearinghouse on Counseling and Student Services.

Sanders, K., & Davis, S. Improving prenatal care for low-income African American women and infants. *Journal of Health Care for the Poor and Underserved, 9,* 14–29.

Scanzoni, J. (1971). *The black family in modern society.* Boston: Allyn & Bacon.

Scarr, S., & Weinberg, R. (1978). The influence of family background on intellectual attainment. *American Sociological Review, 43,* 674–692.

Schaie, K. (1965). A general model for the study of developmental problems. *Psychological Bulletin, 64,* 92–107.

Schofiled, J. (1995). Review of research on school desegregation's impact on elementary and secondary school students. In J. A. Banks, & C. M. Banks (Eds.)., *Handbook of research on multicultural education* (pp. 597–617). New York: MacMillian Publishing.

Schouten, F. (2003, January 19) School segregation growing. *Gannett News Service,* p. A2.

Schwartz, J. (1982). Dialect interference in the attainment of literacy. *Journal of Reading, 25,* 440–446.

Scott, J., & Marcus, C. (2001). Emergent literacy: Home school connections. In J. Harris, A. Kamhi, & K. Pollock (Eds.), *Literacy in African-American communities* (pp. 77–97). Mahwah, NJ: Lawrence Erlbaum.

Scott-Jones, D. (1994). Ethical issues in reporting and referring in research with low-income minority children. *Ethics and Behavior, 4,* 97–108.

Seccombe, K. (2000). Families in poverty in the 1990's: Trends, cause, consequences, and lessons learned. *Journal of Marriage and Family, 62(4),* 1094–1113.

Seitz, V. (1990). Intervention programs for impoverished children: A comparison of educational and family support models, *Annals of Child Development, 7,* 73–103.

Semaj, L. (1980). The development of racial evaluation and preference: A cognitive approach. *The Journal of Black Psychology, 6,* 59–70.

Serbin, L. A., Sprafkin, C., Elman, M., & Doyle, A. B. (1984). The early development of sex differentiated patterns of social influence. *Canadian Journal of Social Science, 14,* 350–363.

Seyfried, S. (1998). Academic achievement of African American preadolescents: The influence of teacher perception. *American Journal of Community Psychology, 26,* 381–402.

Shujaa, M., & Ratteray, J. (1992). Expanding "schools of choice" for African Americans: Independent neighborhood schools in New Jersey. In *New Jersey Public Policy Research Institute, Blacks in New Jersey, 1987; Crisis in urban education* (pp. 39–50). Absecon, NJ: New Jersey Public Policy Research Institute.

Shweder, R. A., & Bourne, L. (1984). Does the concept of the person vary cross-culturally? In R. Shweder & R. Levine (Eds.), *Culture theory: Essays on mind, self, and emotion* (pp. 158–190). New York: Cambridge University Press.

Shweder, R. A., Mahapatra, M., & Miller, J. (1987). Culture and moral development. In J. Kagan & S. Lamb (Eds.), *The emergence of morality in young children* (pp. 1–83). Chicago: University of Chicago Press.

Simpkins, G., Holt, G., & Simpkins, C. (1977). *Bridge: A cross cultural reading program.* Boston: Houghton Mifflin.

Sin, M., Kang, D., & Weaver, M. (2005). Relationships of asthma knowledge, self-management, and social support in African-American adolescents with asthma. *International Journal of Nursing, 42,* 307–313.

Singer, L., Eisengart, L., Minnes, J., Noland, Jey A., Lane, C., et al. (2005). Prenatal cocaine exposure and infant cognition. *Infant Behavior and Development, 28,* 431–444.

Singleton, L., & Asher, S. (1979). Racial integration and children's peer preferences: An investigation of developmental and cohort differences. *Child Development, 50,* 936–941.

Slaughter-Defoe, D., & Rubin, H. (2001). A longitudinal case study of Head Start eligible children: Implications for urban education. *Educational Psychologist, 36,* 31–44.

Smetana, J. G. (1995). Morality in context: Abstractions, ambiguities, and applications. In R. Vasta (Ed.), *Annuals of child development: A research annual* (Vol. 10, pp. 83–130). Bristol, PA: Jessica Kingsley Publishers.

Smith, C. A., Krohn, M. D., Chu, R., & Best, O. (2005). African American fathers: Myths and realities about their involvement with their firstborn children. *Journal of Family Issues, 26*(7), 975–1001.

Snarey, J. R. (1994). Cross-cultural universality of social-moral development: A critical review of Kohlbergian research. In B. Puka (Ed.), *New research in moral development. Moral Development: A compendium, Vol. 5* (pp. 268–298). New York: Garland.

Snowden, L. (2001). Barriers to effective mental health services for African Americans. *Mental Health Services Research, 3,* 181–187.

Sochalski, J., & Villarruel, A. (1999). Improving access to health care for children. *JSPN, 4,* 147–154.

Spence, S. (1990). Black adolescents seeking prenatal care. *Child and Adolescent Social Work, 7,* 285–300.

Spencer, M. (1984). Black children's race awareness, racial attitudes, and self-concept: A reinterpretation. *Journal of Child Psychology and Psychiatry, 25,* 433–441.

Spencer, M. B. (1982). Preschool children's social cognition and cultural cognition: A cognitive developmental interpretation of race dissonance findings. *Journal of Psychology, 112,* 275–296.

Spencer, M. B. (1985). Cultural cognition and social cognition as identity factors in Black children's personal-social growth. In M. B. Spencer, G. K. Brookins, & W. R. Allen (Eds.), *Beginnings: The social and affective development of Black children* (pp. 215–230). Hillsdale, NJ: Lawrence Erlbaum.

Spencer, M. B., Dupree, D., & Hartmann, T. (1997). A phenomenological variant of ecological systems theory (PVEST): A self-organization perspective in context. *Development and Psychopathology, 9,* 817–833.

Spencer, M., Kohn, L., & Woods, J. (2002). Labeling vs. early identification: The dilemma of mental health service under-utilization among low income African American children. *African American Research Perspectives, 8,* 1–14.

Spurlock, J. (1985). Assessment and therapeutic intervention of Black children. *Journal of American Academy of Child Psychiatry, 24,* 168–174.

Stangor, C. (2004). *Research methods for the behavioral sciences* (2nd ed.). Boston, MA: Houghton Mifflin Company.

Staples, R. (1986). *The black family: Essays and studies* (3rd ed.). Belmont, CA: Wadsworth Publishing.

Steele, C., & Aronson, J. (1995). Stereotype threat and the intellectual test performance of African Americans. *Journal of Personality and Social Psychology, 69,* 797–811.

Sternberg, R. J., & Grigorenko, E. L. (2004). Why we need to explore development in its cultural context. *Merrill-Palmer Quarterly, 50,* 369–386.

Stevens, J. H. (1984). Black grandmothers' and black adolescent mothers' knowledge about parenting. *Developmental Psychology, 20,* 1017–1025.

Stewart, W. (1969). On the use of Negro dialect in the teaching of reading. In J. Baratz & R. Shuy (Eds.), *Language differences do they interfere* (pp.156–219). Newark, DE: International Reading Association.

Stockman, I. (1999). Semantic development of African American children. In O. Taylor & L. Leonard (Eds.), *Language acquisition across North America.* San Diego: Singular Publishing Group.

Strickland, D. (2003). Early intervention for African-American children considered to be at risk. In S. B. Neuman & D. K. Dickinson (Eds.), *Handbook of early literacy research* (pp. 93–110). New York:Guilford Press.

Strutchens, M., & Silver, E. (2000). NAEP findings regarding race/ethnicity students' performance, school experiences, and attitudes and beliefs. In E. A. Sliver P. A. King (Eds.), *Results from the seventh mathematics assessment of the National Assessment of Educational Progress* (pp. 45–72). Reston, VA: National Council of Teachers of Mathematics.

Sudarkasa, N. (1997). African American families and family values. In H. P. McAdoo (Ed.), *Black families* (3rd ed., pp. 9–40). Thousand Oaks, CA: Sage Publications.

Sue, S. (1999). Science, ethnicity, and bias: Where have we gone wrong? *American Psychologist, 54,* 1070–1077.

Sullivan, H. S. (1953). *The interpersonal theory of psychiatry.* New York: Norton.

Sunderman, G. L., Tracey, C., Kim, J., & Orfield, G. (2004). *Listening to teachers: Classroom realities and No Child Left Behind.* The Civil Rights Project: Harvard University.

Sutton, P. (2003). Births, marriages, divorces and deaths: Provisional date for April 2003. *National Vital Statistics Reports, 52,* 6.

Synder, T., Tan, A., & Hoffman, C. (2003). U.S. Department of Education (Publication Number NCES 2005025) Digest of Education Statistics (www.nces.ed.gov).

Taylor, O. (1999). Cultural issues and language acquisition. In O. Taylor & L. Leonard (Eds.), *Language acquisition across North America.* (pp. 21–37). San Diego: Singular Publishing Group.

Taylor, R., & Thornton, M. (1996). Child welfare and transracial adoption. *Journal of Black Psychology, 22,* 282–291.

Taylor, R. J., Tucker, M. B., Chatters, L. M., & Jayakody, R. (1997). Recent demographic trends in African American family structure. In R. J. Taylor, J. S. Jackson, & L. M. Chatters (Eds.), *Family life in Black America* (pp. 14–62). Thousand Oaks, CA: Sage Publications.

Telfair, J. (2003). An evaluation of state perinatal community-based programs in Alabama: Overview. *Public Health Reports, 118,* 484–486.

Terling-Watt, T. (2001). Permanency in kinship care: An exploration of disruption rates and factors associated with placement disruption. *Children and Youth Services Review, 23(3),* 111–126.

Thorton, M., Chatters, L., Taylor, R., & Allen, W. (1990). Sociodemographic and environmental correlates of racial socialization by Black parents. Special Issue: Minority Children. *Child Development, 61,* 401–409.

Tillman, L. C. (2002). Culturally sensitive research approaches: An African American perspective. *Educational Researcher, 31,* 3–12.

Trent, W. (1997). Outcomes of school desegregation: Findings from longitudinal research. *Journal of Negro Education, 66,* 255–257.

Trotman, M. (2001). Involving the African American parent: Recommendations to increase the decreasing level of parent involvement within African-American families. *Journal of Negro Education, 70,* 275–285.

Tucker, C. M., & Herman, K. C. (2002). Using culturally sensitive theories and research to meet the academic needs of low-income African American children. *American Psychologist, 57,* 762–773.

Tucker, C., Harris, Y., Brady, & Herman, K. (1996). The association between selected parent variables and the academic achievement of African American children and European American Children. *Child Study Journal, 26,* 253–277.

Tulkin, S. R. (1972). An analysis of the concept of cultural deprivation. *Developmental Psychology, 6,* 326–339.

Tuma, R. (2006). Psychosocial prenatal intervention in African American women improves infant birth weight. *PAS 2006 Annual Meeting Abstract 3724.7.*

Turiel, E. (1983). *The development of social knowledge: Morality and convention.* New York: Cambridge University Press.

Turiel, E. (1998). The development of morality. In W. Damon (Series Ed.) & N. Eisenberg (Vol. Ed.), *Handbook of child psychology: Vol. 3. Social, emotional, and personality development* (5th ed., pp. 863–932). New York: Wiley.

Turiel, E. (2002). *The culture of morality: Social development, context, and conflict.* Cambridge: Cambridge University Press.

U.S. Census Bureau, 2006 Statistical Abstracts of the U.S.

U.S. Census Bureau. (2003a). *The Black population in the United States: March 2002* (Current Population Reports, P20–541). Washington, DC: U.S. Government Printing Office.

U.S. Census Bureau. (2003b). *Children's living arrangements and characteristics: March 2002* (Current Population Reports, P20–547). Washington, DC: U.S. Government Printing Office.

U.S. Census Bureau. (2004). *Children and the households they live in: 2000* (Census 2000 Special Reports, CNSR-14). Washington, DC: U.S. Government Printing Office.

U.S. Department of Health and Human Services, Health Resources and Services Administration, Maternal and Child Health Bureau. (2004). *Child health USA 2004.* Rockville, MD: U.S. Department of Health and Human Services.

U.S. Department of Justice. (2006). *Violent felons in large urban cities. NCJ Publication No 205289.* Washington, DC: U.S. Government Printing Office.

Van Keulen, J., Weddington, G., & Debose, C. (1998). *Speech, language, learning and the African American child.* Needham Heights, MA: Allyn & Bacon.

Vergon, C. (1990). School desegregation: Lessons from three decades of experience. *Educational Policy, 23,* 22–49

Walker, L. J., de Vries, B., & Trevethan, S. D. (1987). Moral stages and moral orientations in real-life and hypothetical dilemmas. *Child Development, 58,* 842–858.

Wallace, I., Roberts, J., & Lodder, D. (1998). Interactions of African American infants and their mothers: Relations with development at 1 year of age. *Journal of Speech Language and Hearing Research, 41,* 900–912.

Ward, J. V. (1988). Urban adolescents' conceptions of violence. In C. Gilligan, J. Ward, and J. Taylor (Eds.), *Mapping the moral domain* (pp. 175–200). Cambridge, MA: Harvard University Press.

Ward, J. V. (1995). Cultivating a morality of care in African American adolescents: A culture-based model of intervention. *Harvard Educational Review, 65,* 175–188.

Ward, M. (1986). *Them children: A study in language learning.* Prospect Heights, IL: Waveland Press.

Washington, E. D., & McLoyd, V. C. (1982). The external validity of research involving American minorities. *Human Development, 25,* 324–339.

Washington, V., & Miller-Jones, D. (1989). Teacher interactions with nonstandard English speakers during reading instruction. *Contemporary Educational Psychology, 14,* 280–312.

Wasik, B., Karweit, N., Bond, M., Woodruff, L., Jarger, G., & Adee, S. (2000). Early learning in CRESPAR, *Journal of Education for Students Placed At Risk, 5,* 93–107.

Watkins, A. (2002). Learning styles of African American children: A developmental consideration. *Journal of Black Psychology, 28,* 3–17.

Way, N. (1996). Between experiences of betrayal and desire: Close friendships among urban adolescents. In B. J. R. Leadbeater & N. Way (Eds.), *Urban girls: Resisting stereotypes, creating identities* (pp. 173–192). New York: New York University Press.

Weese-Mayer, D., Berry-Kravis, E., Maher, B., Silvsestri, J., Curran, M., & Marazita, M. (2003). Sudden Infant Death Syndrome. *American Journal of Medicine General, 117,* 268–274.

Westinghouse Learning Corporation. (1969). *The impact of Head Start: An evaluation of the effects of Head Start experience on children's cognitive and affective development* (preliminary draft). Columbus: Westinghouse Learning Corporation, Ohio University.

Wettzman, M., Gortmaker, S., Sobol, A., & Perrin, J. (1992). Recent trends in the prevalence and severity of childhood asthma. *JAMA, 268,* 2673–2677.

Whaley, A. (1993). Self-esteem, cultural identity and psychosocial adjustment in African American children. *Journal of Black Psychology, 19,* 406–422

White, J. L., & Parham, T. A. (1990). *The psychology of blacks: An African American perspective.* Englewood Cliffs, NJ: Prentice-Hall.

Wigg, N. (2001). Low level lead exposure and children. *Journal of Pediatrics Child Health, 37,* 423–425.

Willis, M. (1992). Learning styles of African American children: A review of the literature and intervention. In A. K. Burlew, W. C. Banks, H. P. McAdoo, & D. A. Azibo (Eds.), *African American psychology: Theory, research and practice* (pp. 260–278). Newbury Park, CA: Sage.

Wilson, W. (1996). *When work disappears.* New York: Knopf.

Wise, P. (1984). Infant mortality in the United States. *Science for the People, 16,* 23–36

Wodrich, D. (1997). *Children's psychological testing.* Baltimore: Books Publishing.

Wolfram, W. (1979). Test interpretation and sociolinguistic differences. *Topics in Language Disorders, 3,* 21–24.

Woods, L. N., & Jagers, R. J. (2003). Are cultural values predictors of moral reasoning in African American adolescents? *Journal of Black Psychology, 29(1),* 102–118.

York, R., Tulman, L., & Brown, K. (2000). Postnatal care in low-income urban African American women: Relationship to level of prenatal care sought. *Pernatology, 20,* 34–40.

York, R., Williams, S., & Munro, B. (1993). Maternal factors that influence inadequate prenatal care. *Public Health Nursing, 10,* 241–244.

Young, R. (1988). A process for developing more effective urban schools: A case study of Stowe Middle School. *Journal of Negro Education, 57,* 307–334.

Zahn-Waxler, C., Radke-Yarrow, M., & King, R. A. (1979). Child rearing and children's initiations toward victims of distress. *Child Development, 50,* 319–330 .

Zieger, E., & Hall, N. (2000). *Child development and social policy.* Boston: McGraw-Hill.

Zielgler, E., & Muenchow, S. (1992). *Head Start: The inside story of America's most successful educational experiment.* New York: Basic Books.

Zimmerman, B. J., & Levy, G. D. (2000). Social cognitive predictors of prosocial behavior toward same and alternate race children among White preschoolers. *Current Psychology, 19(3),* 175–193.

Zimmerman, M., & Arunkumar, R. (1994). Resiliency research: Implications for school and policy. *Social Policy Report: Society for Research in Child Development, 8,* 1–17.

Zinser, O., Rich, M. C., & Bailey, R. C. (1981). Sharing behavior and racial preference in children. *Motivation and Emotion, 5,* 179–187.

Zionts, L., Zionts, P., Harrison, S., & Bellinger, O. (2003). Urban African American perceptions of cultural sensitivity within the special education system. *Focus on Autism and Other Developmental Disabilities, 18,* 41–50.

Index

AAVE. *See* African American Vernacular English

ABC. *See* Carolina Abecedarian Intervention Project

Abecedarian Project, 106–107, 126

Adoption, 6, 7–8, 177

Adoption and Foster Care Analysis and Reporting System (AFCARS), 177

African American Vernacular English (AAVE)
Black Dialect, 111, 122, 126, 130
code-switching, 114
comparisons with SE, 114–117, 121–124
Ebonics, 112–114
history of, 111
in home environment, 199
lack of research on, 117
language intervention programs, 124–127
linguistic rules of, 122–124
Oakland Unified School District use of, 112–114
socioeconomic status and, 119–120
testing tools for speakers of, 128
text sample, 125
training in, 128

African Language Systems. *See* African American Vernacular English

Afrocultural values, 141

AIDS, 49–50, 62, 63, 177

Alcoholism and pregnancy, 43–45, 63

Alcohol Related Neurodevelopmental Disorder (ARND), 44

American Psychological Association (APA)

Afrocentric views in graduate training, 71
journals and study characteristics, 23
policy on culture and diagnosis, 70

Anglocultural values, 141

APA. *See* American Psychological Association

Arizona Test of Articulation Frequency, 128

ARND. *See* Alcohol Related Neurodevelopmental Disorder

Asian American children, 2, 57, 173, 175, 176

Assessment, nondiscriminatory, 93

Association of Black Psychology, 71

Asthma, 56–58

Augmented family structure, 176–178

Baby Your Baby Campaign, 48

Barbarin, O., 68

Barker, N. C., 178, 179

Bayley Mental Development Index (MDI), 44

Bioecological Systems Theory (Bronfenbrenner), 32–34, 76, 77, 170, 171

Black Dialect. *See* African American Vernacular English

Black English. *See* African American Vernacular English

Blindness, 52

Body mass index (BMI), 58–59

Bone marrow transplants, 53–56

Bravado identity, 181

Bridges Reading Program, 126

Bridging the Achievement Gap (Mathis), 103

Bronfenbrenner, Urie, 32–34, 76, 77, 170, 171
Brown v. Board of Education (1954), 85–89, 103

Call and Response, 126
Care perspective, 139–140
Carolina Abecedarian Intervention Project (ABC), 106–107, 126
Ceballo, Rosario, 151–161
Census Bureau, U.S., 103–104, 173, 174, 175, 176
Centers for Disease Control, 43, 45, 49, 53
Cerebral palsy, 52
Chelation therapy, 52–53
Child Health Insurance Program (CHIP), 60
Children's Defense Fund, 174–175
Child Trends Data Bank, 49–50
Chronosystem ecological models, 171
Civil Rights Act of 1964, 74, 85, 103
Clark, Kenneth, 72–74
Clark, Mamie, 72–74
Cocaine, 44, 46
Code of the street, 148–150
Cognitive models of racial identity development, 76
College enrollment rates, 11, 88, 102, 105
Comer, James, 97–98
Communalism, 141, 144
Communication barriers, 123
Community outreach organizations
    educational programs, 104, 127
    health services, 49, 53, 56, 58, 187
    literacy intervention programs, 127
    mental health services, 97
Compartmentalization hypothesis, 75–76
Comprehensive assessment (Comp.), 128–129
Conceptual frameworks, 24–25
Conjugal bonds, 170
Consanguinal bonds, 170
Consortium on Racial Equality in Child Welfare, 7

Contrasting Linguistic Features (CLF), 128
Council of Independent Black Institutions (CIBI), 101
Council of the Great Schools, 102
Council on African American Affairs, 61
Covictimization, 147, 151
Cultural deficit perspective, 17, 28, 134, 142, 161, 165–166
Cultural diversity, 32, 186
Cultural equivalent family model, 168–169
Culturally deviant family model. *See* Pathological family model
Cultural relevancy
    in assessment, 68–70
    in children's books, 124
    in research, 23–31
Cultural theorists, 140–141
Culture and Empathy Model (Humphries), 141, 144

Defining Issues Test of Moral Development (DIT), 139
Demographics, 1–13. *See also* Census Bureau, U.S.
    economic conditions, 9–11
    living arrangements, 4–8
    population statistics, 2–3
Depression
    child exposure to violence and, 152
    child illness and, 55
    in children and single parent families, 66
    clinical, 66
    incidence of clinical depression in children, 66
    in mothers in high crime neighborhoods, 45
    in parenting grandparents, 177
Desegregation. *See* School desegregation
Detroit-Wayne County Infant Health Promotion Coalition, 48
Developmental psychology, 17–18, 25–27
Developmental Psychology

race-comparative studies and, 16
on social class assessment in
    studies, 22–23
Diagnostic and Statistical Manual
    (DSM-IV), 69–70
Dialects, 111, 122, 126, 127–129, 130
Diana v. Board of Education (1970), 92
DIT. *See* Defining Issues Test of Moral
    Development
Doll studies, 72–75
Domain theory (Turiel), 141–142
Dropout rates, 88, 89, 175
Drugs
    cocaine, 44, 46
    drug trade in inner city, 150
    effects of during pregnancy, 63
    effects of in pregnant women, 43–47
    fetal addiction, 44
Dual identity, 169

Early education intervention, 103–107
Ebonics. *See* African American
    Vernacular English
Ebonics Resolution, 112–114
Ecology family models, 170, 171
Edmonds, Ronald, 97, 98–99
Educable mentally retarded (EMR)
    students, 91–93
Education, 83–109. *See also* Public
    school system; Teachers
    Abecedarian Project, 106–107, 126
    academic self-concept, 95
    demographic comparisons, 88–91,
        94, 102–105, 118, 119–120,
        122–123
    early intervention, 103–107
    Head Start, 103–105
    High/Scope Perry Preschool Project,
        105–106
    in Independent Black Schools,
        99–103
    parental alienation from education
        system, 95–96
    peer influence, 95
    public school models and
        effectiveness, 96–99

special education classes, 91–93
Educational apartheid. *See* School
    desegregation
Effective Schools Model (ESM)
    academic achievement, 99
    community-like learning
        environments, 98
    flexible assessment and instruction, 99
    pedagogical attitudes, 98
    principals, 98
    professional staff, 99
Eisenhower, Dwight D., 86
Emergent family model, 169–170
Employment
    achievement gap and, 91
    of African American males, 150
    Head Start parents and, 105
    lack of job opportunities, 10
    parental employment and effect on
        children, 171
    prenatal care availability and, 47
    special education students and, 92
Empowerment theory, 160
ESM. *See* Effective Schools Model
Essays on Moral Development
    (Kohlberg), 136
Ethic of Care (Gilligan), 139–140
Ethic of Justice (Kohlberg), 134,
    137–139
Ethics in child research
    additional consent, 30
    anonymity, 30
    confidentiality, 31
    deception, 30
    implications of findings, 31
    incentives, 30
    informed consent, 29
    informing participants on findings, 31
    mutual responsibilities, 30–31
    non-harmful procedures, 29
    parental consent, 29–30
    participant well-being, 31
    personal misconduct, 32
    reporting results, 31
    scientific misconduct, 31–32
    unforeseen consequences, 31

Eurocentric values, 15, 17
European American children. *See*
    White American children
Exosystem ecological models, 171
External validity, 16, 21–23, 138

Family functioning behaviors
    (Barker and Hill), 179
Family stress model, 173, 174
Family structure
    augmented family, 176–178
    demographics, 173, 175, 176
    nuclear family, 172–174
    single parent family, 174–176
Family systems theory. *See also* Social
    contexts
    circularity, 170
    equifinity, 170
    interdependence, 170
    subsystems of, 170
FAS. *See* Fetal Alcohol Syndrome
Father-headed households, 5–6, 10,
    173, 175–176
Faubus, Orville, 86
Fetal Alcohol Syndrome (FAS), 44, 45
Foster care, 6–7, 177–178
Frazier, E. F., 167
Freedom Schools, 101
Friendships and development, 180–181

Georgia Board of Education, 86
Gibbs, J. C., 140
Gilligan, Carol, 138, 139–140
Gilligan's theory: The Ethic of Care
    Caring for both self and others,
        139–140
    Caring for others, 139–140
    Caring for self, 139–140
Gore, Albert, Sr., 86
Grandparent-headed households
    augmented families, 176–178
    child adjustment to, 177
    coparent role, 177
    custodial care of children, 6, 196
    poverty levels in, 10
Grigorenko, Elena, 25–27

Hall, Kathryn, 40–41
Hall, Prince, 101
Harford Heights model, 99
Head Start, 103–105
Health, 39–64
    access to health care, 59–61
    AIDS and treatment of, 49–50
    Asthma and treatment of, 56–58
    demographic comparisons, 49–50,
        52, 56–58
    infant care, 47–49
    infant mortality, 40–49
    obesity and treatment of, 58–59
    plumbism and treatment of,
        51–53
    sickle-cell anemia and treatment of,
        53–56
Health care access, 59–61
Health insurance, 59–60
Healthy Baby/Healthy Start program,
    48, 60
Healthy families, 179
Helms, J., 145–146
High Intensity Targeted Screening
    project, 53
High school graduation rates, 88
High/Scope Educational Research
    Foundation, 105
High/Scope Perry Preschool Project,
    105–106
Hill, J., 178, 179
Hispanic American children
    AIDS incidence in, 50
    demographics, 2–8
    economic conditions, 10
    family structure, 175–177
    poverty rates of, 173
    school segregation, 84
HIV/AIDS, 49–50, 177
Hood, James, 86
Hot stove encounters, 78
Housing and Urban Development
    Department, U.S., 51
Humphries, M. L., 141, 144
Hydroxyurea, 55
Hypermasculine identity, 181

Immanent justice, 135
Immersion schools, 99–100
Immigrants and immigration, 2–3
In a Different Voice (Gilligan), 138
Independent Black Schools (IBS), 99–103
  academic structure, 101
  diverse socioeconomic student
    backgrounds, 101
  founder of, 101
  immersion schools, 100
  Ngusabo principles, 101
  teachers as surrogate parents, 101
Infant care and mortality, 40–49
Institutional Review Boards (IRBs), 28
Integrative Conceptual Model, 34–35
Interdisciplinarity, 24–25
Interference hypothesis, 122–124
Internal validity, 18–23
IQ tests, 92
IRB. *See* Institutional Review Boards
Irvine Foundation, 40

Johnson, Lyndon B., 59–60, 86, 104
Journal of Educational Psychology
  race-comparative studies and, 16
  on social class assessment in
    studies, 22–23
Journal of Negro Education, 97
Justice Statistics Department, U.S., 147

Kefauver, Estes, 86
Kennedy, John F., 86
Kohlberg, Lawrence, 134–139
Kohlberg's theory: The Ethic of Justice
  criticism of, 137–139
  heteronomous morality, 136–137
  instrumental purpose and ex-
    change, 136–137
  in moral development, 134–135
  mutual interpersonal, expectations,
    good relations, 136–137
  prior rights and social contract, 137
  social systems and conscience
    maintenance, 136–137
  universal ethical principles, 137
Ku Klux Klan, 85

Language and literacy, 111–131
  challenges of, 122–124
  intervention programs, 124–127
  language assessment, 127–129
  language intervention programs,
    125–127
  language learning, 117–122
  language socialization, 118–122
  literacy intervention programs, 127
  oral and written communication in
    home, 119
  parental expectations and, 118
  SE vs. AAVE in home, 119
  use of AAVE in schools, 111–117
Language assessment
  comprehensive assessment
    (Comp.), 128–129
  contrasting linguistic features
    (CLF), 128
  dialect vs. speech disorder, 127–128
  other forms of discourse (Dis.), 128
  spontaneous speech samples (SS),
    128
  training in AAVE, 128
Language intervention programs,
    124–127
Larry P. v. Wilson Riles (1971), 92
Law enforcement accountability,
    149–150
Leach, M. M., 146
Lead poisoning, 51–53
Lead Poisoning Prevention Outreach
    Program, 53
Lee Elementary School, 99
Linguistics and Education (Rickford and
    Rickford), 126
Literacy. *See* Language and literacy
Living arrangements, 2–8
Lucy, Autherine, 86

Malone, Vivian, 86
Marital patterns. *See also* Family
    structure
  consanguinal vs. conjugal bonds, 170
  divorce rate, 5
  trends, 171–172

Maternal risk factors, 43–47
MDI. *See* Bayley Mental Development Index
Medicaid, 60
Mental health and racial identity, 65–81
    assessment and diagnosis, 68–70
    demographic comparisons, 66, 71
    doll studies, 72–75
    racial identity, 72–79
    risk factors, 65–68
    treatment of mental health disorders, 70–72
Mental model, 95
Meredith, James, 86
Mesosystem ecological models, 171
Methodology in research
    cross-sectional, 18–20
    cultural deficit models, 17, 28
    cultural sensitivity, 19, 22, 24, 28, 69
    design limitations, 166
    in developmental research, 15
    experimenter's race, 21
    external validity, 16, 21–23, 138
    interdisciplinarity, 24–25
    internal validity, 18–23
    longitudinal designs, 18–20
    race-comparative studies, 16–17, 21
    race homogenous studies, 16–17
    role of context, 25
    selection bias, 18–19
    selective dropout, 19
    social status, 22
Modifiability studies, 75
Moral development, 133–163
    community violence and, 147–161
    Gibbs' Sociomoral Reasoning Model, 140–141
    Gilligan's theory, 139–140
    Humphries' Culture and Empathy Model, 141, 142
    Kohlberg's theory, 134–139
    morality and racial identity development, 145–146
    overview, 133–134
    Piaget's theory, 134–139

    prosocial behavior, 142–146
    Turiel's domain theory, 141–142
Moreland, C., 146
Mother-headed households
    advantages of, 169
    demographics, 4–5
    depression incidence in children, 66
    poverty levels in, 9–10
    single parent family, 174–176
Moynihan, Daniel Patrick, 166–167, 168

NAACP. *See* National Association for the Advancement of Colored People
National Assessment of Educational Progress (NAEP), 87
National Association for the Advancement of Colored People (NAACP), 84
National Asthma Association, 56, 58
National Center for Health Statistics, 43, 46
National Council for Adoption, 8
National Organization on Fetal Alcohol Syndrome, 45
National Safety Council, 53
Native American children, 2, 57
NCLB. *See* No Child Left Behind
The Negro American Family (Moynihan), 167, 168
Neighborhood Club intervention program, 151–161
    bilingual translation, 154
    curriculum topics, 154–159
    incidence of violence, 151–152
    mental health diagnosis, 152
    PTSD and community violence, 152, 154
    theoretical considerations, 160–161
    treatment and intervention issues, 152–153
Nigrescence models
    dissonance or encounter stage, 145
    immersion-emersion stage, 146
    internalization-commitment stage, 146
    internalization stage, 146
    pre-encounter stage, 145

961-Baby, 48
No Child Left Behind (NCLB), 102–103
Nuclear family structure, 172–174

Oakland Unified School District,
    112–114
Obesity, 46, 58–59
Office of Minority and Women's
    Health, 45
Other forms of discourse (Dis.), 128

PAF. *See* Psychocultural Adaptive
    Functioning
Pan-African-Communication Behaviors.
    See African American Vernacular
    English
Parents
    alienation from education system,
        95–96
    children in Head Start and, 105
    culturally relevant books and, 124
    family language situations and
        learning, 118
    mental health assessment of, 69
    neglect and foster care, 178
    prosocial behavior development, 143
    racial socialization of children,
        77–79
    research parental consent, 29–30
    role in language socialization,
        118–122
Pathological family model, 167–168
Peabody Picture Vocabulary (PPVT),
    105, 128
Peer relationships and development
    in educational experience, 95
    heteronomous thinking and,
        135–136
    importance of, 178–179
    in Independent Black Schools, 102
    peer culture vs. school culture, 95
    race awareness, 179–180
    special education stigma, 92
Person and number in AAVE/SE, 116
Phenomenological Variant to Ecological
    Systems Theory (PVEST), 34

Phonology in AAVE/SE, 114
Piaget, Jean, 134–139
Piaget's theory
    autonomous morality, 135–136
    criticism of, 137–139
    heteronomous morality, 135–136
    in moral development, 134, 135–136
Plumbism, 51–53
Pluralization in AAVE/SE, 116
Police accountability, 149–150
Population statistics. *See* Census
    Bureau, U.S.; Demographics
Possession in AAVE/SE, 116
Posttraumatic stress disorder (PTSD),
    152, 154
Poverty, 9–11, 66, 172–173, 175, 185
Pragmatics in AAVE/SE, 117
Pregnancy, 43–49
Prenatal care, 46–49
Principals, 98
Private schools, 99–103
Project Follow Through, 107
Prosocial behavior, 143–145
Psychocultural Adaptive Functioning
    (PAF), 70
PTSD. *See* Posttraumatic stress disorder
Public assistance. *See* Welfare
Public school models, 96–99
Public school system. *See also*
        Education; School desegregation
    academic gaps, 89–91
    children from poor urban areas, 89
    Effective Schools Model, 98–99
    Freedom Schools, 101
    immersion schools, 99–100
    IQ tests and special education, 92
    learned helplessness, 95
    NCLB, 102–103
    parental alienation from, 95–96
    Project Follow Through, 107
    School Development Program,
        97–98
    special education classes, 91–93
PVEST. *See* Phenomenological
    Variant to Ecological Systems
    Theory

Race awareness, 179–180
Race-social class confound, 21
Racial identity, 8, 72–79, 145–146.
    See also Mental health and racial
    identity
Read and Rise Literacy Campaign, 127
Relational aggression, 181
Relational cognitive style, 94
Research issues, 15–37. *See also*
    Methodology in research
    conceptual frameworks, 24–25
    culturally relevant research, 23–24,
        138–139
    demographics and norms, 18, 21,
        166, 168
    developmental psychology, 25–27
    developmental research methods, 15
    ethical considerations, 27–32
    gender bias, 138
    Integrative Conceptual Model, 34–35
    role of context and interdisciplinarity,
        24–25
    social class, 22–23
    theories, 32–36
Resegregation. *See* School desegregation
Resiliency models, 67–68

St. Jude Children's Research Hospital, 56
School desegregation, 83–96
    court-ordered busing, 87
    federal legislation in support of,
        85–87
    freedom of choice, 87
    negative impacts of, 87–89
    open enrollment, 87
    resegregation in public schools, 89
    resistance and refusal of, 85–87
    Supreme Court rulings, 84–87
    test scores and, 87–88
School Development Program (SDP)
    academic achievement, 98
    governance and management teams, 97
    mental health teams, 97
    parent participation, 97
    staff development and training, 98
SE. *See* Standard English

Self-concept, 75–76, 95
Self-esteem, 67–68, 95
Self-hatred, 73
Semantics in AAVE/SE, 117
Sickle-cell anemia, 53–56
Sickle-Cell Anemia Disease
    Association, 56
Sierra Health Foundation, 40
Similarity-attraction hypothesis, 180
Single parent family structure, 174–176
Sleep disturbances, 52
Social contexts, 165–183
    cultural equivalent family model,
        168–169
    ecology family model, 170, 171
    emergent family model, 169–170
    external systems and family, 171
    family structure and child
        development, 171–178
    family systems theory, 170–171
    in friendships, 180–181
    pathological family model,
        167–168
    in peer relationships, 178–180
Society for Research in Child
    Development (SRCD), 28–32
Sociocultural theory (Vygotsky), 32
Socioeconomic status (SES)
    cultural deficit models and, 17
    cultural sensitivity and, 24
    diversity of in IBS, 101
    internal validity and, 20
    lack of parental school participation
        and, 95–96
    maternal language and, 120–121
    pathological family model and,
        167–168
    pregnancy and health correlations,
        45–47
    prosocial behavior and, 144
    research issues and, 134, 166
    Standard English and, 119–121
    use of AAVE and, 114
Sociomoral Reasoning Model (Gibbs)
    exchanging and instrumental
        reasoning, 140

mutual and prosocial reasoning, 140
unilateral and physicalistic
    reasoning, 140
Southern Manifesto, 86
Special education, 91–93
Speech disorders, 127–129
Spencer, M. B., 34
Spontaneous speech samples (SS), 128
SRCD. *See* Society for Research in
    Child Development
SS. *See* Spontaneous speech samples (SS)
Standard English (SE). *See also* African
    American Vernacular English
    comparisons with AAVE, 114–117,
        121–125
    in home environment, 119
    language intervention programs,
        125–126
    socioeconomic status and,
        119–121
    as test requirement, 128
Standardized tests
    alternative language assessments,
        128–129
    Ebonics Resolution, 112–114
    Effective Schools Model's use of, 99
    in Head Start program, 105
    IBS student achievement and,
        101–102
    legality of IQ tests, 92
    SE requirement, 128
Stereotype threat, 95
Sternberg, Robert, 25–27
Stowe Middle School, 99
Street culture, 148–150
Strokes, 53–54
Sudden Infant Death Syndrome, 45
Sue, Stanley, 21
Supreme Court rulings, 84–87
Syntax in AAVE/SE, 115
Systems approach research, 170

Teacher expectancy theory
    in education system, 88, 93–95
    in special education classes, 92
    teacher's race and, 93

Teachers. *See also* Teacher expectancy
    theory
    AAVE and attitudes toward,
        123, 125
    Bridges Reading Program, opposed
        by, 126
    cultural incongruence and
        attitudes, 94
    demographics, 94
    in immersion schools, 100
    in Independent Black Schools, 101
    NCLB and, 102–103
    need for cultural issues training,
        129–130
    Neighborhood Club impacts on
        students, 161
    pupil performance driven, 99
    school desegregation and, 89
    in special education classes,
        91–93
    teaching styles and student
        achievement, 94
    teaching techniques in inner city
        classrooms, 94
    training choices, 98
Terry (diagnostic tool), 69
Test of Early Language Development
    (TOLD), 128
Troubled families, 179
Turiel, E., 141–142

University of North Carolina, 126
Urban League, 127

Verb tense in AAVE/SE, 115–117
Violence in community
    children's mental health and, 66
    covictimization, 147, 151
    incidence of, 147, 151–152, 154
    moral development and,
        147–161
    Neighborhood Club intervention
        program, 151–161
    police accountability, 149–150
    street culture, 148–150
Vygotsky, Lev, 32